Thomas Morgan Evans is a Henry Moore post-doctoral fellow. He has a PhD in art history from University College London and has taught there and at the Courtauld Institute of Art. He has written criticism for *Art History* and *The Burlington Magazine*, and has worked for the Tate, the ICA and for LUX.

'*3D Warhol* is a fascinating exploration of a facet of Warhol's work that is often ignored. Thomas Morgan Evans examines Warhol as an artist rather than a media personality, comparing his work to a wide selection of contemporaries including Basquiat, Mel Bochner, Wolfgang Tillmans, Donald Judd, Carl Andre and Jeff Koons. This book is indispensable for anyone interested in the work of Andy Warhol… highly recommended.'

Gary Comenas, Founder of Warholstars.org

'By critically investigating the artist's underappreciated sculptural work, *3D Warhol* fills a crucial gap in Warhol scholarship. And it does so with aplomb, delving confidently into a wide range of familiar and unfamiliar objects, illuminating the ways in which they exploit and undermine traditional sculptural aesthetics. At once erudite and accessible, *3D Warhol* provides an ideal introduction to the depth and breadth of Warhol's remarkable career.'

Anthony Grudin, Associate Professor of Art History,
University of Vermont

3D WARHOL

ANDY WARHOL AND SCULPTURE

THOMAS MORGAN EVANS

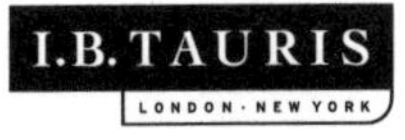

Published in 2017 by
I.B.Tauris & Co. Ltd
London • New York
www.ibtauris.com

International Library of Modern and Contemporary Art 24

ISBN: 978 1 78453 427 1 HB
978 1 78453 428 8 PB
eISBN: 978 0 85772 874 6
ePDF: 978 0 85772 827 2

A full CIP record for this book is available from the British Library
A full CIP record is available from the Library of Congress

Library of Congress Catalog Card Number: available

Typeset by Newgen
Printed and bound in Great Britain by T.J. International, Padstow, Cornwall

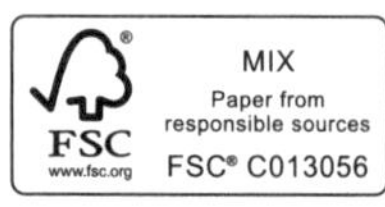

Contents

List of Figures

List of Plates

All Andy Warhol Artworks © 2016 The Andy Warhol Foundation for the Visual Arts, Inc. / Artists Rights Society (ARS), New York and DACS, London

Acknowledgements

In writing this book I have received a great amount of support and assistance. I know how lucky I have been to benefit from the knowledge, suggestions and kindness of all those who have helped me; without them this book could not have been written at all and the certain inadequacies of this text reflect on myself solely.

I should not have been able to proceed in the first place without the financial support of a Henry Moore Foundation post-doctoral fellowship. I am especially grateful to the Henry Moore Institute's Head of Sculpture Studies, Lisa Le Feuvre, for her belief in my project early on. The commitment to research and scholarship at the Henry Moore Institute was humbling from the start. It provided a friendly, grounded environment in which to develop my work in termly seminars and presentations. I am grateful to all those who attended these sessions for their contributions in testing my ideas out and encouraging their development, particularly Jon Wood and Pavel Pys. I hope I reciprocated with my own contributions to the discussions in my time there.

At the Department of the History of Art, UCL, my long-time home from home, my work has continually been supported and advocated to the wider world, primarily through the figures of Professors Frederic Schwartz, Briony Fer and Andrew Hemingway. To them, and to the staff at the department in general but, especially, Charles Ford, I owe a great deal for their friendly guidance and their interest in my progress from BA student to published author. Special thanks also goes to UCL's Art Librarian, Liz Lawes and to Daniela Tanner Hernández for her help with the index.

Matt Wrbican, the archivist at the Andy Warhol Museum, Pittsburgh, is the foremost authority on Andy Warhol. It is through his great generosity and the kindness of the staff at the Warhol, especially Greg Burchard, that this book has much of its content. Geri Amanda at the Menil Collection; Dominic Molon and the staff at the Museum of the Rhode Island School of Design; and Mark Francis of the Gagosian, London, were all key friends and supporters of the project.

Likewise, I want to thank Gary Comenas author of Warholstars.org for his assistance. Warholstars is really something special, an invaluable resource for anyone interested in Warhol and those around him. In correspondence with Gary, I have learnt a huge amount and, through his support for my project, he has gained my lasting affection.

As part of a wider network of young scholars in universities in the UK and abroad, my understanding of Warhol's work and times was improved enormously by conversations with James Boaden, Alex Taylor and Elisa Schaar. In addition, for crucial feedback and encouragement, at many different stages of this book's development, I owe thanks to the readership and support of John Jervis, Anthony Grudin and Mark Stuart-Smith.

I want to acknowledge a list of Warhol ex-associates and champions who have all contributed their time and knowledge to my research. My thanks goes to Bob Colacello, Vito Giallo, Thomas Kiedrowski, Benjamin Lui, Gerard Malanga, Billy Name, John O'Connor and Paige Powell.

My heartfelt thanks also goes to Elizabeth Murray Finkelstein, Bettina Funcke, Seth Price, Richard Prince, Jason Sapan, Arthur Tress, Wolfgang Tillmans and Kelley Walker.

Finally my editors, Baillie Card and Anna Coatman, made I.B.Tauris the best possible place to take my work. Their faith in the book and stewardship of the project meant that the, at times, harrowing experience of going to press was also a rewarding and even fun experience.

This book is dedicated to the memory of my father; to my family, my mother Mary and my brother Ja; but especially to Cadence Kinsey on whose caring, careful support and companionship I have depended these last few years. She has given meaning to (and allayed a lot of nonsense from) both this book and its author's life, her contribution has been and continues to be fundamental.

Introduction: Portraits

Gretchen Berg: 'I'm simplifying.'
    Andy Warhol: 'Yeah.'[1]

Rain machines, alarmed kosher pickle jars filled with gemstones, replica cornflakes boxes, 'disco décor', time capsules, art bombs, birthday presents, perfume bottles, and floating silver pillows that are clouds, paintings, and films at the same time. Museum interventions, collecting and curating projects, expanded performance environments, holograms. This is a book about the vast array of sculptural work made by Andy Warhol between 1954 and 1987, a period that begins long before the first Pop paintings and ends the year of his death.

Warhol made sculptures that he called 'abstract' and 'invisible', as well as ones which were perfectly true to life, heavy and handcrafted. Though some of these works were part of families, with similar physical attributes and names, generally there was little continuity of this kind between the sculptures that he made. Each were designed for different occasions: some were intended to be shown privately, some publicly, others somewhere in-between. Unlike the painting and film work, which relied on a limited core group of assistants and collaborators, Warhol's sculpture brought different persons, institutions, media (including newly emerging technologies) and disciplines together. These sculptural projects crowned pinnacle moments in Warhol's career, but also occupied downtime and periods of artistic and personal change; junctures in his more commercially orientated practices. In an overview of the sculptures produced in the period 1970–72, Neil Printz observes that these were made during a period of 'crisis and transition', following the assassination attempt on his life in June 1968 and the move from the 'silver' Factory of 47th Street to 33 Union Square in the same year.[2] Warhol's sculpture also represented different aspects of factory life: its birthdays, unique projects, visitors, open-ended commissions, and the 'leftovers' from other works. The *Time Capsules* project, an enormous archive of clutter (1974–87), is the superlative example in this regard. Like *Screen Tests*, his series of film-portraits (1964–66), or the *Andy Warhol Diaries*, the filmic and textual equivalents of *Time Capsules*, Warhol's sculpture recorded Factory time.

This diverse body of work can be divided according to art historical labels: portrait busts intended for display on plinths, Institutional Critique, archival and collecting projects, eco-art, a continued dialogue with Minimalism and environment work, multimedia and participatory *Gesamtkunstwerk*, and the recent category of 'studiowork'.[3] When Warhol bought a large property in the exclusive Montauk area of New York, he teased his new neighbour by telling him that he was going to dig up some of the surrounding grounds as part of an earth-art project. In fact, this may be the only post-1960 category of sculpture to which Warhol cannot be tied.[4] Yet despite all the ways the work can be associated with the discourses that surround sculpture, it can equally be seen as resistant to sculpture as a category, existing almost in spite of it. In 1996, Warhol's friend and one-time assistant, Christopher Makos, characterised this relation to sculpture while considering a tricksy late concrete work that Warhol had given him as a gift:

> The Warhol sculpture—I think it's from 1982—was a Christmas present. Andy would use big holidays as reasons to purge his creativity. Andy was always asking me and his other friends, 'What can I do for sculptures? What's unusual?' Those were hard questions for Andy because he thought in very linear terms. He didn't think in three-dimensional terms at all. Photographic terms, canvas terms, flat terms. He couldn't figure out what you do to do something sculptural.[5]

Warhol made sculpture to 'purge creativity', not to put it to use. There is a suggestion here that sculpture was not considered work or even artwork at all. Yet, at the same time, Makos' statement sums up the dynamic at the heart of this book: the dual direction of travel between Warhol's relation to sculpture and sculpture's relation to Warhol. It proves that Warhol was very much concerned with sculpture and, in some way, orientated himself around it. But what I want to suggest, and what Makos does not, is not just that this dynamic existed but that it was incisive in both directions. Warhol did something unusual with sculpture, something radical to do with sculpture emerging from those 'hard questions', and in tension with the traditional notion of the 'three-dimensional' that Makos describes. With its many incarnations, its unresolvedness, its reflection of personal and working life, and its sheer complicated difficulty, Warhol's sculpture can also offer unique access to a figure whose work is notoriously hard to read and explain, and whose motivations were well-guarded. Contained within Makos' words are two tendencies that I propose broadly categorise Warhol's sculpture: first, in relation to Warhol's 'purge of creativity', there is a dynamic between waste and production and, second, there is an antipathy between the image—the 'flat' or 'photographic' terms—and the sculptural object.

These themes are present in Warhol's own most explicit statement on sculpture, which both echoes a sense of him acting from behind a veil and the potential of sculpture to lift it. It occurs in *The Philosophy of Andy Warhol: From A to B and Back Again* (much of which was ghosted by either Pat Hackett or Bob Colacello): 'My favourite piece of sculpture is a solid wall with a hole in it to frame the space on the other side.'[6] For a study that puts sculpture first, it is not a great start. Here sculpture is essentially demoted, made to defer to the status of the image and the 'terms' in which Makos recognises that Warhol thought. Yet this 'wall with a hole in it' is, nonetheless, one that suits our purposes: Warhol's sculpture is a glory hole which offers access back to the space where he stands, a portrait of Warhol which would otherwise be hidden and which entails a certain trespass onto a secluded space.

In the formulation 'Warhol, sculptor' we therefore already have a picture, a portrait, of Warhol himself that reaches beyond the idea made famous in the oft repeated words of Gretchen Berg's 1966 article 'Andy

Warhol: My True Story': 'If you want to know all about Andy Warhol, just look at the surface: my paintings and my films and me, and there I am'.[7]

Berg's article was based on an interview conducted in 1966, and appeared in three versions between 1966 and 1967. It is a classic portrait of Andy Warhol as a picture of cool: 'against interpretation' and yet presenting himself, as much as his work, as something to be viewed. Though designed to grab its contemporary audience, the quotation still reverberates and is worth some consideration. The words are, in fact, Berg's and not Warhol's, but they are credited to him.[8] His role in this case (as in many others) is to be a reflective surface, a mirror and, in allowing the words to be put into his mouth, Warhol acts out the very characteristics attributed to him. Since the publication of this interview, Berg's characterisation has become historically important, both as evidence ('the truth about Andy Warhol') and as an influential approach to writing about Warhol. It concedes that what is beneath the surface is unreachable while what is on the surface is transmittable, exchangeable and reproducible. Perhaps the wall with a hole in it from *The Philosophy* is also part of that surface, a screen. If it was, it nonetheless proves there is something behind it to be looked at and understood, and suggests that sculpture provides a way in.

If Warhol is usually associated with the short period between 1962 and 1966, two of the works from this time whose impact was greatest, and above all else established his place at the forefront of artists working in America, are sculpture. These include the *Brillo Boxes*, from 1964, and *Silver Clouds* shown in 1966 — described by Brian O'Doherty as 'one of the sights of the 1960s', which 'changed every particle of the gallery space.'[9] In addition, *Rain Machine* (c.1970), shown at the 1970 Expo in Japan, represents one of Warhol's largest commissions, while *Raid the Icebox I* (1970) is significant for the way in which it anticipates major new forms of artistic practice that are still current today (in this case, 'artist in the museum' works). Given the prominence of these sculptural works it is remarkable that there has not been a serious study of Warhol's sculpture outside of the three (soon to be four) volumes that make up the, albeit excellent, *Catalogue Raisonné*.[10] In the history of art, the sense that Warhol's sculpture was not essential to his work or to how he operated is pervasive: the sculptural is a 'hard question' for art historians working on Warhol, much as it was for Warhol himself.[11]

Faced with this question, as this book is, it has more often than not been those books which record and inventory Warhol's output that have therefore been vital. They reflect a life spent recording, collecting, delegating, collaborating, socialising and making in all media and, in studying Warhol's sculpture through archival sources, we get a sense of just how interconnected the various aspects of Warhol's life were. Amongst these there are a few representative publications including Callie Angell, *Andy Warhol Screen Tests: The Films of Andy Warhol Catalogue Raisonné* (2006); Georg Frei, Neil Printz and Sally King-Nero, *The Andy Warhol Catalogue Raisonné, Volumes 1–3* (2002–2004); Kenneth Goldsmith, ed., *I'll be Your Mirror: The Selected Andy Warhol Interviews* (2004); John Smith, Mario Kramer and Matt Wrbican. *Andy Warhol's Time Capsule 21* (2004). Further, much of the detail in this book about Warhol's less well-known sculptural work has been gleaned from sources in which it features coincidentally, such as diary entries, interviews and recordings whose object, again, was to record what happened or was happening. Careful analysis of installation shots, first-hand accounts and interviews have been vital for understanding the work's meaning.

Taking a broader interest in Warhol's work, there are, of course, a great many other resources on which to draw, many of which feature the more famous sculptures. However, it is rare that the status of these works as sculpture, and their distinct function in that regard, influences an overall thesis or is placed in proper context. One exception would be Thomas Crow's analysis of the 'absconded subjects' of Pop.[12] Meanwhile, the literature on Warhol's films, paintings and biography—the various sites which Warhol, in Berg's text, names in regard to a 'surface'—has become vast and hugely varied and it is notable how many of these readings produce portraits of Warhol that have become influential from narrow studies of short periods, single series and even single works. In much of this literature, Warhol's work has been considered a demonstration of postmodernist theory, especially in terms of the impact of the ubiquitous mechanically reproducible, screened, and non-embodied image. Roland Barthes, Jean Baudrillard, Michel Foucault, Gilles Deleuze and Frederic Jameson all wrote on Warhol between 1966 and 1997, influencing the historical reception of Warhol's work as a point of contrast to Minimal and post-Minimal art's orientation around the subject in space, around the body—both as a space and in space—and around the physical and material conditions of the work itself.

Branden W. Joseph has observed that the idea of Warhol's art and persona as presenting an unyielding surface,

> has inflected much of the critical and art historical commentary on Warhol, where a dialectic frequently unfolds between the attempt to define the artist's meaning and the tacit assumption that neither he nor his art will provide the means to do so. In a large portion of the writing on Warhol, the result is an analysis that cedes to projection, with the overall impression being one of an ineffectual and unenlightening hermeneutic spinning out of control.[13]

For Joseph, wariness of Warhol's mimicking, slick surface is at the root of sophisticated arguments about the work. Despite their differences, this is certainly true of the work of Benjamin H. D. Buchloh (1989), Hal Foster (1996) and Douglas Crimp (1999) who all take care to avoid the trap that Joseph describes, of merely seeing oneself and one's own preoccupations reflected back in the mirror Warhol holds up. To an extent, these writers agree that the crux of Warhol's work is in its reproduction of the modern socio-economic phenomenon of mechanised capitalist production and the entanglement of the subject within it, leaving all that is holy—desire, death, identity, and art as a potentially radical endeavour—in peril. In Crimp's text, his own agenda in writing about the complexities of 'getting the Warhol we deserve'—a phrase appropriated from Hal Foster—is to advance the work of cultural studies as a discipline, and to encourage a queering of our understanding of the work and its context. Indeed, one way that the literature on Warhol might be divided is between disciplinary approaches: between the context of art history, both a particular history and the particular toolkit for doing it, and the wider context of visual culture and cultural studies. In Crimp's analysis, Warhol's mirror surface is a projection by art history that disguises the blatant issue of unstable identities. In this way, Warhol's queerness, and the importance of it for his work, is both there on the surface and hidden for Crimp.

One might likewise reflect on the queer status of sculpture within the discourse on Warhol. It too is there for all to see in his work but is, at the same time, masked. And while the observation that Warhol made sculpture is one that privileges an art historical category, and arose from my own art historical approach, I shall argue that the work nonetheless underlines the importance of a context wider than art history. It acts to collapse and undermine the category of sculpture as it is traditionally understood and, importantly, as it was reinventing itself in the 1960s. It is an approach based on conventional art historical categorisation and formal analysis that nonetheless clashes with conventional understandings of art's history so that, ironically, it is Crimp's account of cultural studies—to 'supplant the rarefied art history with other histories'—that describes the work in this book.[14] Warhol was a photographer, pornographer, author, cinematographer, publisher and even philosopher; he was a Pop artist, conceptual artist, abstract artist, mogul and queer revolutionary. An attempt to understand his sculpture explicitly calls for *all* of the Warhols at our disposal. Looked at from the other way, the works enhance our understanding of different aspects of Warhol's art and his other business and private interests, subject matter and social groups. Warhol's sculpture is vital in thinking through his collaborative experiments in mixed media and in the media; his influence on contemporary artists; the relationship between his painting and film works; and his explorations of the institutions of art and social space.

How Warhol's work sits within art history is therefore central to the book, yet to consider it in terms of sculpture is to already place it within a fraught and much-contested territory. This is especially true in the context of the 1960s and the rise of Minimalism, where writers have tended to treat Warhol, in relation to this dominant narrative, as a complement to, or counterpart of, Minimal Art, as per the work of James Meyer (2004), Briony Fer (1997 and 2009), Alex Potts (2001) and Hal Foster (1996). However, one context that does remain vital is that of Pop. Though many of the sculptural works in this study appear far from the paintings generally associated with Pop, the themes that arguably characterise Warhol's Pop, such as unnaturalness, trespass, bringing the outside in and mis-registration, are nearly always present and are often elaborated in his sculpture. Yet reading the infinite number of blurbs for the infinite publications centred on Warhol, many beginning with lists of Warhol's diverse activities, we find they hardly ever include sculpture as a distinct category of work. Thus, as a study of Warhol's sculpture, this book's deviation from other approaches to Warhol's work is directed by a Pop ethos of de-sublimation. This book argues that attention to Warhol's sculpture, and the certain kind of attention to spaces of reception and display that the study of sculpture brings, also helps put into relief the complexity and sophistication of Warhol's Pop Art.

One of the key themes in this respect, which will be developed throughout this book, is that of the 'off-register'. The off-register is that which does not cohere with the predetermined systems of representation. In being that quality of fragmented or diverted presence, a transgression of boundary lines, or simply the quality of something 'not lining up', it thus concerns both formal and socio-political observations. The off-register was always a part of Warhol's work. Benjamin Buchloh has argued that 'lapses' and 'hiatuses' of registration were a formal procedure that blurred the lines between Warhol's commercial illustration work and the later Pop Art.[15] While an advertising illustrator in the 1950s (though the work continued to sustain him into the early 1960s) Warhol made drawings using a blotted, transfer technique, which gave a messy, carefree impression. Colour was applied to these drawings with little regard for the discipline of 'staying within the lines'. With this off-register work, Warhol enjoyed enormous success at a time during which photography was, according to a late interview, 'sending art down the drain'; its increasing dominance putting many other illustrators out of business.[16] The mechanically produced image is itself considered in terms of registration in Hal Foster's analysis of Warhol's *Death and Disaster* (1962–3) series: here, that which is off-register provides moments of drama. He describes the 'pops' or tears in the image-screen as a 'slipping of register', describing in paint the psychic process through which a subject realises, with horror, that an event one fears to be real has passed unnoticed, without registering.[17]

The subject as off-register, as 'beside' itself, might also pertain to ideas of performance and role play. Integral to Crimp's analysis of the queer aesthetics of Warhol's films is 'the separation of actors from their roles', of working at 'cross purposes', and abrupt 'jump' cuts or splicing. With its refusal of any fixed or determined identity, this constantly de-centring work is also determinedly off-register. As I have suggested already, Crimp's analysis equally finds the discourse on Warhol, with its failure to grapple with the queer status of the work, as much off-register as he finds the films themselves. Again, this condition of Warhol's queer cinema is akin to the situation with Warhol's sculpture: neither the idea of 'Warhol, sculptor', or the 3D work he made, fits into the parameters that art history has assigned for Warhol; both are out of register with the conventional parameters for the reception of his work. Moreover, and proving Crimp's point, the mis-registrations in Warhol's work had a meaning that was immediately apparent for a circle of artists and writers, all of whom were gay. During this time, Warhol's mis-fitting line took on a special significance: for William S. Wilson, who wrote for Mario Amaya's *Art and Artists* magazine (1965–8), the off-register was symbolic of a means of figuring and refiguring identity. In a preface to the re-publication of a piece written on Warhol in 1968 he spelt it out:

> Mario Amaya, Ray Johnson, Paul Thek and Joseph Raffaele felt misrepresented in a society in which they were discouraged from representing themselves as men who loved men (in that specific decade). Such themes of misrepresentation were emerging in the art of Andy Warhol, whose off-registration of silk-screen images was an aesthetic elaboration of the off-registrations in his daily life.[18]

Warhol's mis-registration signals, I think it is possible to say, estrangement from norms, being missed and missing, but as such it registers or represents those who have been estranged.

These themes of estrangement and fitting in can be seen in many of Warhol's works. His *Dance Diagrams* (1962), painted in large-scale and displayed on the gallery floor, are among the most innovative of the early paintings whose subject is the attainment and mis-attainment of certain standards. Other paintings of this time, such as the *Do It Yourself* (1962) colouring-in paintings, the *Before and After* (1961) nose-job painting and the *Cover Before Striking* (1962) match books, also all seem to share a single commanding voice, instructive about how to fit in. The original diagrams used for the *Dance Diagrams* were taken from a book of common dance steps whose pages also bore written instructions about what to do. It was imperative at that time, for many hoping to gain social acceptance, that one could take part in dances at such social meets as organised by neighbourhood churches and so on: dancing could be a fraught subject. Michael J. Golec has written on these works in terms of this kind of social inclusion, using as an example *Dance Diagram Fox Trot* (1962) with its missing instructions and cropped seventh step.[19] Here, a missed step signifies a failure to remain in registration, but on the part of a subject who is going to some lengths to conform. Ideas of stepping on toes and the crossing of lines that signify social norms relate to another central theme of my book, that of trespass, both in terms of gaining the entitlement to enter social space and the deviations of missteps. While Buchloh has argued that the work signals the kind of participatory aesthetics that capitalist society offers – proscriptive, limiting, even punitive – for Golec, this source of social anxiety is more textured and it is here that an idea of the 'artworld' comes into play. This idea, introduced in Chapter 2, is something that will be vital to my analysis throughout the book. Golec argues that although social participation was an aspiration for those 'left out', the artworld audience stands self-consciously apart from the mainstream. The gallery changes the work's message; it can skew how one sees things. Thus, though the *Dance Diagrams* represent the aspiration to conform to social norms, the off-register could also be emancipatory. Warhol's ability to occupy a space with his work that appears to be on both sides of social boundaries – the artworld and the real world – is crucial to the criticality of the work I want to highlight in this book, and is essential to Warhol's Pop aesthetics.

If the registrations of these 'command' paintings might be read predominantly in terms of class, in another pair of early paintings the role-play of social class and sexuality both share space and do so more explicitly in relation to the artworld. These are the portraits that Warhol made of Robert Rauschenberg in 1962–3, a period overlapping with Rauschenberg's first career retrospective and the year before he became the first American artist to win the Grand Prize at the Venice Biennale. Yet Warhol reframes the artworld's darling in a context that was meant to jar. The title of one of these works refers to James Agee's and Walker Evans' 1941 book: *Now Let Us Praise Famous Men*. In this work, we see Rauschenberg in family photos, a biographic quarter cycle that reveals humble Southern origins. Class and sexual identities entwine with one another here, as they did in Rauschenberg's own life. Warhol, I think, makes Rauschenberg's less-than-emphasised social origins also stand for his equally camouflaged sexual orientation.[20] Though I do not think that Warhol is 'outing' Rauschenberg (who was wary of the 'swish' Warhol) he does cast a shade over the more famous artist's public face. Recalling

William S. Wilson's comments, cognition of social difference needed to be suggested, but not explicit. In Warhol's other portrait of Rauschenberg we see the artist assuredly staring into the middle distance through varying levels of inky haze. This painting is called *Texan*; Warhol again ungenerously puts Rauschenberg's socio-geographic origins before his status as an artist, and again, claims to 'reveal' something about an aspect of the homosexual Rauschenberg's 'real' identity.[21]

At this time, Abstract Expressionism had established a monopoly on interiority, profundity and deeper meaning (things which Berg had posed as the opposite to 'surface' in her famous article), equating these things with art's ultimate purpose and value. This was done via a model of the artist as a heroic persona, one who, in practice, was also 'profoundly' and 'deeply' homophobic, machismo and intellectually idealist. Surface, in this sense, was a boundary between art and the social world, with all its ills. At the time when Warhol set out to begin painting, around 1960, the values privileged by Abstract Expressionism were in a kind of perfect registration with the values of the artworld: their interiorities coalesced, their boundaries mapped over one another. In the first pages of *POPism*, his account of the 1960s, Warhol writes that Abstract Expressionism had 'become an institution', while, in contrast, Pop's subject was 'all the great modern things that the Abstract Expressionist tried so hard not to notice at all.'[22]

Pop therefore proposed a competing worldview that was art-historically and institutionally off-register with the reactionary template of the art-world. In his early book on Warhol, Rainer Crone took seriously Warhol's persistent denial of having a critical agenda regarding the content of his images. Crone contends that whereas works such as the 1964 *Race Riot* paintings do not contain a critical message intrinsic to their image, they 'become criticism as soon as they are received into the machinery of the art market and thus accepted by society *as viable artworks*.'[23] The critical-ity of work such as the *Race Riot* paintings comes not in the visibility of their images—the visual and critical attention they would receive in the gallery context—nor in the accusation that these images from the media, perused at America's breakfast table, go unnoticed in the 'real world'. But rather that, within an art institution at the time of Abstract Expressionism's reign of 'trying not to notice', these images—commodities also—blown-up to 17 feet tall like road side billboards, went unseen on some fundamental level precisely by those who made it their business to 'look'. It is in these ways that Warhol's Pop stands for, very fundamentally, the work of setting content against framework, whether it be the framework of class, of gender and sexuality, the institution, style or the technology through which that content is communicated. The off-register is fundamental to the notion of Pop Art; it is there in its name—'Pop Art'. The two things are historical antinomies, as is the idea of Warhol and sculpture.

Another origin myth in *POPism* gets to the crux of the matter of class, the ultimate site of the clashing of registers in Warhol's Pop work. This myth tells the story of how Warhol settled on his famous clipped, hard, painting style for the paintings of soup cans and Coke bottles that were so important in establishing his work. Warhol explains how he presented the filmmaker Emile de Antonio with two versions of paintings of Coke bottles. In one, an image of a Coke bottle competes against a hashed, messy homage to Abstract Expressionism. The other, Warhol describes as 'just a stark, outlined Coke bottle in black and white'—a 'cold, no-comment' painting.[24] The first of these de Antonio scorns: it was 'a piece of shit, simply a little bit of everything', he is reported to have said.[25] The other, with the gestural paintwork dumped, de Antonio calls 'remarkable—it's our society, it's who we are'.[26] Warhol's subtraction of painterly gesture paints a picture, a portrait, of 'society' that many would argue *should be* more like the 'little bit of everything' of the first picture. Warhol's new portrait of American society, represented by the singular and untarnished commodity image, is very different to the one Ralph Ellison gives in the Epilogue of his novel *Invisible Man*: 'America is woven of many strands. I would recognize them and let it so remain'.[27]

The work of Anthony E. Grudin has helped deepen our understanding of the significance of de Antonio's proclamation. Grudin uses the example of *Superman* (1961), first displayed in the window of the Bonwit Teller department store. Here, Grudin observes that in photos of this installation the works appear without the funny, messy crayon scrawls and the partial erasure of text that they acquired in later versions.[28] Grudin argues that these additions are an elaboration of the trials that the working class undergoes to keep within the lines, to assimilate with the American ideal of a 'classless' professional middle class like that represented by Clark

Kent. In his analysis, Grudin concludes that stylistic imperfections were neither an 'Abstract Expressionist holdover' nor 'accidents', as many have ascribed them, but a qualifier to the myth that one might gain entrance into American society through various forms of assimilation and cultural reproduction: 'at its best and most incisive, Warhol's art was […] about the possibility of mass-cultural participation within capitalism.'[29] At the same time, Grudin persuasively argues that the brands that Warhol borrowed in his early paintings—those of Coca-Cola, Brillo, Campbell's and so on—were specifically associated with the working class, who were the target audience of these companies at the time. Again, what these brands harnessed was an *attempt* to associate with a core American identity on the part of a population excluded from it.

Thus, in Grudin's reading, Warhol's messy, off-register elements highlight the difficulties of assimilation through tracing the signifiers that stood for real social, institutional and physical spaces. Indeed, these real spaces and their representations frequently overlap in Warhol's work. We see this in the *Dance Diagrams* which map over floor space but, I would argue, it is best realised in Warhol's sculpture. As early as 1989, Benjamin Buchloh highlighted the importance of not allowing iconographic readings of Warhol's work to overshadow an approach that belongs, historically, to the sculptural.

> The endless discussion of Warhol's Pop iconography, and even more, those of his work's subsequent definition in terms of traditional painting, have oversimplified his intricate reflections on the status and substance of the painterly object and have virtually ignored his efforts to incorporate context and display strategies into the work themselves.[30]

Buchloh thus redirects consideration of Warhol's work. He opens up the possibility that this kind of thinking about materiality might also be transversally connected to the material conditions through which the social world that Warhol was part of, and represented, is negotiated: where spectatorship and participation bleed into one another. This saves Warhol's work from the macro scale at which iconographic readings have tended to operate and is crucial for thinking about many of the works in this book, which are specific to the worlds that Warhol inhabited. It shows how the act of taking one's place, as audience or author, bore a relation to all kinds of social negotiations. The work could be about entitlement as much as it could be about aspiration, and could target individuals as well as social groupings. Indeed, arguably, the question of the significance of Warhol's art is redundant without a prevailing concern for the symbolic space in which Warhol 'deployed' it. If Rainer Crone has made the case that seeing Warhol's work in terms of theatre is a productive way of looking at it, this book could be said to be all about 'scenes'.[31] Certainly I make no apologies for writing about Warhol's 'shows', as his opening nights were often unprecedented social events. The aforementioned symbolic space in question was, predominantly, the artworld but I argue that more care needs to be taken about the particularities here. Charles F. Stuckey's work on 'Warhol in Context' certainly sets a precedent for this focus on what he calls Warhol's 'wry sense of conceptual contextual gesture'.[32] For example, Stuckey suggests that the installation of *Brillo Boxes* at the Stable Gallery was 'a parody of the happenings and installation exhibitions that had been organized by the artists associated with the Hansa, Judson, Reuben, and Martha Jackson galleries including Jim Dine and Claes Oldenburg'.[33] Key to Stuckey's observation is not just the importance of the influence of happening and environment artists on Warhol but the idea that his approach to this influence is parodic.

Yet the idea of a theatrical Warhol, very much the artist-decorator and artist-set designer (as well as court fool), is one that puts the already fragile sense of a 'Warhol sculptor' in jeopardy. In the case of the installation of *Brillo Boxes*, object and environment literally come to be pitted against one another: if the impact of the work came through there being a critical mass of boxes, this impact would be diminished as the boxes (as individual works of art) got bought up. Yet, at the same time, the effect of taking over the gallery, and making it appear more like a warehouse than a space for an elite form of commerce, had an impact on the commodity status of the *Brillo Boxes*. Perhaps the failure of this exhibition, in terms of sales, was also a mark of its success. Indeed, further to this, if this environmental Warhol is one better understood by thinking of him in 3D, through an approach in many ways most appropriate to sculpture, there are, on the other hand, no clay or plaster works in this book, no bronzes; little that would connect Warhol to sculpture's traditions. And while Buchloh's invitation to think of Warhol materially and in terms of an encounter is foundational, there is little either in his own work or in work that follows his lead, despite Stuckey's contribution, that accounts for Warhol's sculpture as a body of work.

The overall contention of this book is that Warhol's sculpture constitutes a series of critical, oppositional recodings of the institutions of art. The work attempted to undermine what was most anti-social about these institutions, particularly their containment of social distinction within select spaces. It did so through a series of interventions into the artworld that singled out the reification of objects on which these institutions rested and through which they expressed their sense of their own value. Warhol's strategies for doing this can be divided approximately into three, though none of the works in this book exclusively relies on any single one. First, was the proposition of the anti-object: the insertion into the artworld of objects that failed to reflect the value mutually upheld between the spectator and the gallery or museum. These were objects in which value was absent or fleeting, or which parodied the values, or valued objects, of the particular context in which the work was shown. If this co-constitution of value between the spectator and the work was in dynamic, this relationship relied on maintaining categorical distinctions, particularly between real and representational space and, indeed, sculptural object and image. And this leads us to the second strategy: Warhol's sculpture supplanted and confused such categories and was, therefore, capable of being representative in more than one sense. Lastly, Warhol's work with sculpture was about invasion and trespass. It shows an acute awareness of the striations of social space and the way in which privilege, entitlement and social standing defined and delineated one's access and belonging to its many levels. All of the major exhibitions in this book were also major events, and these invasions of the sedate space of the artworld all defined moments of social mixing and social force that Warhol had carefully orchestrated. In the following chapters, the different pathways through which Warhol engaged with these aspects are thematised. This means that the same works are discussed at different times if they provide readings relevant to the different themes, and chronological order falls away so that each chapter spans large periods of time.

The first chapter, then, begins with some of Warhol's earliest works: the development of the hand-painted *Campbell's Soup Cans* (1962). There is a tension between some of the works in this group, where the material or haptic qualities of the cans are communicated, and others, indeed those that would finally be shown, in which there is a systematic reduction of these qualities that anticipates Warhol's later silkscreen technique. My argument here is that an understanding of sculpture can be seen as emerging from the qualities that were 'cast-off' in the development of Warhol's 'no comment' style: something haptic, spatial, and outside of the metaphysical frameworks of image reproduction or circulation. The sculptural can act as a refuge for what does not meet the conditions of the reproducible image and which is also, at this period in Warhol's work, synonymous with the commodity form. The work discussed in this chapter is collected both through the poetics of failure and the unfinished, as well as the formal tropes of the discarded and waste. It begins with Warhol's first solo artistic exhibition in New York City in 1954, remembered by Warhol and his associates as the 'crumpled paper show'. Crumpled paper becomes a subject that Warhol would revisit again as late as 1983 in the work *Abstract Sculpture*, made of newspaper print on Mylar. Such work has both important art historical forebears and progeny. In 1953, Marcel Duchamp exhibited a crumpled paper poster for his exhibition at the Sidney Janis Gallery, and in 2005 Seth Price began displaying 'Mylar crumples' bearing an image from a banned newsfeed.

The second chapter begins with the development of Warhol's epoch-defining sculptural statement, his 1964 exhibition *The Personality of the Artist*, which featured *Brillo Boxes* amongst other facsimiles of packaging. Uniquely, the chapter considers this work as an event of critical and insti-tutionally reflexive installation art. Key here is the analysis of the themes of trespass, entitlement and agency in the 'artworld', a term used by Arthur C. Danto in his 1964 article on the same exhibition. Important to my argument about this work and, more broadly, for the book at large, *The Personality of the Artist* takes place at the same moment as Minimalism. This central chapter contains a re-reading of Warhol's most famous sculp-tural work in tension with the art historical paradigms that emerged in parallel with it.

The third chapter looks at sculptures, from the 1960s and 1970s, which bring together Warhol's painting and film work, and the two different 'worlds' to which they belonged. These works are: *Large Sleep* (1965), *Silver*

Clouds (1966), *Rain Machine* (*c*.1970) and a holographic portrait from 1976. They exemplify the tendency within Warhol's sculpture towards collaboration and technological innovation. *Silver Clouds*, which marked his so-called retirement from painting in 1966, was made in collaboration with the scientist Billy Klüver, who had worked on the Bell Labs/NASA Telstar satellite launch in 1962. *Rain Machine* was shown at the Osaka World Fair in 1970, and emerged from the *Art and Technology* initiative run by LACMA. These works constituted the major focus of Warhol's efforts during the period when they were made. Their interest—and also, I suggest, the reason for their neglect in art history—lies in their hybridity and the disruption of categories that they threaten to cause. In these works Warhol reaches beyond the limits of the imaging technology available to him. Expressed through an idiom that is, in the last instant, sculpture, he fuses film and painting whilst simultaneously critically reflecting on the values attached to the media he attempts to leave behind.

The fourth chapter looks at Warhol's *Shadows* exhibition from 1979. This work, installed at the Dia Beacon, has been preserved for the public in a way that the earlier *Personality of the Artist* show has not. However, little has been said about what *Shadows* says in relation to the art of this time. My analysis of the work considers how, in league with the polemical thrust of contemporary movements Pattern and Decoration and Photorealism (movements that art history has endeavoured to sweep under the carpet), Warhol at once produced a rebuke and satire of Minimal aesthetics and a reassertion of what he called Pop's 'commonist' challenge to the artworld. That this vast painting-environment, commissioned and displayed by one of Minimalism's great patrons, was one in which Warhol associated himself with 'the art across the street', could be said to be characteristic of the attitude of Warhol's work not just in the case of *Shadows*, but more generally. In my reading of the exhibition of *Brillo Boxes*, *Silver Clouds* and *Shadows*, the three moments together provide a new appraisal of the artist that considers the importance to his work of sculpture and installation, and his critical engagement with Minimalism over an extended period of time

The final chapter begins with an appreciation of Warhol's overlapping collecting and art making. He collected objects, people and images, and all were used and reused in his artwork. Returning to the 'waste paper' with which the book begins, I read this recycling of 'junk' as a prototypical means of re-dissemination which engendered further collecting and consuming activity. Warhol's artist-curator project *Raid the Icebox I* (1969–70) forms the centrepiece of this chapter. Though the work finally received scholarly attention in the mid-1990s, its importance, particularly for Institutional Critique and the work of artists such as Fred Wilson and Andrea Fraser, is still under-established. The truth is that *Raid the Icebox I* is an entirely remarkable work, one of the first 'artist in the museum' works ahead of similar, canonical, projects by John Cage and Joseph Kosuth. In this chapter, I shall argue against assumptions that the exhibition was an apolitical piece of theatre: at the Rhode Island School of Design Museum, Warhol expanded the ground of sculpture, orchestrating assemblage and installation across media and institutions. Though *Raid the Icebox I* is the primary work cited in this chapter, a discussion of the 612-part *Time Capsule* project, and his collecting more generally, as well as some experiments with concrete and chocolate, all emerge from this study.

The above has, I hope, introduced the variety of works that will be considered in this book and how collecting them together under the category of sculpture relates to the existing literature on Warhol's work. This aspect has been a primary concern in my research because, by way of an art history of Warhol's sculptural output, what I attempt to provide here is also a picture — a portrait — of Warhol's place in art history that goes beyond two dimensions.

1

Locating the Sculptural

The paintings of Campbell's soup cans brought Warhol his big break. They were his first major multiples and the single subject of his first Pop exhibition at the Ferus Gallery in the summer of 1962. They helped to define, and still define, Warhol as a Pop artist, both in his own right and, crucially at the time, as distinct from Roy Lichtenstein with whom he had previously shared the subject of comic book characters. The paintings were presented either on one canvas, as in *200 Campbell's Soup Cans* (1962), or in tight series in which the key variable is the flavour of the soup. In either, there is no other sign of life, no other relationship to the world. They exist in an abstract space, with no shadows and no sense of human scale, thus they speak of a larger condition of alienation from the objects of our experience and hence from the embodied, sensory self. They are signs more than objects: detached, immaterial, ungrounded. And, more than any other images in the history of art, they have become mascots for theories of the post-modern, a theoretical territory in which Warhol's work more generally has become a touchstone. In these paintings, commodity fetishism powerfully unifies sign and object in a new immaterial hyper-reality. But we might also say that this sense of abstraction also suggests a reconfiguration of painting under the serial and uniform order of the mass produced commodity object. Thus, painting too comes to be at a remove from itself, it becomes 'painting': a frame within a frame from which the commodity appears.

Yet, in these works that reject painting as a harmonious space of mediation between the subject and the world, there is an uncanny sense of substanceless presence: they are like ghosts. As Benjamin Buchloh writes, 'these paintings are imbued with an eerie concreteness and corporeality, which in 1961 had distinguished Piero Manzoni's *Merda d'artista*. But Warhol differs here [...] in that he transferred the universality of corporeal experience onto the paradoxical level of mass-cultural specificity.[1] This aesthetic—what Roland Barthes calls a 'residue of a subtraction' of the individual—stands in contrast to Abstract Expression's earlier anthropomorphism.[2] These paintings mark the beginning of a moment of wider resistance to the centring and reflection of the subject that Abstract Expressionism might be seen to stand for. And yet, in Warhol's early Pop Art, what goes hand in hand with a refusal to situate the subject within the image is the idea that the images, as Emile de Antonio said of *Coca-Cola*, represent 'us': modern subjects of consumerism.

But what of works from the same year such as *Big Torn Campbell's Soup Can (Pepper Pot)* (plate 1.1)? In marked contrast to their more famous counterparts Warhol also painted images of soup cans that are recognisably from life, appearing as if happened upon at the kitchen counter, half ultra-modern still life, half dishevelled object of desire. This proximity to life suggests that these cans are not just real *things*, but that there is, or might be, a subject with whom their reality was interconnected. In one painting from this series, a can opener hovers in position, as if guided by an invisible hand. In another, a pencil and watercolour study, the can is used to house a wodge of dollar bills. If this early series of paintings and drawings of soup cans imply a ready consumer, we, of course, know who that was. According to David Bourdon's biography of Warhol, 'Warhol's mother habitually served Campbell's soup at home, and Andy grew up on the product.'[3]

Beneath the labels in a few of the torn soup can paintings (particularly *Big Torn Soup Can Pepper Pot* and *Vegetable Beef*, both 1962) the silvery surface of the tin has been rendered by a marbleising technique. It suggests a reflective surface that can carry images by itself like a mirror but its messy, going-no-where grey also provides a striking contrast to the regal red of the label and the bold shapes of its letters. If the side of the can could be considered a mirror surface, one could say that it bears images as a consequence of its materiality, while at the same time the label is just barely material as a consequence of its image needing somewhere to be. There is a state of dissolution and fragility in this painting then, a sense that painting itself is unravelling and rent. Work backwards and re-fuse the two elements that Warhol has drawn apart, and painting as it was to earlier generations of painters is regained: the duality of material self-sameness and cultural signifier in a single whole. But, with the development of his paintings of factory-fresh cans, supermarket shelf cans, and the whole-scale introjection of the commodity sign into the space of painting, there was no going back.

As the torn and used can works were developed in parallel with the 'supermarket shelf' images of soup cans, we have to be careful about inferring that the more famous paintings emerged after the traces of thingness, use and the subject had been cast aside. David Joselit's excellent analysis avoids this kind of storytelling. For him the tearing of the image from the object in *Big Torn Campbell's Soup Can* only illustrates the trauma more obliquely inferred by the others: 'Even in ostensibly straight-forward works like his 1962 series of Campbell's soup cans,' he writes, 'the commodity is divided against itself.'[4] Joselit sees in both types of painting the same tension between figure and ground, image and object that map on the 'extra-optical dimensions within a postmodern media-saturated consumer society.'[5] However, even as equivalent, there is left the question of what to do with what has been left out by the shifting framework that the commodity has brought on representation. If painting as it was is torn apart, what can one say of the scraps? In these less famous works, the shadows, as it were, of the paintings of 'clean' soup cans, the capacity of painting to contain and construe aesthetic value seems to have been made vulnerable, in parallel with—perhaps even as a consequence of—the defaced can's own uncertain status with regard to value.

In these cases it is sculpture that emerges as the conceptual container for this matter, the ravaged paper and the stripped or spent cans. These disassembled components, and what Warhol did with them, become an important counterpoint to Warhol's painting as it evolved. The paintings of used and abused cans are not sculptures, of course, but if painting becomes something else at this moment, taking on the order of the mass produced commodity image, they are not that. Outside of the perimeters set by the multiple, mechanically reproduced image and the commodity object, these works are defined by a condition of negation that links them to the three-dimensional work that follows in this chapter. If the torn cans have gone through a transformation that, in their depiction, metaphorically can be seen as also between painting and sculpture, what follows is a consideration of sculptures actually produced by similar kinds of transformation. Processes of crushing and crumpling especially are means through which sculpture emerges out of image space in the work that will be featured in this chapter. Yet, in this work, it is not so much the sculpture's materiality that comes to be emphasised—images also require material supports—but an inability to conform to the conditions of production that define the modern image and the modern commodity. In the example of the paintings of the soup cans, this non-conformity is also the state in which the subject—and traditional ideas about artistic production and expression—reside, while the image becomes a representation of forces which are ostensibly antithetical to these. In this chapter I show that, in examples of Warhol's sculpture and in a history of significant practices that followed, the analysis of Warhol's series of *Soup Cans* helps to reveal something about the condition of sculpture today but only in so far as this stretches our understanding of what the sculptural is 'after Warhol'.

***

In the book *Unseen Warhol* (1996), Benjamin Liu and John O'Connor, who both worked for Warhol in the 1980s, talk to (among many others) Vito Giallo and Nathan Gluck, two of Warhol's early associates from the 1950s. In their interviews with Liu and O'Connor (whose combined voice is italicised in the following conversation), both men describe Warhol's first solo show in 1954 at the Loft Gallery, run by Giallo and Jack Wolfgang Beck. In their accounts of this exhibition, a sense of the young Warhol as radically innovative hinges upon an idea of the sculptural nature of his work. Beginning with Giallo:

> [Warhol] would start with a square piece of paper. He would take the paper and he would fold it, and somehow he got a lot of pyramids out of it. Then he would open it up one way or

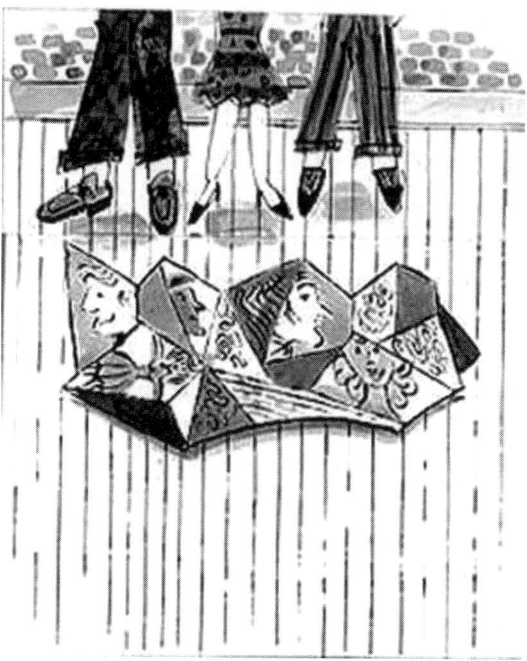

Fig. 1.1. Vito Giallo, *Andy Warhol's Folded Paper Show*, pen and ink on Strathmore paper, 2013. Courtesy of Vito Giallo.

another, and some pyramids would be sticking out. Next, he would do drawings of heads and people on parts of the pyramids, and he did a lot of marbleizing, oil on water. Finally, he'd hang them up so that they were sticking out from the wall. We used pushpins to hang them up, and they kept falling down; I must have picked those pieces up a hundred times.

O'Connor / Lui: *What happened to all of them?*

I think he threw them all out. He never sold anything at the gallery. Very few of us did. But I know nobody who even looked at this show. I thought it was fascinating. I was so amazed. It was his turn to do a one-man show, and I thought it would be drawings and paintings, something straightforward. And then when these things came in I was just shocked.[6]

Gluck's account of the same show differs slightly, describing a more forthright artistic statement:

Andy did these strange marbled things, and then he crumpled them up and just left them around on the floor.
They were on the floor? I thought they were pinned to the wall but they kept falling to the floor.
Oh, that's a theory. But I thought Andy had installed them on the floor. Well, maybe by the time you came to see the show it was all on the floor.[7]

Warhol was a commercial illustrator when he displayed these home-made marbleised patterned papers, approximately 12 in number, to which he had added figures in ink.[8]

I am going to consider Giallo's as the fuller account here, as he remembers pinning the drawing/sculptures up 'a hundred times', but I think it is also important to include that of Gluck (who in the end concedes it might have been the case that the work originated on the wall) because it gives a sense of the impact the work made on the gallery visitor.

According to Giallo, the intention of this exhibition had been to showcase Warhol's dainty, folded and illustrated papers. However, in the event these intricate wall-mounted drawings, on folded, coloured paper, kept coming unstuck and, after several attempts to re-mount the work, Warhol instructed Giallo to leave them on the floor where they were trampled by visitors who did not realise that they were standing on 'the work'. The exhibition was thus re-conceptualised and became known, retrospectively, as the *Crumpled Paper Show*. In a recent correspondence with the Warhol scholar Thomas Kiedrowski, Giallo made a drawing of how he remembered the work on the floor of the Loft Gallery, prior to being stood on (fig. 1.1). The example of the *Crumpled Paper Show* places some of the tensions between registers of commodity, image and material object, identified in the paintings and drawings of soup cans, in an explicitly sculptural context. In doing so, the work presents sculpture as a category for what begins as image but which cannot be withheld by it. It exists outside of the frameworks of both the image and of traditional sculpture. The expectations of the viewers, the chance event of the work's falling to the floor and the reimaginging of the work after the event are what truly establish this work as sculpture, I propose, rather than its mere material heaviness and three-dimensional qualities. It is as if the work's irreconcilability with the condition of the image, rather than the heaviness of the paper, results in the collapse onto the floor, and it is only there that the work is reconceived. The *Crumpled Paper Show* became the work it did by being made in the moment of its unmaking, the authorial touch so small a thing as to virtually be a nothing, produced by Warhol finally *not* allowing the work to be restored to the wall and considered a 'made' entity. Yet this artistic touch, so different from what distinguished his work as an advertising illustrator, is a crucial part of the picture of sculpture I am presenting. And what it lacks in craft it makes up for as a gesture. Like 'scrunched', the term 'crumpled' calls to mind rejected bits of paper tossed into wastepaper baskets. It is suggestive of frustration, dismissal and rejection; it is 'abstract expressionist' in a very literal sense. If this process of naming and reconstituting the work in retrospect is as determined as I am claiming, Warhol might have had some art-historical inspiration for doing so. In 1953—the year before the *Crumpled Paper Show*—he is likely to have seen Marcel Duchamp's *"Dada: 1916–1923," Sidney Janis Gallery, New York, April 15 to May 9, 1953* at the show of the same title (fig. 1.2). This work consisted of the poster for the coming exhibition scrunched tightly into a ball.[9] Like *Crumpled Paper Show* Duchamp's crumpling is equally an abstraction, an act against a previously established legibility that occurs in the poster's transition from two dimensions to three. Likewise, there is a play with tenses in these works: if Warhol's is partially a retelling of the story, Duchamp make a gesture of denouncement using the material announcing his exhibition, and does so from a point before the event.

In Warhol's work more broadly, we are faced with incidences of abstraction where in paintings and prints, for example, images are transferred off-register or else mis-register completely. We might think of the *Crumpled Paper Show* in these terms, as failing to register both on the wall where they were placed and with the gallery visitors as scrunches of intricately produced waste-paper on the floor. Likewise, in Warhol's early films, such as *Kitchen* and *Vinyl* (both 1965), accidents create dramatic moments of discord, shocking viewers out of their lulled states when carelessly placed bodies and objects interact on the screen. These moments occur, for example, when a drink falls on the floor or a harsh sound interrupts a scene from off-set. In Peter Gidal's words, in these moments 'gestural super-reality converges with overtones of dada-absurdity [...] overpowering the visual and aural concentration of the viewer.'[10] The sense is that, much like the paper

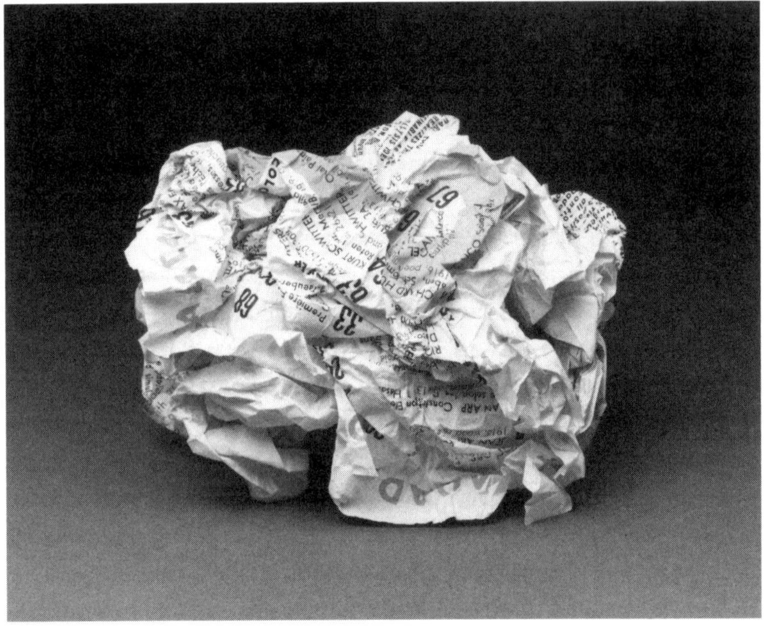

Fig. 1.2. Marcel Duchamp,*"Dada: 1916-1923," Sidney Janis Gallery, New York, April 15 to May 9, 1953*, 1953. Letterpress exhibition catalogue and poster designed by Duchamp; crumpled version. Philadelphia Museum of Art, Gift of Jacqueline, Paul, and Peter Matisse in memory of their mother, Alexina Duchamp, 1998-4-49. Copyright: © Artists Rights Society (ARS), New York / ADAGP, Paris / Estate of Marcel Duchamp.

crumples, also a kind of decoration, through accidents and moments of discontinuity props and materials that would otherwise be backdrop insist on their status as contingent, affective and as objects. As has already been considered regarding the paintings of soup cans, here too (and as I will argue of his sculpture and installation more broadly) Warhol can be seen as reversing the figure-ground relationships that supported ideology.

Between Gidal's analysis of the occurrences of accidents in Warhol's film and *The Crumpled Paper Show* there are, however, important distinctions. If the accidents on set shock, the crumples go unnoticed. And while we might think of both incidences in terms of a reality, in defiance of the framework of representation, there is also a sense in which the crumples are abstract, indecipherable, and outside of the awareness and expectations of the viewer. In 1983, Warhol made two quite different sculptures both called *Abstract Sculpture* and, as their shared title suggests, they help us get a better sense of what Warhol understood by this term and what its relationship to sculpture was.

The first of these *Abstract Sculptures* I want to consider in tandem with another work, *Crushed Newspaper*, also 1983. These two works, in turn, are tied to Warhol's long retinue of hand painted and silkscreened images of newspaper pages. *Abstract Sculpture's* content is from the *New York Post* and *Crushed Newspaper's* is from the *Daily News*, both date from October 1983 (24 October and 19 October respectively). These works stand out from the series of newspaper works to which they belong as they are printed onto sheets of Mylar, the same shiny material used for Warhol's *Silver Clouds*, whereas their partner works are prints on canvas. In the case of *Crushed Newspaper*, the Mylar has been tightly crumpled—crushed—and has then been flattened out for display. *Abstract Sculpture*, however, has been crumpled and has then been mounted in a Plexiglas case so that the contorted sheet stands up and the silvery surface of its verso can be seen from the other side of the translucent case (plate 1.2). This crumple could well have been done in one movement, exactly the same gesture with which one would discard any sheet of paper, but the effect here is to make a dramatic sculptural object.[11] Looking at *Abstract Sculpture* from the reverse side of the vitrine-like case, we indeed see inside an abstract sculpture, a distorting and contorted reflective surface. In three dimensions, it replays the way Warhol traditionally accompanied his silkscreen paintings with equal sized monochromes, producing diptychs for which he could charge more. Warhol's 'blanks' have been considered by Benjamin Buchloh as a correlative of the theme of the off-register, writing that both techniques 'identify with failures or resistances to comply with the rigors of the symbolic order.'[12] In both *Abstract Sculpture* as well as *Crushed Newspaper* this disruption is carried further by the action that has obscured the newspaper text. This is also true of Warhol's earlier *Death and Disaster* works. Yet between these works and the *Death and Disaster* paintings, there are parallels beyond the blanks that accompany the printed portion of the work. These also reproduced images from news media and the content is as grisly as *Suicide*, *Race Riot* or *Ambulance Disaster*. *Abstract Sculpture* shows page three of the *New York Post* after a terrorist attack on a Beirut US Marine barracks in October 1983. According to the paper, 172 had been confirmed dead but the headline announces that number could 'top' 200.

Crushed Newspaper, like *Race Riot*, refers to another racially motivated act of terrorism by the state against its own citizenry, in this case the student, artist and close friend of Keith Haring, Michael Stewart. Stewart was brutally murdered while in police custody in September 1983. A report of his death in the *Daily News* newsprint, dwarfed by an advertisement for a sale at a clothes retailer.[13] That these crumpled works signify angry, dismayed responses to the news that they contain adds another dimension to the understanding of their status as off-register and abstract. In the case of *Crushed Newspaper*, Warhol's reaction does not cohere with the rational order that allots the announcement of Gimbel's sale a dominant space on the page. In *Abstract Sculpture* it competes with the legibility of the print by remaining in 3D.

Stewart's death is also the subject of the other sculpture called *Abstract Sculpture* made around this time (plate 1.3). The work is a sizeable assemblage that relies for its structure on a large canvas that had been smashed up and then fixed into place. The work thus reflects, in different media, the action of crumpling or screwing-up that occurs in the Mylar works. On the structure, multiple smaller canvases by other artists have been attached. *Abstract Sculpture* was produced in collaborations with Jean-Michel Basquiat and Italian painter Francesco Clemente between 1983–4. Basquiat was already working on a series of large collaboration paintings in Warhol's studio at this time. Two of Warhol's assistants, Jay Shriver and Agusto Bugarin both also played some part in creating this work. Italian painter Francesco Clemente and two of Warhol's assistants, Jay Shriver and Agusto Bugarin, all also played some part in creating this work.[14] Matt Wrbican has confirmed, however, that it was Warhol's idea to smash the large stretched canvas (a task Shriver and Bugarin undertook) commenting that this reflected both the violence of the police and the artists' anger. Basquiat, who also created *Defacement* (1983) in response to Stewart's death, was responsible for pouring pink paint all over the sculpture and Shriver attached smaller paintings to the larger canvas, including the same print of newspaper with the story of Stewart's death used for *Crushed Newspaper*. With at least three authors, this is a work of multiple points of view sutured together on a picture plane that is shattered and frozen.[15]

In the examples above, sculpture seems to emerge out of the practice of painting unable to accommodate or account for the relation between the artist and the subject matter. It becomes a platform and an answer to precisely the 'defacement' of reality that goes on in the media. Yet, as in the story of Stewart, the whitewash is equivalent to death and, in these works, Warhol's feeling about death's own abstraction is entwined with these ideas. Looking at other sources, for example *The Andy Warhol Diaries* (1989), there is a clear sense that death, for Warhol, was abstract. Over the pages of *The Diaries* he frequently cuts short his meditations on his own and others' mortality with the resigned and exasperated expression 'it's so abstract!'[16] As the 1980s proceed, and age, drug use and AIDS claim more of the lives of those he knew, death features more frequently, and we are confronted with a paradox: death seems to become *more* abstract as it becomes more of a reality for Warhol and those around him. Crumpling up the Mylar newspaper as if to throw it away can therefore be read as physically acting out this attitude toward what one cannot get to grips with. It is the index of a process in which an abstract idea becomes an abstract form. Yet, at every step of that process, there is an accompanying and very explicit reality, one that can be quantified ('172 dead') and preserved. Indeed, perhaps the crucial aspect of the reality of these works is their relation to their times. Warhol's work 'tells the time', reflecting the world and the people that surrounded him. The two works called *Abstract Sculpture* are exemplary of the understanding of sculpture proposed in this chapter: a modality, in dialectic with image culture through forms of negation such as accidents and acts of destruction, that themselves have a relationship to the subject which can be both abstract while, at the same time, realist.

If Warhol's *Abstract Sculptures* refuse the structures of value inscribed by the institution of visibility and, more directly, the institutions of the media, gallery and the artworld that hold them in place, he is not alone in exploring the alternatives. Nor has art history neglected to consider the metaphorics through which these possibilities might be understood. We might, for example, consider Briony Fer's conception of 'the unmade' discussed in relation to Eva Hesse's studiowork: part-productions to accompany the part-object, and engaged in the metaphorics of the cast and cast-off which we might easily apply to Warhol's expressive, and expressively passive, gestures above.[17] However, Warhol's place in this history of sculpture has not been fully evaluated, nor have these themes been fully thought through with regard to his work. In itself this reflects a further tendency to think of sculpture as anomalous within discussions of image production and circulation, ones which Warhol's painting work has otherwise been taken to illustrate perfectly.

Yet in a history only recently coming into relief, for artists working with image production, reproduction and circulation technologies, sculpture has been shown to be a vital context for the understanding of their work. Mel Bochner's *Color Crumples* (1966), for example, demonstrate for Fer how 'conceptually close' Eva Hesse and Bochner were at the time.[18] In these, and Bochner's later *Surface Dis/Tension* (1968), photography's readability and reliability came into question. Photographs of crumpled grids cut to shape produce the illusion of three dimensions, especially when re-photographed. Yet, though these works share a formal vocabulary with Warhol's Mylar works, perhaps we might consider them closer in kind to the paintings of torn soup cans where the sculptural is suggested in the unravellings of the image's relation to the certainties of mechanical reproduction. Luke Skrebowski writes, in the context of 'photography after conceptual art', that: 'Bochner's early concern with the "phenomenology of the photograph" tipped over into its deconstruction, its unmaking, through a process that included the manipulation of the crumpled, sculptural surface of the image.'[19] Unlike Bochner, however, Warhol's experiments should not be described as a concerted 'manipulation'. Instead, a much greater sense of vulnerability, to violation and to accident, characterises his approach, precisely as it does the subject of the work. To this extent, Warhol's work is in kind with more recent artists who have explored the failures of mechanical reproduction. As slips of registration are increasingly rarely made by image technologies, they, symbolically at least, become more fraught, as, at the same time, these the automated processes become more enmeshed with our sense of self.

With Warhol's folded and crumpled papers in mind we might think of Tillmans's *Lighter* series, beginning in 2005 (plate 1.4). These are photographic prints of abstract 'colour fields' produced by being 'carefully folded', 'crumpled' and 'buckled' and put through the process of development variously before and after this treatment.[20] Like Warhol's crumpled floor sculptures, they began with an accident, in this case a printer jam, producing what would normally (or certainly in the eyes of the printer) have been considered a reject. This notion of the detritus of image production processes or exchange frameworks is an important model through which to view Tillmans' experiments with medium, which might also include Tillmans's *Silver* works, beginning in the late 1990s. These are prints made with the hazardous waste products of chromogenic processing, containing sediment impurities and tiny particles of other prints that would normally cause imperfections in development. Hence, they present not only that which is the fallout of the production of the image, but also that which both constitutes and obscures the image.

Displayed in Plexiglas boxes, the *Lighters* are uncontestably abstract, sculptural works, as well as works which echo closely the arrangement in Warhol's *Abstract Sculpture*. Tillmans describes the *Lighters* as a form of 'concrete' photography which act as antidotes to our inundation with images and to what Tillmans describes as a 'compulsion' to represent.[21] Yet, at the same time, the work might be seen to extend the photographic process into the gallery, the Perspex cases refracting and bending new light onto surfaces of the print. Variations in the visual qualities of the work are now as much to do with what Tillmans has emphasised as the 'real' conditions of shade and exposure caused by the work's relief. This conception of realism as non-representational, indeed as strategically posited against representation, disrupts the contemporary ease with which pictures are produced and disseminated. This is not about the photograph considered as a discrete object, however, but rather an emphasis on that object's contingency in contrast with the controlled conditions in which the image tends to be received and which it itself represents. Tillmans' folds and crumples leave the picture open, they allow for a porosity whereby the influence of light, which, for a limited period, 'shapes' the photographic image, now also continues to do so in the gallery and in three dimensions. It is notable that for a long time Tillmans did not frame his work and mostly still does not. The frame protects the image from any risk to its value, but also the value of the cultural norms and commercial properties it is supposed to uphold. Like Warhol therefore, whose act of crumpling was an 'answer' in another register to what he read in the newspaper, Tillmans's work dwells on that which the image refuses by presenting and celebrating the waste products of the image economy. In opposition to the frame and its function of exclusion, Tillmans engages in an ethical practice of inclusivity.

Also related to Warhol through a shared sensitivity to the off-register are the scanned and printed paintings by Wade Guyton which similarly draw attention to the fallibility of the transfer of images. Again, Guyton works with (or against) the photomechanical printer, neglecting it, leaving things to chance, dragging the prints out rather than letting them fall. 'Tracks' in the print, strips of extraneous pigment and absences of pigment reveal the weakness of the idea of a direct transfer of images, and emphasise the physical process of the paper being rolled out. Scale is clearly important for this work, in Guyton's later works, huge scale threatens the status of painting itself, something in Chapter 4 I will argue Warhol also set out to do with *Shadows* (1979). In conversation with Rachel Kushner, Guyton, dismissing installation or architecture as alternative categories, agreed that the work reveals itself to be 'sculpture in a photographic skin. In drag as painting.'[22]

For these more recent artists, technologies of image reproduction are less likely to 'screw up'. Today the state of the image—which Roland Barthes described as a 'floating chain of signifieds' and which Warhol, as Barthes acknowledged, did so much to bring to our attention—has entered a state of liquid dissolution, superseded as digital has superseded analogue.[23] No longer does the image swim in the fixing solution of the darkroom; information streams are now constituted by waves of images. Discussing the work of contemporary artist Kelley Walker, Scott Rothkopf has written: 'images today are never really ours, just slippery emblems that keep moving and morphing as they pass from one incarnation to the next.'[24]

Neither object nor image, sculpture emerges in the examples above as something incompatible with the totalising register of the image. It represents contingency and destabilisation that threatens both modern production and distribution, and suggests a collapse of the distance of both to the modern subject. In the contemporary artist Seth Price's work, this contingency is harnessed as a form of resistance in a strategy of 'dispersion'. Dispersion is a system of re-circulation, diverting content from established circuits of distribution online.[25] As with Warhol's *Crumpled Paper Show* and Tillmans's folds, Price's sculptural work also expresses an idea of fall-out, but what spills out of the screen in Price's work is an abjection that is far more integral to the structures of circulation themselves. An important example is his *Hostage Video Still with Time Stamp* of 2005 (plate 1.5). In this series of works, images are screen-printed on what he describes as 'Mylar crumples'. These sheets of transparent plastic carry downloaded low-res website images of the decapitation of a Jewish-American businessman by Islamist militants, which were at first distributed online but became subject to censor. When exhibited, the rolls of Mylar are fitted with grommets which allow the sheets to be attached to the wall, although all that is specified in the work's provision to galleries is that the arrangement of the sheets should further distort the image, hence their being crumpled. It is important to Price that Mylar is also the material used to protect books and paper for archival storage, so that this highly sculptural matter, sometimes left as huge bolts of free-standing material, is made from a kind of frame or protective barrier against damage that might occur over time. This idea of preservation contrasts with the image's relation to a 'live' image economy through which the censored image is eroded into near inde-cipherability.[26] On the floor, a place all of the work in this chapter is in dynamic with, Price's sculptures represent the fallout from the contem-porary image-frame of mass circulation on the World Wide Web, yet his is a strategy of reclaiming a relation to content from media similar to Warhol's reaction to newspaper reports in the eighties; ones whose expression also took the form of sculpture.

We might think of these artists, dragging their work into the world, as contesting the frameworks constituted by the delimiting structure of techno-corporate entities, of media and the category of the image bounded to these. As with Warhol's paintings of torn soup cans, the work in this chapter refers to something cast off or cast out of those established relays of consumption and receptivity. In doing so it confounds the ways in which we engage with work through traditional categories and conventional understandings. Warhol's earliest sculpture, and work featured here that echoes it, locates an institutional boundary that becomes a platform for critique. In the following chapter, the literal boundaries, this time of the gallery, become this platform.

2

'Sublime but compulsive negation':
Brillo Boxes

> The most striking opening of that period was definitely Andy's
> Brillo Box show [...] You could barely get in, and it was like
> going through a maze. The rows of boxes were just wide enough
> to squeeze your way through.
>
> (Robert Indiana)[1]

The *Brillo Boxes* had their gallery premiere at a show of box art at the
Dwan Gallery in Los Angeles in February 1964. But it was their exhibition
en masse, at Eleanor Ward's Stable Gallery between 21 April and 9 May
that year, which constituted the next big step in Warhol's art career. It is to
this exhibition that Robert Indiana refers in the quotation above and on
which my analysis will focus in this chapter. As well as the famous *Brillo
Boxes*, the work on show at this exhibition, titled *The Personality of the
Artist*, included facsimiles of packaging for Motts Apple Juice, Del Monte
Peach Halves, Kellogg's Cornflakes, Heinz Tomato Ketchup and Campbell's
Tomato Juice. There were also earlier, slightly smaller, yellow *Brillo Boxes*
(1964) on show, although these were far fewer in number. The total num-
ber of boxes on show was between 300 and 400.

Combining the technical developments of his silkscreen painting with
his obsession with common, all-American packaging, in many ways Warhol's
Brillo Boxes were the pinnacle of his painting up to that point, as much as

they introduced a new sculptural dimension to his art. Unlike other silkscreen works of this time, Warhol made sure that the *Brillo Boxes* were perfectly in-register, and touched up fine details with a brush; a return to the 'clean' commodity aesthetic that made for painstaking work.[2] Indeed, these sculptures emerged directly out of investigations connected with the early Campbell's soup paintings: the idea for painted boxes originated with Warhol's 1962 *Campbell's Soup Box*, an attempt to extend his stacked, multiple soup cans into three dimensions by painting them onto a wooden box (plate 2.1). Warhol wanted to give the illusion of a perfectly cuboid stack of cans. Looking at the top of this box sculpture, one sees a grid of silver discs—the lids of the cans—while the side view looks very much like one of the two-dimensional stacked soup can paintings. At this time, Warhol's close friend Ed Wallowitch was photographing stacked and variously arranged supermarket goods.[3] Therefore, like the work discussed in the previous chapter, this was sculpture formed in dynamic with seamlessly readable and reproducible images: a painting in sculptural dimensions, both traditions subordinate to the powerful new realism that Wallowitch's photographs and Warhol's work pursued. Warhol's evaluation of the box painting was that it was a failure, that it 'looked funny because it didn't look real.'[4]

In the same year as *Campbell's Soup Box*, Warhol experimented with a series of silkscreen works, *Statue of Liberty* and *Optical Car Crash* (plate 2.2), which were also attempts to create new realistic, three-dimensional effects in paint. In these works, an illusionistic three-dimensional field is produced through Warhol's classic operation of 'mis-registration'. In order to produce this optical effect, the image on the canvas was deconstructed into two off-set, chromatically opposite coloured images. Special 3D viewing glasses isolate each image behind the correspondingly coloured lens and the whole thing is then reconstructed in the mind's eye where it appears in 3D.[5] Like these 3D-effect 'optical' paintings, and the rather less interesting multicoloured *Mona Lisa* (1963), but unlike most other paintings of this period, the *Brillo Boxes*, also 3D paintings of sorts, were made using multiple screens of different colours, one after the other, rather than the standard single screen, usually black, used in most of the silkscreen work at this time.

The *Brillo Boxes*, therefore, were a continuation of Warhol's investigations in painting. One key difference between them and the other painting work, however, is their lack of any relation to an accompanying abstract space. It is in such a space, for example, that the *Campbell's Soup Cans* seem to float, and in other work is provided by the blank colour-coordinated canvases that accompanied his silkscreens. Warhol said these blanks enabled him to charge more money for the work but if, in this case, Warhol's blanks represent the empty value-space of art and, indeed, art's empty values, it will be my argument in this chapter that the importance of the *Brillo Boxes* was that they cast the gallery in this role.[6] And, elaborating on this analogy, if *Campbell's Soup Cans* draw a parallel between the artwork and the popular commodity, Warhol's packaging boxes draw a parallel with the packaging in which we find the work of art.

The Artworld

It was indeed as the location of something abstract and valuable that Arthur C. Danto considered the gallery space in his 1964 article 'The Artworld', published in the *Journal of Philosophy*. And it was precisely because of how real Warhol's *Brillo Boxes* appeared that Danto looked to something more abstract than the visual object to define the important leap in art history that he felt the boxes brought about. In his article, the philosopher argued that the question 'what is art?' could no longer be answered in terms of aesthetic attributions of likeness or representation. The *Brillo Boxes*' irreducible sameness with their commonplace counterpart, for Danto, could only be resolved by the understanding that one existed in the 'real world' and the other in the 'artworld'. And it was the work's self-conscious reference to its place there that, from then on, would define what art was, according to Danto. But 'artworld' did not mean, exactly, Eleanor Ward's Stable Gallery. Instead, for Danto the artworld is 'a theory that takes [Warhol's *Brillo Box*] up into the world of art and keeps it from collapsing into the real object which it is.'[7] Suggesting some alternative ways of presenting a Brillo box as art, Danto writes:

> But the question is, What makes art? And why need Warhol *make* these things anyway? Why not just scrawl his signature across one? Or crush one up and display it as *Crushed Brillo Box* ('A protest against mechanisation [...]') or simply a Brillo carton as *Uncrushed Brillo Box* ('A bold affirmation of the plastic authenticity of industrial [...]')?[8]

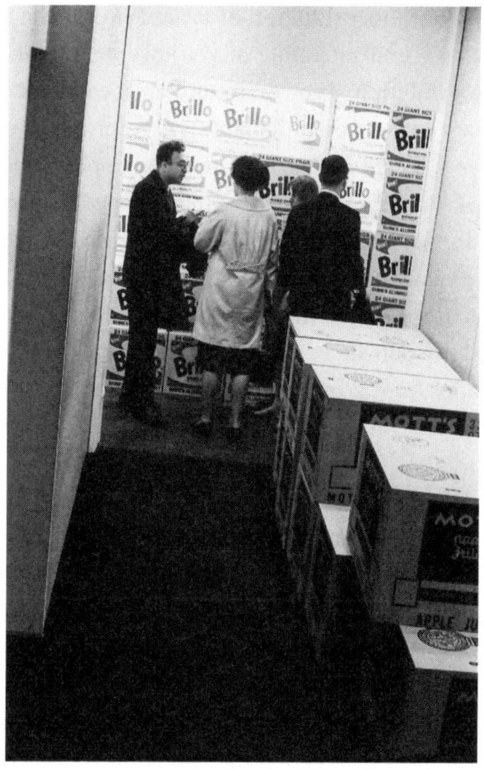

Fig. 2.1. Billy Name, *Stable Gallery (Wall of* Brillo Boxes), 1964. Courtesy of Billy Name.

Danto's crushed Brillo box more or less outlines the argument of the previous chapter: the prevailing 'reality' of the mechanisation and reproducibility of the visual world might induce artists to operate against it, concentrating instead on what falls from circulation. His crushed Brillo box is like the paper crumples of Warhol, Price and Tillmans: crumpled and crushed matter caught in a dynamic with mechanical reproduction. But Danto does not dwell on these manoeuvres; instead, he is more concerned with art as a category that belongs, not so much to the object, as to the world apart in which the object is placed. Thus, he ponders the *Brillo Boxes* as he finds them: art objects that seem indistinguishable from pieces of commercial trash, yet with entirely different values attached to them.

Like Danto, Warhol's exhibition of *Brillo Boxes* at the Stable Gallery is vital for my own understanding of Warhol's work. And, likewise, my reading of the exhibition revolves around an idea of the artworld as a conceptual space that, at this moment, was reconceived in a couple of important ways— including Danto's—in order to protect its values from what Danto calls 'collapse'. But, in complete opposition to Danto, what I will suggest in this chapter is that Warhol's work, far from helping to consolidate the values that Danto scrambles to protect, instead brilliantly exposed the territorialism of those who associated art's value with themselves, above those outside in the real world. Thus, I will draw very different conclusions from Danto about Warhol's boxes—not least that they should primarily be considered as representational sculpture rather than conceptual works.

Having assumed that the *Brillo Boxes* are identical to their real-world counterparts, Danto suggests that Warhol's re-pose the question 'what is art?' by bracketing what he calls the 'red herring' of visuality. However, once he has established for himself that the answer to the question 'what is art?' has to do with the way the work itself rhetorically asks that question, he then lets visual concerns seep back into his account. 'Why live with dull anaesthetic objects? Why not objects as beautiful as *Brillo Boxes*?' he asks.[9] Further, in more direct contradiction of his thesis, Danto describes the moment he first saw the boxes *in situ* and was struck by how real they seemed, 'piled high, in neat stacks, *as in* the stockroom of the supermarket'.[10] He continues:

> [Warhol] […] piles them high, leaving a narrow path; we tread our way through the smooth opaque stacks and find it an unsettling experience, and write it up as the closing in of consumer products, confining us as prisoners […] true, we don't say these things about the stockboy. But then a stockroom is not an art gallery.[11]

The idea that the gallery had been transformed into a warehouse or stockroom was common in reviews at the time and Warhol intended precisely this effect (figs. 2.1 and 2.2). The installation followed the development of environment works such as Allan Kaprow's *Yard* (1961) and Claes Oldenburg's *Store* (1961) and, in the October following *The Personality of*

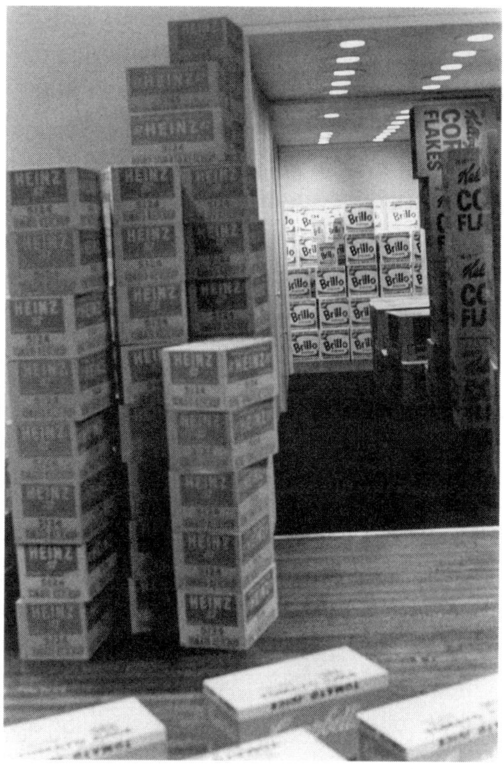

Fig. 2.2. Billy Name, *Stable Gallery*, 1964. Courtesy of Billy Name.

the Artist, the group exhibition *The American Supermarket*, which included Warhol's work alongside Oldenburg's, was held at the Blanchini Gallery. However, crucial to Danto's argument is the conviction that 'we cannot readily separate the Brillo cartons from the *gallery* they are in.'[12] Danto imagines a stockroom, not noticing that this accredits the *Brillo Boxes* with the very representational effects that he claims his paradigm shift has left behind.[13]

Anthony E. Grudin has, likewise, brought to our attention Danto's speculations on the impact of the arrangement and great number of the boxes, remarking that the Brillo box has undergone a 'sublime transfigura-tion' into an aesthetic object in Danto's description, only to be relocated (in the description already quoted above) in the 'stockroom' of Danto's imagination—complete with 'stock-boy'.[14] Grudin considers the *Brillo*

Box in an analysis of the iconography of Warhol's early Pop work, and has argued that 'class permeated Warhol's work during this period from two directions: it infused both its motifs (no matter how "American" or "universal" some of them may now appear) and the technique and style of their execution.'[15] This, Grudin points out, is something that is generally under-explored in writing on Warhol. In Danto's text, the 'stock-boy' walks among the gallery-goers like a ghost in Danto's mind, so that the classed subject that has been repressed by the elite artworld—more specifically by the new idea of the artworld as theorised by its philosopher—returns. Grudin goes on:

> The artworld, for Danto, was precisely the place where one could reflect upon modernity's indignities without having to consider the particular class positions that suffered these indignities most directly […] In his subsequent writings on Warhol, Danto has continued to deploy the first person plural as an alternative to class analysis or specificity. A recent monograph refers to 'the bare declarative aesthetic of the proletarian representations [Warhol] began to favor,' but then claims, pages later, that Warhol's 'mandate was: *paint what we are*.'[16]

We might say that it is not just reality from which Danto defends the idea of art, therefore, but a specific kind of social reality: a working class reality. Of course, superficially, Danto's words echo Emile de Antonio's response to the Coke bottle paintings discussed in the Introduction. According to Warhol's account in *POPism*, de Antonio also said that the 'clean' renditions represented 'who we are,' and dismissed Warhol's messier 'hash marked' painting of the same subject as 'shit'.[17] Yet, in Warhol's account, de Antonio is defending this sign of 'who we are' against artiness and affectation, precisely the opposite of Danto's argument about the *Brillo Boxes* which, first and foremost, is a defence of art as a category. If he, like de Antonio, is against the kind of packaging that art had come in up to that point, it is only because Danto, the philosopher, sees an opportunity to shift the terms of engagement with elite culture to those which were more compatible with his own expertise and better protected against devaluation. Juxtaposed against de Antonio's valorisation of common identities, Danto's philosophy of the *Brillo Box* evidently renders meaningless the space of social reality in which those identities are formed: he assumes that what is common has no value to protect. Danto uses the site of common identity to construct a new theory of art.

Elsewhere, Grudin focuses on Warhol's choice of brands as a subject for his works. He writes:

> The brand images Warhol borrowed—the so-called 'national brands', advertised and distributed nationwide under brands owned by their manufacturer or distributer, like Coca-Cola, Campbell's Soup, and Brillo—were, during the late 1950s and early 1960s, being targeted specifically at working class consumers.[18]

Thus, there was a concerted effort on Warhol's part to define a class identity through his choice of subject matter. In the case of the *Brillo Box*, that choice was made as early as 1962 while Nathan Gluck was still Warhol's assistant. This ties the work to the slightly earlier moment of activity to which Grudin predominantly refers. Gluck, Warhol's first assistant, recalls:

> When he wanted to do his box sculptures, he sent me across to the A&P and said, 'Get me some boxes.' I came back with things that were very artsy, maybe a Blue Parrot pineapple box or something like that. And he said, 'No, no, no. I want something very ordinary, very common.' So he went back and got a Brillo box.[19]

Warhol's choice of Brillo boxes itself, therefore, recalls the tension between the real world and the artworld. 'Arty' packaging boxes would have added to or reflected the value and values of the artworld. They would have fallen 'in line' when what Warhol wanted was the off-register effect of an object that was simultaneously utterly common and utterly other and alien: as if misplaced in the context of the artworld. In a review for *Arts Magazine* Sidney Tillim described this clash, brought about by the intrusion into the art gallery of the *Brillo Boxes*, as a work of 'sublime but compulsive negation' and as an 'ideological tour de force'.[20]

When stored in the Factory prior to exhibition, all the boxes had been kept wrapped in plastic and Warhol wore latex gloves during the installation of the work at the Stable Gallery. The layers of protective plastic and the gloves were used because Warhol wanted the *Brillo Boxes* to be pristine: an effect amplified by the fact that they are painted with white grounds, in contrast to the rather thick yellow and grey-brown of the other box sculptures with which they were exhibited. The Stable Gallery consisted of two rooms, one larger than the other, with an entrance corridor between these two rooms. For the exhibition, the boxes were arranged in hierarchy, with the simplest, largest and least contrasting—namely the *Kellogg's Cornflakes Boxes* and *Mott's Apple Juice Boxes*—piled in areas that were between the exhibition spaces in the gallery.[21] This narrowed passageway served to make visitors more aware that they were entering a particular space, one that they might perhaps have to push to gain entrance to. The bright, bold Brillo facsimiles—whose contents in the real world were designed to scrub pots and pans to a bright shine—were stacked floor-to-ceiling in the smaller room so densely that it would have been impossible to enter unencumbered. George Frei and Neil Printz state: 'it would have been impossible for a visitor to enter the south gallery where the *Brillo Boxes* were shown.'[22] This sense is clearly illustrated in Billy Name's photograph of gallery visitors confronted with a wall of *Brillo Boxes* (fig. 2.1). The effect of the arrangement was to create a tight aperture as one entered the gallery space as best one could (or more likely stood in the doorway), as well as to frame a view of the room's central space and starkly blank wall. Framed by the corridor, this room looked almost like one of Warhol's paintings. Again, as in the previous chapter, here we see sculpture in Warhol's work 'framing' or acting as a material support for the conventional space of representation by occupying the negative space surrounding it, especially the floor.

In photographs of the other, larger room, mock Del Monte boxes are stacked on the windowsill on one side and the floor is covered by *Campbell's Tomato Juice Boxes*, with a stack of *Heinz Tomato Ketchup Boxes* on the immediate right obscuring the view of one corner of the room. In the large quantities in which they were shown, these boxes brought disorder by impeding the movement of visitors around the gallery. George Frei and Neil Printz continue: 'even when Warhol chose not to mass them […] his sense of sculpture as a spatial obstruction is striking […] visitors were required to thread their way around the Campbell's boxes, along the perimeter of the gallery, or wedge themselves in the narrow intervals between them.'[23] However, although the obstruction to the flow of visitors was particularly bad in the room of *Campbell's Tomato Juice Boxes*, which had been laid out regimentally on the floor rather than stacked, this did not cause all the visitors to the gallery to behave in the way George Frei and Neil Printz describe. Ken Heyman's photograph from the opening night of *The Personality of the Artist* illustrates this point. Here, the *Campbell's Tomato Juice Boxes* are in disarray, having been kicked and shunted out of line (plate 2.3).

Michael J. Golec, who has written on the 'aesthetics, design and art' of the Brillo box, writes that 'Warhol predicted the disturbance of his installation such that it wrought a gap for social action that was at odds with the proper conduct of behaviour in the gallery.'[24] For Golec, like Grudin, the Brillo box represents the social order of the time. But, in Golec's very detailed dismantling of the Brillo design, what this represented is considered less in terms of class than in terms of the buttoned down and normative social conventions of the period. With its graphics evocative of a wiping action, Golec describes the design as 'normative in its diagrammatic prescription for the proper movements of the housewife.'[25] In the gallery, this normativity was redoubled by the almost radiant white brightness of the *Brillo Boxes*, their hierarchical relation to the other boxes, and the careful and precise layout of the exhibition overall, particularly in the Campbell's room. However, Golec argues that, although the Brillo box design unified the consumer and the commodity by incorporating the consumer's 'embodied articulations', Warhol also guaranteed the disruption of any scenario of identification in which the role of the consumer could be seamlessly articulated within the commodity.[26] Instead, Warhol's *Brillo Boxes* expose 'mass culture's systematic management of the public sphere […] and [they] thus constituted a refusal to concede to the disciplining pressures of the normal.'[27] He describes how, while the 'real' Brillo boxes 'overemphasised the "image of cleanliness" and […] rationalizing tendencies […,] Warhol took issue with these discourses as they resulted in disciplinary or normalising behaviour'.[28] This resistance against such tendencies in Warhol's re-presentation of the boxes was, for Golec, expressed through the eventual state of disorganisation of the work in the gallery space which Warhol had carefully orchestrated and that 'undermined the organisational nature of […] housekeeping and [its] mutual collusion with normative ideologies in the early 1960s'.[29] Here, it is the artworld, conceived as a sculptural space, which enables the prising apart of the synthesis between consumer and commodity in the Brillo design.

Golec's understanding of how the installation worked to produce social interaction fits with remarks that Warhol himself made about his early 'Minimalist' films which were made at the same time as the *Brillo Box* show were being planned. Like the extension of the box work into the viewing space of the gallery goer, the invasive and extended quality of the ultra-long running times of Warhol's 1963–5 movies prompted an activation on the part of the spectator that affected the experience of viewership. If, during the six-hour screening of *Sleep* (1963), for example, one should need to step out, or want to begin a conversation, or shift in one's seat in response to an ache, or simply start thinking about something else—even blink, those things become dramatic disruptions in contrast with the monotony of viewing what was very undramatically unfolding on the screen.[30] Indeed, in her article from 1966, Gretchen Berg reports Warhol saying that his early films, such as *Sleep* (1963), were made to 'help the audience get more acquainted with themselves. Usually when you go to the movies, you sit in a fantasy world, but when you see something that disturbs you, you get more involved with the people next to you.'[31] In Golec's reading this conversion of aesthetic engagement into social, and perhaps erotic, interaction is duplicated at the Stable Gallery. Golec describes a scenario whereby the installation created 'an alternate pattern of culture,' one where people became 'less interested in the art than in one another.'[32] The spectators disengage from a particular type of expected viewership (and, more broadly, subjecthood) as the *Brillo Boxes* disrupt and prohibit modes of viewing but, at the same time, these negotiations themselves become alternative patterns of culture based on the audience getting involved with each other. Turning away from the work, to the spectacle it has created in the gallery or cinema, provokes the heating up of relations among the viewers. Becoming diverted from the spectacle they, as Warhol described of *Sleep*, start getting 'involved with themselves'.

In these examples the activation of the spectator is directly related to a de-activation of the idea of the work as a source of particular kinds of aesthetic engagement. And, if the activation can be characterised as a heating up, it is appropriate that we speak of a cooling down, at this time, of the art object. This, indeed, was a *moment* of 'coolness', a word used to describe a new attitude, particularly in association with what was becoming known as Minimalism. In 1965, both Barbara Rose, in the essay 'ABC Art', and Irving Sandler, in the essay 'The New Cool Art', included Warhol in discussions of works by the likes of Donald Judd and Carl Andre. Coolness described the dis-engagement of the spectator but, at the same time, a new awareness of the environment, its inhabitants and the work's relation both to the space and the body. This new self-consciousness can be seen to be at play in both Danto and Golec's readings of the *Brillo Boxes*; in Warhol's statements about his intentions for his film; and in the early reception of Minimalism. Cultural engagement is figured as a kind of revolving door, feeding new patterns, a new aesthetic sensibility. In Golec's reading, he positions his aesthetic of sociality, and the idea of the spectator as a self-determining agent, at the threshold of spectacle. It is as if the spectator had rebounded from an art that refused to accommodate it.

If this was the case, by the end of the 1960s the new aesthetic attitude had had an effect on viewership. In another interview, published in 1969, Warhol again claimed that *Sleep* made audience members 'get involved with themselves and [...] create their own entertainment'.[33] But this time the claim followed the statement that 'when people go to a show today they're never involved anymore'. Although the two statements, from 1966 and from 1969, are very similar, they indicate a change in modes of reception and two very different models of viewership which we might characterise as having gone from 'hot' to 'cool'. In the first, the model is an ideal consumer of spectacle, tailor-made to 'sit in a fantasy world'. In the second, the viewer is already predisposed to be watching at a remove, to be not 'involved'. Comparing the two statements, we might say that while they are almost the same in relation to how Warhol's work 'disrupts' viewership, they are also opposed: in the first he sees the work as disengaging, but in the second he is actually attempting to create a kind of engagement. These statements chart a changing account of the sensibility of the cinemagoer (if not of the filmmaker, who, by the later point, was heading in a much more commercial direction). While, at first, the cinemagoer is an absorbed consumer of spectacle, the gloss then begins to wear off the familiar forms of mass entertainment.

Yet, if Warhol's films caused the spectator to revert to social interaction and Golec describes a similar situation that, at the Stable Gallery,

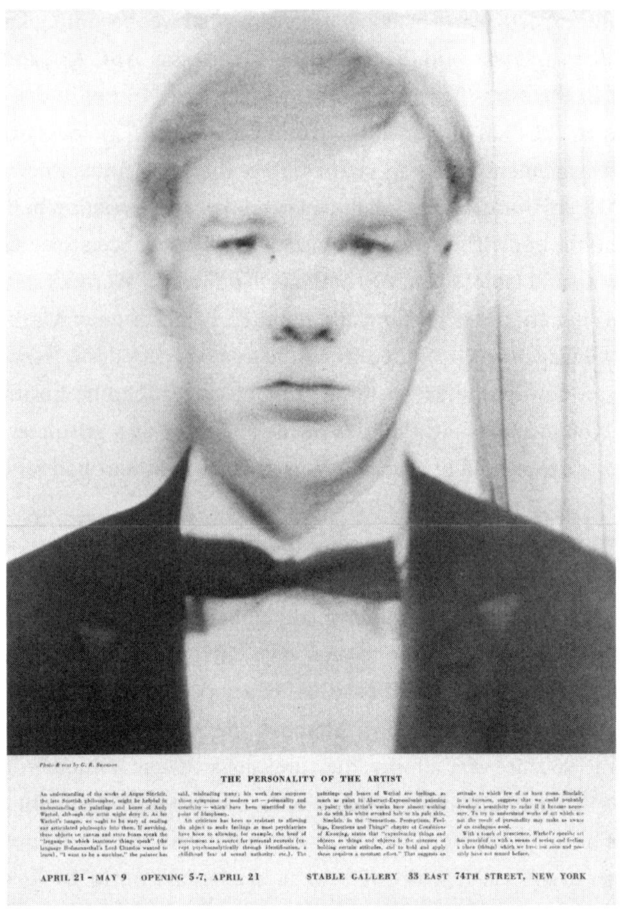

Fig. 2.3. Exhibition Announcement, *The Personality of the Artist / Stable Gallery, New York, 21 April–9 May, 1964*. Collection of The Andy Warhol Museum, Pittsburgh.

liberated the viewer from the constraints of social norms, I would suggest that, there, Warhol had another agenda, more cold than cool. Warhol's opening statement in *POPism* describes a diversion of aesthetic attention that compares to those described above: Pop Art 'took the inside and put it outside, took the outside and put it inside'.[34] But this also describes a reversal of the order of the artworld that literally took place with *The Personality of the Artist*. True to his claim that Pop put the inside on the outside (as well as putting the outside on the inside), the mass of boxes constrained viewers to the margins of the space they were accustomed to occupy while the *Brillo Boxes*—that 'great modern thing'—trespassed in its new setting. Gerard Malanga remembers the 'long line of people' queuing to get into the gallery: this was not necessarily indicative of especially high numbers of visitors that night—but rather a situation in which those that did turn up had trouble negotiating the entrance crammed with boxes.[35] In this scenario, Warhol's installation, far from acting on behalf of the gallery goer, inciting interpersonal relations and new patterns of culture, was instead impersonal and antisocial; a work of what Sidney Tillim described at the time as 'aggressive passivity'.[36] It is this attitude we see written on Warhol's face in the advertisement for the show. It made no reference to the boxes but, instead, had a page-sized photobooth mug shot of Warhol, beneath which was the title: *The Personality of the Artist* (fig. 2.3). The image has much in common with the police mug shots used for the work *Thirteen Most Wanted Men* (1964), which was contemporaneous with the Stable Gallery exhibition. Having been commissioned to create a mural for the New York Pavilion, Warhol's painting of the state's most wanted criminals was censored almost immediately. Apart from a very different attitude to that suggested in Golec's reading, what is also suggested by Malanga's anecdote and the poster image is a very different set of relations to the spectator, based, not on aesthetic attention and convivial interaction, but on the underlying social structures of property and class. In this reading, the boxes were trespassing on a territory which, formally, had protected the artworld against the interference of the world outside. Confronted by this situation, Arthur Danto's interpretation of the exhibition, as securing the status of the artworld, not surprisingly rests on an analysis of the single object isolated in philosophically neutral space. As if in response, Tillim wrote: 'one wondered if a single box, or a few boxes would reproduce the effect of the ensemble in a gallery where they could so successfully repudiate any art quality whatsoever'.[37] This repudiation counters the idea, in both Danto and Golec's readings, that Warhol's work redeems the artworld; instead, it condemns it. Yet, as single commodities, the purchase of the boxes might also be seen as confirming the collapse of supermarket and gallery Danto attempted to prevent: the latter did not merely *look* like a warehouse, it actually was one. *New York Times* critic Grace Glueck's gleeful report that the 'biggest buyers spurned the smaller

Brillo cartons marked "3¢ off" which sold for $200 to plunk down $6,000 for 20 of the regular size' only confirms the point.[38]

If Warhol's boxes occupied the space of spectatorship so that they became viewer-substitutes, the work of Marisol supports this idea to some extent. Marisol also exhibited at Eleanor Ward's gallery and was close to Warhol at this time. Her plywood box figures, which include a portrait of Warhol himself (*Andy*, 1963), were begun exactly in the period Warhol was devising *The Personality of the Artist* exhibition. In these works, plywood boxes act as proxies for body form and body space. Her show of such works at The Stable Gallery, the same year Warhol showed the plywood *Brillo Boxes*, was a huge hit with both the public and critics. Elsewhere in art history, the occupation of the space of spectatorship by proxies—in Warhol's case, boxes—is suggested in relation to the work of George Segal in a famous reading by Brian O'Doherty. For O'Doherty, Segal's tableaux with plaster figures, *Cinema* (1963) for instance, suggest the usurpation of the spectator by a lifeless and somehow banal other, much as I am arguing of Warhol's boxes. O'Doherty writes:

> The spectator in the tableaux somehow feels he shouldn't be there. Segal's art makes this clearer than anyone else's. His objects—great lumps of them—wear a history of previous occupancy […] Their familiarity is distanced by the gallery context and by the sense of occupancy conveyed by the plaster figures […] Since the environment is occupied already, our relationship to it is partly pre-empted by the figures which have the blush of life completely withdrawn from them […] the effect on the spectator who joins them is one of trespass. Because trespass makes one partly visible to oneself, it […] tends to substitute the Eye for the Spectator.[39]

Warhol's *Brillo Boxes* function in a similar way. In being moved (and in being arranged with the intention that they might be) the *Campbell's Tomato Juice Boxes* became indices of the people who moved them. The obfuscation of Warhol's message, using sculptures of packaging waste rather than figures, might be seen as a greater debasement of the figure of the spectator, while at the same time as providing one reason O'Doherty did not call on Warhol's work here.[40] Nonetheless, both intrusions are classed: O'Doherty's description recalls Marx's 'lumpenproletariat', while Warhol's stand-ins were factory made objects that represented a kind of lowest common denominator of American identity. Like the 'trespass' O'Doherty identifies in Segal, the *Brillos Boxes'* invasion of the gallery space puts the viewer at a self-aware remove but, in Warhol's work, a different kind of 'scene' developed than the slightly embarrassed, polite renegotiation that O'Doherty's spectator faces. At *The Personality of the Artist*, viewers damaged and disturbed the uncanny, pristine dry goods in order to venture into occupied territory. The 'real world' trespassed onto the 'artworld'; but, in turn, the spectator, eager to reclaim that space of entitlement, disturbed and trespassed on the space now occupied by the work. Warhol had laid a trap. The installation incited multiple acts of violence in retaliation on the part of those who nudged the *Campbell's Tomato Juice Boxes* aside to establish themselves in the room—it was all part of the fun anyhow. Yet one implication was that the work could not qualify as 'art' without first establishing a reciprocal, perhaps narcissistic, engagement with an artworld subject.

For O'Doherty, Segal's work acknowledges a spectatorial subject that is ignored in the cerebral, 'optical' reception of modernism. It does so by making the spectator conscious of its own presence through its trespass on the space already inhabited by the plaster figure. O'Doherty describes this embodied spectator—no doubt the very spectator who was negotiating Warhol's boxes—as blundering and painfully corporeal. In O'Doherty's text this leads to a discussion of Minimalism. With Minimalist art, O'Doherty describes a moment of exchange of information between bodily sense and disembodied connoisseurial looking, each acting on the other's distinct experience of the encounter. For O'Doherty this reintegration of modalities is a means of overcoming the self-reflexive remove of aesthetic appreciation native to the white cube: the same remove of snobbish self-alienation that Warhol had recognised as Abstract Expressionism's elected state. But if Warhol's Pop attacked this idealised observer instead of reconfiguring it, this does not mean that it showed a less comprehensive understanding of the situation. What Minimalism's success does indicate, however, is its willingness to re-accommodate, or better accommodate, the observer into the artworld. In the following section, I will argue that Warhol used the very developments attributed to Minimalism to undermine this new form of accommodation.

O'Doherty's suggestion is still familiar in debates and historical narratives: Minimalist art sought to reconcile the two modes of viewership, 'the spectator' and 'the Eye', activating the space of encounter in so doing, and entangling artwork and viewer in a codependence.[41] This quality of Minimalism is given a central role today in defining the trajectory not just of sculpture but of a whole history: the re-evaluated role of the subject and the ensuing movements of Process Art, Institutional Critique and Post-Minimalist art.

Donald Judd's famous 1965 essay 'Specific Objects' (first composed the year before, the same year as the *Brillo* show) played a crucial role in forming these understandings of Minimal Art. Here, the notion of the encounter as grounded in the 'real space' of the observer (something crucial for O'Doherty) was given its most lasting platform. The legacy of 'Specific Objects' was guaranteed after Robert Smithson embroiled Judd in the debate with Michael Fried, a few years later, about what Minimalism actually was and was not, something that Judd's original essay does not address. Rather, in 'Specific Objects' Judd discusses the possibility of a three-dimensional art-object that is defined through the refusal of traditional categories: it is 'neither painting nor sculpture' he writes.[42] In Judd's essay, the real space of the object is equivalent to that in which the exhibition space and the bodily space of the spectator exist. We might think of their existence as being on a single register, with no break between the illusionary and the actual:

> Three dimensions are real space. That gets rid of the problem of illusionism and of literal space, space in and around marks and colors—which is riddance of one of the salient and most objectionable relics of European art.[43]

Judd's conception of 'new three-dimensional work', proposed in the article, was of a new anti-image, anti-illusionary art. Judd emphasised the importance for the spectator to encounter the work in real time and in its environment, and for that time and environment to delimit the spectator's appreciation of the work according to its specific qualities. Judd's work functioned from the surface outwards, in a recursive relationship to its environment. Thus, one might think of the gallery space 'answering' the objects' statements. While Judd conceived his work as apart from sculpture and painting, the Minimalist object nevertheless embodies something of what the sculptural stands for: its emphasis on matter, real space and time.

During the January before the *Brillo Boxes'* Stable Gallery show in spring 1964, Warhol was contacted by Samuel Wagstaff Jnr who was organising what is reputed to be the first Minimalist show, *Black, White, and Gray* at the Wadsworth Atheneum.[44] He attempted to convince Warhol to submit a 'stack' of white boxes. Wagstaff may have come across something very like these in Warhol's studio as early as 1963 while Warhol was in the process of producing the *Brillo Boxes* or, perhaps, Wagstaff simply reimagined the finished packaging boxes as monochrome.[45] Warhol did not comply with the request but the white *Disaster* paintings he sent instead were included in the show. These contain many of the attributes that Wagstaff sought, namely a treatment of the subject detached and mediated to the point of obscurity, a reduced monochrome palette, and an enlarged scale.

Of course, packaging boxes painted in bold colours would not do for *Black, White, and Gray*. Their exclusion pairs them with the work of Donald Judd who was also not included. Works by Judd, such as *Untitled (Record Cabinet)* produced the year before for his first major show at the Green Gallery, disqualified him because, although it was monochrome, it was painted with bright 'cadmium red light'. Nevertheless, like Warhol, Judd came to embody the 'new attitude' that Wagstaff wanted to display. From the sidelines, in his work as a critic, Judd recognised this new attitude in his otherwise disparaging review of the exhibition.

The box works made by Judd and Warhol during 1964 were closer than they have more recently been represented. Both artists were pushing developments in their painting into three dimensions, almost in spite of the already established category of sculpture. Judd's early box works are conspicuously 'painted'; the specific 'cadmium red light' included in the work's list of materials. As with the *Brillo Boxes'* perfectly registered painting, Judd's use of a particular red rendered these works—their areas of shade, the precision of their lines, their 'object-hood'—literally 'high definition'.

In 1964, many of the people important to Minimalism's critical reception surrounded Warhol at the Factory. In his film *Batman Dracula*, for example, which was made that year, Wagstaff appears alongside Gregory

Battcock and David Bourdon. Battcock edited *Minimal Art: A Critical Anthology* in 1968 while Bourdon, who featured in Battcock's book, had, in 1964, published on Carl Andre and Robert Morris. In Bourdon's later survey of Warhol's work, he writes:

> Warhol's Boxes paved the way for Minimal sculpture. His ideas concerning irreducible three-dimensional forms, repetition, and semi-mechanical fabrication influenced the thinking of many sculptors who were designing simple polyhedrons with uninflected surfaces, often painted in flat colours. After Warhol's box show it became commonplace for artists to have their work industrially fabricated, to have it manufactured in multiples, and to withhold as much evidence of handcraft as possible.[46]

Bourdon's very sculpted paragraph (it certainly stands out from the text around it) must have been written with Judd's work in mind. It clearly tries to undermine the emphasis that histories of sculpture have placed on Judd's work. Here the notions of 'semi-mechanical fabrication' and the 'industrially fabricated' do the work in the description: these features are made responsible for the coexistence of the other elements. In both Warhol's and Judd's early sculpture, repetition exists within specific works. This is true of the stacked soup cans in the failed early box work, and in the repeated grooves and slats of works by Judd such as *Untitled* (1963), otherwise known as *Record Cabinet*. But it is the aesthetic related to industrial fabrication—something crucial to Warhol's work—that allows both artists to elaborate a tendency for multiple separate units, and hence enables the development of Judd's mature work.

Much of Warhol's sculptural work of this time, including the *Brillo Boxes*, *Silver Clouds* and *Cow Wallpaper*, can be seen as a sabotage of Minimalism's aesthetic of high seriousness and weight; a *détournement* through the parallel use of the gallery's architectural frame of physical interaction, boxes, Plexiglas and Mylar surfaces, and industrial fabrication. While Bourdon's suggestion frames a comparison between Warhol and early Minimalist work in the language of Minimalism's operations, it tilts the balance in Warhol's direction. Indeed, Bourdon might invite one to take a further step: to reject the frequent invocation of Warhol's work as a convenient counter to Minimalist practices—especially Judd's—and instead to position Warhol as the pioneering agent in relation to whose work Judd must be placed.[47] We might also reverse the relationship and 'think Judd' in Warhol's terms. If Warhol's work operates according to the artworld gaze mis-registering real-world content, the off-register image reflecting this situation, Judd's even plane of 'reality'—a facticity that travels unruptured across the surface of the industrially produced object, the architectural space and the spectator's awareness—is a highly manipulated feat of pure registration.

Judd once told an interviewer, 'the thing about my art is that it is a given.'[48] If this position were a philosophical framework—and David Raskin's recent study has presented it as tantamount to one—it would be one in which doubt and negation were absent. Indeed, an art of total 'given-ness' suggests the conversion of negativity, of negative space and of all kinds of otherness and unfixity, into positivity. It seems that art history at this moment, and (as shall be discussed below) in the run-up to Institutional Critique, was replacing the autonomous art object with the autonomous larger physical situation: 'I prefer art that isn't associated with anything,' Raskin quotes Judd as saying.[49]

So conceived, Judd's work and the Stable Gallery show that Warhol installed in 1964 are opposed. While negative space became part of positivist thingness in Judd (or at least potential thingness), Warhol's boxes, as well as representing the negative space 'outside' the artworld, literally occupied and expanded negative space, so much so that the work operated by threatening to negate viewership itself. By this I mean in a literal sense that the work became invisible to those who could not squeeze their way into the gallery as well as, in another sense, that the work undermined the spectatorial role with which the gallery space enfranchised the viewer. The misrecognition of the space as a warehouse or stockroom speaks to an accompanying misrecognition of the viewer's place.

This indistinction is reflected in the title of the exhibition, *The Personality of the Artist*. If Judd vouches for the specific object as mediating between a specific kind of viewer and artist, Warhol's portrayal of a persona of gormless non-specificity is very much contiguous with the work. Warhol challenges the specificity of the institutional artworld environment by filling it up with that which is incongruous, that which does not acknowledge—partly through an act of sheer obstruction—the requirements of the gallery. Duly provoked, visitors to the show disrupted the arrangement of the work in order to re-establish a presence to which they considered themselves entitled. Awareness of the entitlement bestowed on the viewer by the artworld is therefore central to Warhol's understanding of this space, his handling of it, and the idea of trespass in this book. Entitlement makes the artworld metaphysically different from the real world. Bringing the real into the artworld, as Warhol did, renders the subject belonging to the artworld off-register, unable to 'fit in' in his or her own habitat. The viewer is confronted with the threat that their attention, even their proximity and relation to work described at the time as non-art, will displace them in relation to the hierarchical space to which the gallery once granted entitlement.

Warhol's box installation also counters rhetorical claims about Judd's work as 'real space,' and Minimalist art's broader interest in the work's physical relationship to the spectator and the surroundings considered as part of that work's design. What these expansions into the viewer's space do is to enclose the spectator more directly in the constitution of the work's value. At the same time, they police and constrict interpretations of the work through their 'minimal' content; it being no more or less than is materially there. Judd's continual emphasis on the work's 'power' in 'Specific Objects' has already been given deserved attention in feminist critiques. But I see this (in this case) as merely a characteristic trace of an actor whose larger crime is to attempt to refuse other voices.[50] Take the painter Jo Baer's account of her breakup with Judd and Dan Flavin, which:

> came about because of a review that Judd wrote about Kenneth Noland's target paintings. He said that Noland was the best painter working today, but, since Noland's work wasn't that good, it proved that painting was dead. Not long after I read this, Flavin and Sonja and Judd and Julie were at my house one day throwing a football around. For some reason, this subject of the death of painting came up, and I said to Judd something like "your logic is crap. You can't say Noland is the best painter, but he's not very good, so painting is finished. That's ridiculous, Mr Falsum Propositum" [...] And he said, "you don't know what you're talking about. You have no right to speak to me this way, blah blah blah, I'm leaving." He got very angry with me, because

> I was laughing at him. And as he was leaving, he turned around
> and said, "Flavin, are you coming?" And Flavin was standing
> there with the football and looking at Jack and me, and he just
> put the football down. "Sorry," he said to me, and he and Sonja
> went. Out the door, that was that.[51]

Judd seems to have been quite intolerant of others' terms, even from within his own camp. Jo Baer's exit from the scene at the end of the 1960s followed a fight which, whatever her faults, also indicated just how committed establishment players such as *Artforum* (who put a moratorium on her name after this) were to Judd's cause.

Attention to character is justified here for two reasons. First, it seems that Judd's influence really took precedence, and second, that influence is given the authority that comes from being blended into a larger history of formal and social concerns. Warhol's place in this history is one that in various ways ties the psychic predisposition of the individual to the moment—as if to say he got something right, but only because he was a particular kind of person. This treatment particularly characterises the critical reception of the work *Raid the Icebox I*, which will be a key focus of a following chapter of this book. More generally, and very much unlike Judd, Warhol rarely dogmatically influenced the reception of his work, his comments baffled rather than enlightened the critics and he frequently acquiesced, for example, when others voiced their opinions about his works.[52]

Judd's position is aligned to Danto's. Both men, near contemporary graduates of the same philosophy department, theorise a state of art at the same time when both are beginning their working lives, and both men's texts have been read as radical and innovative. They make a series of observations informed by a positivist approach, establishing—in institutional space—a quality of reality that they claim was not present before. But for both, this real quality is depthless in and of itself: it acts as a point of equivalence between the real world and the artworld newly conceived; it becomes a position from which to defend their own work and fend off works that offer something different. In the case of Judd's run-in with Baer, this is the discipline of painting he had only recently abandoned himself.

Minimalism is seen to have established the foundations on which the critical procedures that today shape many of art's discursive frameworks are based: Institutional Critique; notions of a mobile spectator, an antidote to Spectacle's passive receiver; public art and Land Art; performance and video practices. Historical time concertinas, the radical art practices of the 1960s and 1970s do the work of framing and legitimising the choices that contemporary institutions make regarding what artists to support and how to justify these choices. Work such as Mel Bochner's *Measurement: Room* (1969), in which Bochner provides Letraset dimensions of the gallery along the edges of its walls, has been used to illustrate the transition from Minimalism to Institutional Critique.[53] It turns our attention to the real space (in feet and inches) of the gallery, one of many works of this time that analyse what James Meyer has called 'the specular and ideological conditions of the late modernist "white cube."'[54] But in light of the present analysis we might re-diagnose Bochner's project as that of a frontiersman on behalf of this outward, environmental expansion in Minimalism's wake. Barely aware that his is a civilising mission, Bochner travels to the four corners of the white cube world, measuring on behalf of a new establishment order. What history has written up as the institution (for us evoking both meanings) of a radical new platform for critique, might also be seen as a response to a call for greater stability: to ground the artworld's 'reality' in the calculable conditions of production and display, and sure up that ground against any further threats of collapse.

These new engagements locate the 'reality' of the artworld as a palimpsest, layered over the real world: Bochner's measurements would be the same in either, of course. The metaphysical conditions that had previously divided the realities of artworld and real world have come down to a zero point. Bochner saw the measurement itself as revealing 'an essential nothing-ness'.[55] This minimal difference, this 'ultra-thin' space of reception is one not of exchange between worlds, but of takeover. Thus, with Warhol's assistance, we can locate Minimalism as a moment in the history of art when a seismic shift took place in the idea of receptivity. If 'reading' had previously meant vouching for one's experience of a work from a position of authenticity, independence, 'critical distance' even, now the encounter required the viewer to equip themselves appropriately: to get 'in-register' with the art, to perform a subject position built into to the work itself. With the death of the authorial voice in the 1960s (though not of the authority of ownership), one kind of normativity was exchanged for another. It began with a divestment of projection, a moment of non-interpretation, the mere operation of the senses 'receiving' a work that was 'given'. But it nonetheless constituted an acculturation to the sensibilities of the status quo — hence *Artforum's* moves against Baer.

Likewise, for Danto the 'real' Brillo box is seen to collapse into the art-world *Brillo Box*: one's engagement with art is no longer perceptible, or primarily experiential, but is conceptual. The viewer, after Danto, might only turn up to the exhibition to confirm to his or her self that the difference, materially, visually, amounted to zero. But turn up from where? Because this new art required the viewer to belong to the artworld if there was to be anything to be gained from turning up at all: this, therefore, is an art form of vested interest. This proposition of non-difference (what would be called a sleight of hand anywhere else) discounts the values attributed to what art had been before, taking the claim to distinguish and demarcate value away from the real world and making it native to the space of art. The value of art and the value gained from looking at art become located in the artworld. Henceforth, where one cashes the value of art, so to speak, is internal to the artworld, and the subject must be internal to it in order to gain from it. Crucial, though, is that this move relies on an initial claim about the reality principal of the new work. The implication of Danto's bid is that critique need no longer appeal to a reality belonging outside the artworld to maintain distance and validity, because it can self-regulate. If the viewer feels disenfranchised on exiting the artworld, Danto's reading implies, this is no longer something that good art need be accountable for. If these things are suggested by Danto's theory of art, it is not a reading which I think is true to Warhol's work. Indeed, in arguing for Warhol's art in terms of trespass, the awareness of the real, social difference between the zones of artworld and everyday experience, the private and the public and so on is crucial. The seeming visual similarity of the *Brillo Boxes* threatens the territory of social distinction, the artworld, not by visual non-difference but by rendering that distinction indifferent. Warhol's *Personality of the Artist* is, in my reading, a rebuke to those who have invested a little too much, and are hoping to prevent the bubble bursting. Warhol brings the outside, considered valueless and beneath consideration, in; he threatens to bankrupt those whose capital is uncertain on the outside. Warhol's work—not all of it, but the work in this book—refused to enrich those who had become native to the institution at the expense of those outside.[56]

While *The Personality of the Artist* explores mobility between social worlds, Minimalist art negates the value of this mobility through its claim to locate the same 'real space' within the artworld as outside it: there is nowhere to go, ironic considering the emphasis in key interpretations of Minimalism on active, mobile spectatorship. Instead, viewership is imagined as co-constituted with the work. The viewer is part of the structure that includes the work and the surroundings at each point. Admittedly, the viewer determines this point within the gallery, both in time and in space but, in doing so, must enter both into a structural framework and into the role of a mobile component. The single register and single level of reception of this work, circumscribed by its reduced content, rewards passivity and compliance, which poses as spectatorial mobility.

Sharing its conditions with reality, the artworld only distinguishes its autonomy through the value and values it retains. Ironically, the value and meaning of art, after Minimalism, so often rests on the idea that the work is providing a kind of access to reality, or real experience, as if it was not in abundance elsewhere. Reality becomes a kind of currency therefore through which artworld value is distributed. Art history sustains these economies of value that, while appearing to occupy and be occupied with 'the real world', maintain an autonomy from it. One example is Hal Foster's approach to Warhol's *Death and Disaster* series in his *Return of the Real*, from 1996. In the ordering of the chapters in Foster's book, his reading of Warhol's *Death and Disaster* paintings comes after a section on Minimalism. But it is also after Minimalism in the sense I am arguing. This 'after' is one that both calcifies what Minimalism was and, to a large extent, influences how art is to be understood from this moment. In a particular footnote of Foster's book, he defends Minimalism from Anna C. Chave's feminist critique. His answer is that 'however circumscribed, Minimalism did put the question of the subject in play, and in this respect feminist art begins where Minimalism ends.'[57] As a version of history this might be questioned but, that aside, his comment also reveals something about Minimalism that I want to highlight as problematic. If Minimalism's impact has been to put the subject 'into play', it is only insofar as it requires the spectator to 'assume the position'. The interpretation of the work of art becomes much more a question of how one should be as a subject—a kind of interpretation of selfhood (sympathetic of course to the kind of subject who 'belongs' in art galleries)—so that the work can function as it is designed. Foster's readings of Warhol's images reveal this new burden as essentially modelling the subject to fit with work that upholds the values of the artworld rather than the other way round: i.e. upholding the value of the subject and its social reality through the work.

This new task of interpretation hides its own nature as *work*, an addition to the value of the work of art and its institutions so that, like Danto attempted before, all profits (both cultural capital and, we may assume, literal capital) stay within the artworld and there is no leakage into the real world. Moreover, by 'circumscribing' the spectator it also hides the way in which interpretation is nonetheless still an *act* by a subject who, in real-world terms, is autonomous and entitled, and who expects a return on their investment. Warhol's *Brillo Boxes* are close in operation to such art forms. That they also hinge on an approximation of 'reality' which is exploited at the zero point of non-difference. But if, 'after Judd', value became non-transferable when other conditions became equivalent, Warhol reversed this: opening the artworld out on to the real so as to maintain for the subject a dignified, non-prescriptive autonomy.[58]

3

Atmosphere

The best atmosphere I can think of is film, because it's three-dimensional physically and two-dimensional emotionally.[1]

Andy Warhol

The critic David Bourdon has described Warhol's *Silver Clouds* of 1966 (plate 3.1) in words that make them seem impossibly *full* and heavy with meaning, floating in a remarkably dense art-historical atmosphere. According to Bourdon, the work demonstrates the artist's

> uncanny ability to summarize and comment upon several sculptural ideas that were then in the air. In form, they possessed the simple and irreducible volumes that characterized so much contemporary Minimal sculpture. Although they had no movable parts their unrestricted motion and resistance to gravity clearly related them to the 1960s boom in kinetic works and the earlier air driven mobiles of Alexander Calder. The plumpness and malleability of Warhol's objects corresponded to Claes Oldenburg's innovative 'soft' sculptures. The clouds implicitly encouraged spectators to nudge them gently in order to see them float away; this qualified them as 'participatory' artworks, still another trendy concept in an anti-elitist era that advocated greater 'spectator participation' for a work's fullest realization.[2]

60

Similarly, Benjamin Buchloh suggests that we should see Warhol's *Silver Clouds* in terms of Allan Kaprow's happenings and Robert Rauschenberg's and Frank Stella's use of silver surfaces.[3] None of these references are out of place. One can hardly deny the links that tie Warhol to his contemporaries through the use of similar materials, forms or means of display. But Bourdon does not give all of Warhol's works, his paintings especially, the same treatment. I think we can read art-historical deferral, in this case, as a condition of the works' being an art-historical anomaly; a response to the *Clouds'* art-historical lightness and reflectiveness, one might say, rather than to their weight and the way they absorbed whatever else was 'in the air' at that time.

Besides—and this is something art history has overlooked—the most important references to artworks lie in Warhol's own sculptural productions. In addition to *Silver Clouds*, this chapter will look at three other case studies: from 1965, *Large Sleep*; from 1970, *Rain Machine*; and from 1977, a portrait of Warhol by the holographer Jason Sapan. All of these sculpture works, as I show in this chapter, transport the cinematic environment and cinematic mode of viewing to the gallery space. These works therefore represent an early trespass into the gallery by film, and Warhol makes that invasion with sculptures that reflect critically on artworld aesthetics. In this light one would qualify Rosalind Krauss's catch-all reading of *Silver Clouds* in the essay 'Madness of the Day'—that the work signifies eyesight itself—requiring of it a proviso about the kind of looking that is being done. Indeed, rather than acting as 'strange metonymies of daylight', the *Clouds*, I shall argue, reflect cinema's lack of daylight and the darkness of the underground's perpetual night-time.[4] Warhol's attempt to shift modes of viewership within the gallery space might be seen in terms of the argument in the previous chapter: the transposition of the cinema space to the gallery, like the transposition of supermarket stockroom to the artworld, indicates socially transgressive motives and a critique of that artworld's values. Here, these motives are represented not just by the medium of film and the content of underground cinema, but also by a challenge to the gallery's aesthetic regime. The first thing I want to argue, therefore, is that by the time *Silver Clouds* were being developed, Warhol already had reason to seek alternative devices to painting for what he wanted to say.

Until summer 1964, Warhol had been represented by Eleanor Ward's Stable Gallery, where he had produced the work that features as the focus of the first two chapters of this book. Here he had established himself as foremost among Pop artists. His first show at the gallery in late 1962 included the paintings of soup cans, *Dance Diagrams*, *Elvises* and *Marilyns*, while for his second show in 1964, the gallery space was completely taken over by sculptural facsimiles of packaging cartons, most famously *Brillo Boxes*. As I described in the previous chapter, at *The Personality of the Artist* exhibition, the boxes nearly filled the space, restricting access and free movement. The impact of this show is often underestimated: the gallery was an elite social space, and here it was being reduced to a stockroom. This demotion implied a similar refusal to acknowledge the inhabitants of the space as appropriately highly valued. In order to reassert their position, viewers nudged and kicked the neatly and provocatively lined up boxes out of their way or nonchalantly leaned on them. If this revealed the personality of the artist, it was one whose body, morphed into the *Brillo* or *Kellogg's Boxes*, had become both an obstruction to the sense of entitlement of viewers wanting to enter the space. This spiky attitude was also in evidence that year in the controversial subject matter of Warhol's other achievements. He exhibited his paintings on the subject of *Death and Disaster: Race Riots*, the assassination of a president, suicide, the mangled wrecks of highway disasters; bodies strewn across the surface of the road and the landscape of America. It was also in March of that year that his one subject film, *Blow Job*, was presented at Ruth Kligman's Washington Square Gallery. Lastly, following a high-profile public commission, he emblazoned the external façade of the New York State Pavilion at the 1964 World's Fair with mugshots of the state's most wanted criminals.

Warhol's notoriety helped accomplish a great ambition: that year he joined the Castelli Gallery. Here his peers included Robert Rauschenberg, Jasper Johns, John Chamberlain, Frank Stella, Roy Lichtenstein and James Rosenquist. To mark the 10th anniversary of the gallery in 1968, Warhol made another series of box sculptures, with silkscreen portraits on polystyrene of ten Castelli artists arranged in different coloured rows: *Portraits of the Artists* of 1967 (fig. 3.1). This colourful piece of tongue-in-cheek art memorabilia, featuring the faces of the highest-profile American artists working at the time, made for a collector's item. It points to what will be the

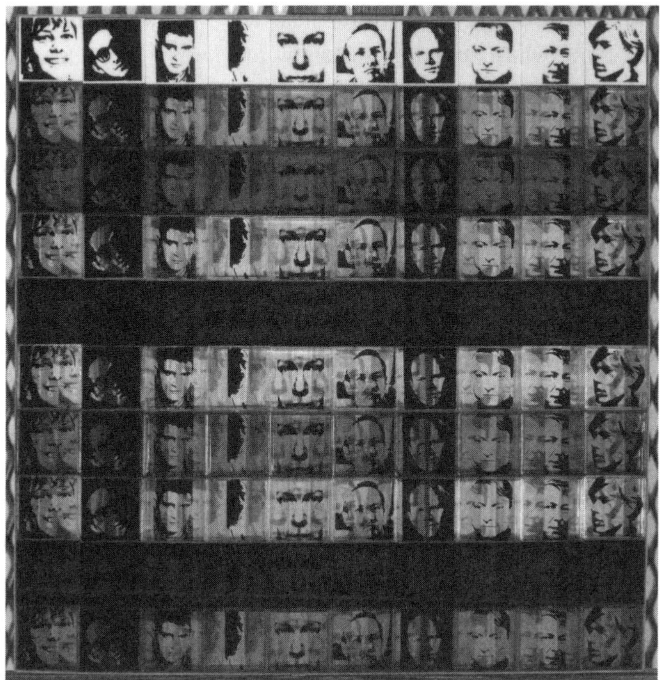

Fig. 3.1. Andy Warhol, *Portraits of the Artists*, 1967. Collection of The Andy Warhol Museum, Pittsburgh.

theme of the final chapter—collecting—but also further defines Warhol's sculpture as so often made in order to mark reflective moments in time. Warhol's move to the Castelli Gallery precipitated some self-censoring. He opened there, at the end of 1964, with *Flowers*, which used part of an image that had won second prize in a photography magazine readers' competition. These could be *fleurs du mal*, or an ironic take on flower power, yet it is no surprise they sold much better than *Ambulance Disasters* or *Electric Chairs*.

Despite his ascendancy, Warhol's longed-for promotion as a painter to the Castelli ranks was not in the circumstances he had hoped. Painting, he complained, was hard work and was becoming unrewarding; the audience was conservative and the break with Eleanor Ward had been acrimonious. Worse, and most importantly, he had begun to think that Pop Art had reached its sell-by date: Minimalism was the new thing. Painting, he later wrote, 'just wasn't fun anymore'.[5] Thus, in Paris in 1965, while attending his show of *Flowers* at the Sonnabend Gallery, he announced that he was a retired artist. The announcement echoed Marcel Duchamp's famous 'retirement' in order to devote his life to chess; Warhol, however, was going to concentrate on films. It was during this time of flux, which had begun in the summer of 1964, that Warhol began work on *Silver Clouds*.

The *Clouds* themselves are made from Scotchpak, a type of reflective silver Mylar, and are essentially pillow-shaped balloons filled with helium (indeed, they were also referred to as *Silver Pillows* because of their shape).[6] For their installation they were carefully weighed down with fishing weights so as to float in mid-air amid the gallery-goers. This balancing meant that the *Clouds* were sensitive and reactive. Small climatic changes in the atmosphere and air currents, including those caused by the comings and goings of spectators and the ambient temperature in the room, would cause the *Clouds*' behaviour to change. In *POPism*, Warhol recalls:

> I preferred to have all the pillows float scattered […] We spent all one afternoon tying fishing weights to them to get them to get moving, floating in between, bumping into each other, but it was impossible to make them sit still in the middle of the air, because one of them would always drift away and start a chain reaction.[7]

The sensitivity of *Silver Clouds* highlights the spectator's presence in the gallery—as the box installation had done—through their movement or their being moved.[8] Together, these works pivot on a sense of being something and nothing. As something, the boxes act as an impediment to access to the gallery, while *Silver Clouds* undermine the rigid structures on which aesthetic relations in the gallery were based. As nothings, the boxes resembled common packaging, of no value, while *Silver Clouds*, flighty and immaterial, threatened disappearance. Each work was designed to provocatively usurp the meaning and identity of the gallery space in one way or another, devaluing it and its inhabitants: an affront to those whose place within the traditional gallery context is a question of entitlement.

The genesis of *Silver Clouds* began with a collaboration between Warhol and the scientist Billy Klüver. Klüver had worked on the Bell Labs/

NASA Telstar satellite launch in 1962. Since then he had become known as the 'artist's scientist' and in 1966 he became a founding member of the organisation Experiments in Art and Technology (EAT), along with engineer Fred Waldhauer and artists Robert Rauschenberg and Robert Whitman. Warhol had first asked Klüver if it was possible to make a floating helium light bulb and Klüver had begun work on this in 1964. It is often said that the idea was inspired by a Jasper Johns drawing that Warhol had bought in 1961. A floating light bulb could not be achieved but, ever open to suggestion, Warhol was shown the recently invented material Scotchpak and immediately decided 'let's make clouds'.[9] Although *Silver Clouds* floated bunched up in a corner of the ceiling at the inauguration of EAT in Rauschenberg's studio, they were not officially made under EAT's auspices.

In the making of *Silver Clouds*, further possibilities for distinct artworks emerged. They were made from segments cut from an enormous tube of Scotchpak, which was inflated at the Factory in 1965. This work even had a name: *Infinite Sculpture* (plate 3.2). There is a sound recording of this event and, in it, Warhol is clearly very impressed with the result of the work. 'Oh! Ah! Oh it's beautiful!' he suggestively croons. Beginning in 1964, Warhol had begun to take his tape recorder everywhere he went, referring to it as his wife.[10] This audio documentation went in tandem with what was to become Warhol's main interest and work in late 1964 and 1965: capturing the events at the Factory on film.[11] The recording makes clear that the project which included *Infinite Sculpture* and the *Clouds* were, from the outset, produced in a collaborative spirit. This working method, like the work itself, was indicative of a change at the Factory at this time which became much more focussed around events and social interaction.

Warhol turned towards full-time movie-making around 1964. From this moment the Factory became an anti-film studio where unstable characters—often heavy substance users, particularly of amphetamine—became the stars and 'superstars' of the films. It was a pharmacologically altered parallel universe of character assassination and sexual deviance, a brutal arena of the exploitation born of narcissistic hungers for attention. If the *Brillo Box* show took the exposition of self-important objects and reversed the focus to self-important people, exposing how value operates through projection and identification in the artworld, Warhol's films, from

1965 at least, objectified people whose affected self-importance had become an art form.

This was in stark contrast to the preceding period during which, on any given day, one was likely to find only Gerard Malanga and Warhol quietly getting on with producing paintings. It was at the after party for the *Brillo* exhibition that the Factory became a quasi-public space, and it was there and then that the 1960s started for many in New York — a 'seminal moment', as Victor Bockris writes in his biography of Warhol:

> The reception was the first time the New York social and art worlds were at the Factory and it was a huge success […] It also marked a turning point in Andy's career. It was the last time he would be photographed in a group with Oldenburg, Lichtenstein, Wesselmann and Rosenquist.[12]

The feature that primarily characterised this moment was the social mixing that took place at Warhol's Factory, at the exhibitions themselves and also at events such as the *Exploding Plastic Inevitable* (*EPI*), which followed in 1966. Of this phenomenon Warhol writes in *POPism*: 'With one thing and another we were reaching people in all parts of town, all different types of people […] it was fun to see the Museum of Modern Art people next to the teeny-boppers next to the amphetamine queens next to the fashion editors.'[13] With Warhol's retirement from painting, occurring the same time as the *Clouds* were being made, film became the driver for the new working method and sociality at the Factory. If the sculptures in this chapter represent film's importance for Warhol at this point, over the larger period covered by this book it was in fact sculpture that provided Warhol with the opportunity to allow social interaction to productively infiltrate his work.

Billy Name's image of Warhol on the Factory roof, barely holding onto the great silver phallus of *Infinite Sculpture*, exemplifies this social mix of overlapping worlds within which *Silver Clouds* were made. Two representatives of important institutions are present in the photograph: Billy Klüver and Pontus Hultén. Klüver we have met but Hultén was the first director of the Pompidou Centre and before that director of Moderna Museet in Stockholm, where he gave Warhol his first retrospective in 1968. Also present are Harold Stevenson and Waldo Diaz Balart. Both important and accepted international artists, they represent avant-garde painting as it then was. Billy Name, Danny Williams and Gerard Malanga were Factory kids and assistants to Warhol. Talented, mixed up and young, they represent the countercultural movement and the underground. Lastly, Paul America can be seen as standing for an entirely new species of person at the Factory: a 'superstar'. He was to become the main attraction that year in the film *My Hustler*, an important work in Warhol's trajectory from art films to more commercially oriented releases. At the soft centre of all of this we find *Silver Clouds*. Even before they were exhibited in 1966 — indeed, before they even became the objects that were exhibited — their production bridged the gap between the two phases of Warhol's work in the 1960s and the two worlds that Warhol operated in at this point: uptown and downtown, the art world and the underground.

Silver Clouds do not just historically and methodologically correspond with the important shift in operations at the Factory, they are also symbolic of that shift. Warhol remarks in *POPism* that 'they meant something special to me: it was while I was making them that I felt my art career floating away out the window, as if the paintings were just leaving the wall and floating away.'[14] Even though they were exhibited at Warhol's second show at the Castelli Gallery in 1966, *Silver Clouds* marked a literally reflective pause to observe the occasion of his 'retirement' from painting and recommitment to film. *Silver Clouds* symbolise the paintings of Warhol's 'art career' floating away, and for this reason can be considered 'paintings' as well as sculptures.

> The new thing I am working on is sculpture because since I don't want to paint anymore and I thought that I could give that up and do movies and then I thought that there must be a way that I had to finish it off and I thought the only way is to make a painting that floats [...] the idea is to, ah [...] fill them with helium and let them out of your window and they'll float away and that's one less object.[15]

Warhol had intended that the *Silver Clouds* would literally float out of the Castelli Gallery's open window which, for him, was a way to 'finish off' painting.[16] As a collection of 'throwaway objects', *Silver Clouds* share the status of Warhol's crumpled paper works from 1954, described in Chapter 1, and the idea of throwaway objects will again be central to this study when, in Chapter 5, we shall consider Warhol's ambivalent relationship to collecting. The art historian David Joselit likewise considers *Silver Clouds* as assassinating painting by 'making an object which is dispensable, which will float out of the window'.[17] But he also reads the work, and its companion work, *Cow Wallpaper*, as travestying painting's organising principals of figure and ground. While *Cow Wallpaper*, jolly images of a dairy cow displayed in the Castelli Gallery's second room, was all background and committed the long-despised crime against avant-guardism of decoration, the floating *Clouds* were 'a figure with no ground'.[18]

In combination with the *Cow Wallpaper*, *Rain Machine* and *Flowers* works, *Silver Clouds* also indicate Warhol's increasing reticence about painting by suggesting a pastoral theme. Such a theme was incongruous for an artist who so self-consciously sought to align himself with what was modern, and hence (in his view) metropolitan, and whose identity as the artist 'Andy Warhol' was set at a great distance from the Warhola roots in the Ruthenian peasantry. We know also that Warhol disapproved of Jackson Pollock's departure from the city to the rural Hamptons. How could a supposedly modern artist abandon New York for a seaside hamlet? Warhol's employment of bucolic kitsch in these works is, then, another way in which the work figured painting as a bankrupt exercise, one put out to pasture. And yet, as it turned out on the occasion of the Castelli show, all but one of the *Clouds* avoided the window. They were intended to mark the 'death' of Warhol's painting but they lingered like ghosts, only to be reincarnated over and over again in later years: sold and remade for Warhol's continuing shows throughout the latter half of the 1960s and appearing in Merce Cunningham's dance work *Rainforest* in 1968. Cunningham's, however, is much more an *urban* jungle, suggesting a merging of the natural world and the new society, emergent in the sixties, around SoHo.

Warhol did not have another Castelli show until 1977, and no other major show of painting until *Mao* in Paris in 1974. Yet he continued to paint primarily, as he used to say, 'to bring home the bacon' and fund his other enterprises. Nevertheless, in the period between summer 1964 and 1965 we find Warhol cultivating a derisive opinion of the traditional art form of painting. Whether they made it out of the window or not, whether painting and Pop were really dead or just playing dead, *Silver Clouds* were the remnants, the cast-offs, the corpses even, of his involvement with the project of modernist painting in the 1960s. In '*Horror Vacui*: Andy Warhol's Installation', Mark Francis has suggested that *Silver Clouds* create a vacuum and, further, that this is something that would be repeated in Warhol's work over and over again.[19] *Silver Clouds* highlight, as well as redouble, the empty space in which art is everything and nothing. Like pillow talk, *Silver Clouds*, or *Silver Pillows*, are empty nothings, easy, floaty words after the fact. But Francis's suggestion of a vacuum implies a more radical negation that includes painting and sculpture as targets but also goes further: a negation that also puts at stake the role of the artist and his work as a visible object. By the time Warhol made *Silver Clouds*, it was the idea of the artwork as an object — a thing at all — that seems to have been resented. 'Every-*thing* is art,' Andy told *Newsweek* in 1964. 'You go to a museum and they say this is art, and the little squares are hanging on the wall. But everything is art, and nothing is art.'[20] By 1966, the year the work was exhibited, Warhol had more to say about this antipathy. In an interview alongside Roy Lichtenstein, conducted by Lane Slate for National Educational Television, painting's object-ness is at issue:

> I don't believe in painting because I hate objects and, uh […] ah […] I hate to go to museums and see pictures on the wall because they look so important and they don't really mean anything […] I think.[21]

It is this enmity, both to art and to objects per se, that frames Warhol's discussion of *Silver Clouds*. Warhol finds intolerable the way art objects demand that the viewer differentiate between them and their surroundings: the little squares of art mounted on the wall of the gallery. These objects force the viewer into engagement and action, at a time when Warhol had adopted an ultra-cold passivity. However, this refusal to judge or engage, in favour of letting things be and watching, was also central to the work. If the *Clouds* were interactive, they were also a spectacle that implied another viewer looking on at a remove. Warhol's work simultaneously establishes both a distanced position for voyeurism and an aesthetics of relation and participation.

These competing senses give the work dual identities, in which conceptual distinctions can be made between the work as sculpture and as cinematic experience. This idea of duplicitousness was compressed in a comment published in his book of philosophy, *From A to B and Back Again*: 'my favourite piece of sculpture is a solid wall with a hole in it to frame the space on the other side.'[22] The film camera performed this role for Warhol, and increasingly so at the time he was developing *Silver Clouds*. However, this framing of space from a non-disclosed position of remove had also been the function of the *Brillo Box* installation in 1964; arguably, one's presence in the elite space of the gallery at that show had become separate from the position of viewership, which was from the imagined position of a lower social class. In Warhol's hands, film was the perfect medium for the passive voyeur, partly because his version of it was so 'hands-off'. For two years, from 1963, he made underground movies with barely a panning shot. With no need for a gallerist or critical approval, film also appealed in that it was relatively free of censor and from the restrictions of elite taste; thus he could once again explore the difficult territory left behind after *Death and Disasters*, *Blowjob*, and *13 Most Wanted Men*. In both production and display, film dissolved everything into charged atmospheres, reminding us of the conditions on which *Silver Clouds* relied to animate them: turbulence and atmospheric changes. It is also the heading in *The Philosophy* under which Warhol describes his favourite sculpture. As we have seen in Chapter 2, a Warhol movie could be no more than a mood setting in the cinema, a background to 'help the audience get more acquainted with themselves.'[23] It is therefore predictable that he disliked, for example, structural film's attempts to make film otherwise, to make cinema an object or a series of physical components.[24] Warhol's earliest films, such as *Blow Job*, *Eat* (both 1964), *Sleep* and *Haircut* (both 1963) (which emulate in film the task-based experiments of Yvonne Rainer's dance work), allow spectatorship to be a conduit for, or mode of 'subscription' to, participation and yet at the same time they make use of the implied distance brought by spectatorship.

In 1965, Minimalism was said to be superseding Pop in the flurry of new movements and Warhol's retirement might be seen as a reaction to Minimalism's apparent takeover of the New York artworld at the moment when Pop was losing its edge. Likewise, *Silver Clouds*, shown only four weeks after Donald Judd's first show at the Castelli Gallery, can be read as a response to Judd's work. It too puts the environment of display, viewer experience and the object on a level plane. Yet Warhol's objects are non-specific; their surfaces are never fixed in relation to the seeing eye and they have no solid, secure relation to the space in which they exist. If a viewer wants to see in the way that Judd described, in terms of the physical relations of encounter, then to see Warhol's works is to do the impossible: to see gravity, air and heat. In this way, Warhol's works reveal the rhetorical glitch in Judd's positivism, which equates the material relations of things with their visibility. *Silver Clouds*, then, are counterpoised to Judd's Minimalist art: they are 'non-specific anti-objects'. As Charles F. Stuckey points out, they are simultaneously paintings, sculptures and moving images (films), but they are also big fat nothings: 'one less object' objects.[25] In David Bourdon's account, with which this chapter began, Warhol's work merely apes Minimalism's irreducible geometric forms. Although Bourdon conveys that the works involve a self-conscious historical positioning, he offers no real discussion of the conflict or the aesthetic stakes with which *Silver Clouds* are invested. He fails to recognise that *Silver Clouds* expose Minimalist operations as reactionary attempts to preserve the engagement between viewer and artwork as one that affirms distinct, stable positions on which to heap social and market values. The categorical indifference of *Silver Clouds* also suggests a moral indifference that is inimical to the social conventions of the art world of the time.

As I have described previously, Warhol's relationship to Minimalism is blurred by the fact that in 1964–5 it was a general term that was sometimes used to describe aspects of Warhol's own work. Indeed, Warhol's films were described as 'Minimalist' right from the moment of their first reception, and with works such as *Empire* (1964) one can understand why.[26] The film is shot in a way that instrumentalises and even industrialises the medium of film: the artist remains detached, not handling the camera and doing only rudimentary editing work. The subject of the film, the Empire State Building, is a single form reproduced on a temporal scale equivalent to the expanded spatial scales on which Judd later insisted. Warhol established this real time both in the duration of the film — the sun slowly rising over the Manhattan skyline — and in the sense that a different kind of watching was required of the audience. Over its eight-hour duration people talked, ate, drank, went to the bathroom, smoked. Life and lifetime went on in front of *Empire*. But Warhol also described *Empire* in homoerotic terms, it is an 'eight hour hard-on. It's so beautiful. The lights come on and the stars come out and it sways.'[27] We might think again of the *Infinite Sculpture* here. That too was a phallic object of near-infinite proportions set against the New York City skyline, and Warhol's reaction to it in the sound clip reveals that it was also orientated around the queer gaze, no less so than *Empire*. With these film and sculpture works, the aesthetic did not merely constitute a counterclaim to the straight norms of a figure such as Judd, nor was it simply positioned as a radical alternative in and of itself (which existed underground with a degree of autonomy, and would later emerge in painting). Rather film, and these sculptures which carry the aesthetics of Factory film into the gallery, acted as a lever with which to prise long-held spectatorial configurations, and what they stood for, out of position. Both constituted by and constitutive of an atmosphere, *Silver Clouds* relinquish the object-subject dynamic by which Minimalism operates.

In 1966 Warhol was not the only artist to subvert the rigorous seriousness of Judd's carefully orchestrated encounter with the specific object, nor the only one to use inflatables to do so. At the same time, the then-anonymous collective IT, which comprised the artists Iain Baxter, Ingrid Baxter and John Friel, made a much more explicit gesture of parody in the direction of Minimalist forms. IT was briefly formed to produce two exhibitions in commercial galleries in Toronto and LA. At these occasions they performed plagiarisms, additions to and corrections of artworks by their elders in Abstraction, Pop and Minimalism. Of course, the inflatable object is an ideal medium of satire, an implicit statement about inflated high-art values (plate 3.3). Other additions to the art history of inflatable sculpture, that today includes Paul McCarthy's *Blockhead* (2003) and Mark Leckey's *Felix the House Cat* (2013), also poke fun at a tendency towards dour seriousness, hinting at a subversive collapse of the border between the art institution and the world outside. These works are connected to Warhol by deep-running and ill-lit waters. Within this history, there appears a moment, in the early 1980s, when bubbles and other kinds of inflatable objects—as well as animated cartoon figures that seemed to float above the ground of the picture plane—became *de rigueur*. They include Jeff Koons's *Inflatables* (1978), Keith Haring's 'bouncing babies' and the bubble paintings of Kenny Scharf. In Scharf's work we see the new machine-age of today: orientated around communication, cosmically expanding, and emphatically and seriously about real possibility, while at the same time wrapped in an infantile bubble aesthetic. The car was an important feature of Scharf's aesthetic vocabulary at this time. His inclusion, in his imagery, of the aerofoils and tail fins of the classic car designs of the 1950s, encapsulates the tradition of an all-American astral future that works (in the same way as much of Warhol's iconography of the 1960s) to point in two directions in time at once. Much of the work from the early 1980s, above, was made in the explicit context of 'fun', in contradiction with the perceived seriousness of the dominant artworld at the time. But this was also a moment when painting's ground was literally in transition with the evolution of graffiti in the downtown scene.[28] That this Pop legacy is a rebuke to monumental Minimal, post-Minimal and conceptual tendencies is suggested by the damning reception the work received in academic circles.

Pop's autophilia is also expressed in John Dogg's 1986 hi-gloss customised spare wheel covers mounted to the gallery wall in otherwise sparse and empty space (fig. 3.2). However, these works, derived from the backside of 4x4s, and the artist Dogg himself, were both actually the creation of Richard Prince, a practical joke executed in collaboration with the gallerist Colin de Land over a short period in the mid-1980s. As a memento of the exercise, Prince has, on view on his website, an envelope from the offices of *Art in America* sent by the writer Deborah Drier for the AWOL artist, c/o Colin de Land. Across the front of the envelope Prince has typed 'I never had a penny to my name, so I changed my name.' This line also appears in the text 'in propia persona' from which we learn most about Dogg (it is also the subject-text of one of Prince's joke paintings). This was a piece of fictional gonzo journalism, written by Prince about Dogg, in which the artist escapes New York and what New York had become after the 1960s and 1970s with the rise of the Neo-Expressionists and graffiti: Schnabel, Basquiat, Haring and Kenny Scharf.[29] Dogg is, we can imagine, a frustrated combination of Warhol and Donald Judd, to whom the name 'John Dogg' refers. Dogg collapses the representational strategies of Warholian Pop, re-representing what was already ubiquitous within culture, with the conflicting sensibility of hallowed reification of Judd. Dogg emerges in the moment (1985) during which the thriving Downtown scene imploded, establishing a new divide between artist-philosopher and artist-entrepreneur that mirrors the earlier one in the mid-1960s, with Minimalism and Conceptualism on one side, and Warhol on the other. Dogg is a cartoon just like many of the inflatable figures featured above. He represents American

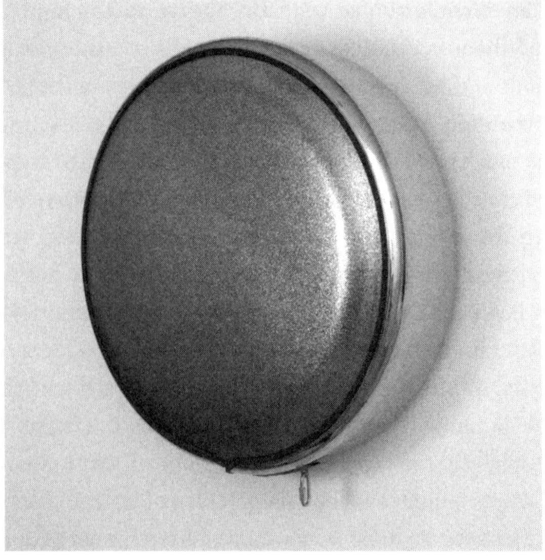

Fig. 3.2. John Dogg, *Untitled (tire)*, 1986. Rubber tire and continental kit, 76.2 x 76.2 x 25.4 cm, ©John Dogg. Courtesy of John Dogg.

masculinity, and is thus a sort of everyman, and it is through bringing that status into the artworld that much of the critical purchase of Prince's prank comes: in the New York artworld ubiquity is also its opposite, non-existent, a nothing; John Dogg is everything and nothing.

Dogg is obsessed with the American muscle car which, like Minimalism and Conceptual Art, had its moment between the mid-sixties and early 1970s, before the oil crises of the seventies made cars with such huge engines an untenable proposition for the blue collar drivers to whom they were originally marketed. The cars are entirely 'specific objects'. They are broken down in Dogg's/Prince's text as spec-lists of measurements and component parts, yet these are, unlike Judd's work but very much like Warhol's, in themselves iconic: the Hemi-Cuda engine, the ram-air hood scoop, the Mustang fastback. Like the work of both Warhol and Judd, the car theme is representative of a moment in American manufacturing, and a certain historical American-ness, that had been substantially lost when the work was made. And the work is a conflicting combination of the two kinds of straightness that a fusion of characterisations of Judd and Warhol and their work ought to be — Warhol's artless delivery of the everyday and Judd's normalising and rationalising attitude; Judd playing 'straight' when, as Paul Thek said, 'the world was falling apart', and Warhol's 'freakish' personhood of non-personality. There is, in Dogg's characterisation of Judd's taciturn, exacting flatness, a suggestion that in the real world Judd would be a typical guy, except that his decision to exist in the artworld distinguishes him as an oddity. The parallel between the artworld and the real world that Prince sets up, and which John Dogg straddles, is of course the subject of much of my analysis in this book. Dogg's approximation of the discourse of advanced art provides a means through which, in the text, Prince can comically attack the value of Judd's work, and its legacies in art, based on realist, proto-architectural spaces and self-consciously critical/ philosophical approaches. An example of this can be seen in him saying 'from where I stand. I really don't see things from where I stand.'[30] Prince also has Dogg speak *as one of Judd's works*, saying 'there's nothing inside me dying to get out.'[31] Judd's work and its ethos is lampooned through a recontextualisation in ultra-banal surroundings throughout the text:

> all the walls were painted flat primer gray [...] Twice a day John watched *The People's Court*. That was "his show." The defendants and plaintiffs were real people, not actors [...] I picked that color blue because it was on sale [...] A lot of my work is about being under the circumstances.[32]

Dogg's character seems to call the bluff of Judd's matter of fact persona, to outdo it and make it absurd. While Dogg's tire covers also suggest inflatables, of sorts, the critique here is more sustained, its tenor unlike the subversive lightness and silliness of the previous examples. We imagine, instead, Judd's seriousness trumped by the all-American machismo of Dogg: drag races, girlfriend ('Breasts. Big thighs, bottom.'), gun collection et al.

Warhol's *Silver Clouds* suggest a scopic and social distance between the gallery and the world that Warhol inhabited at the Factory. Caught on film, its atmospheric and anti-object aesthetic seemed to offer marketable alternatives to the artworld and its institutions. With *Silver Clouds*, Warhol was able to gesture towards this aesthetic in the gallery space: collapsing categorical distinctions and polluting the tightly framed co-constitution of value between viewer and object with the unbounded sensibility and atmospherics of Factory life. In drawing attention to atmosphere the work provided a foil to artworld pretensions, specifically those of Minimalism. However, in another sculpture made by Warhol, that was contemporary with *Silver Clouds*, the differing aesthetic tendencies of Factory and artworld might be presented as in negotiation as well as opposition. In 1965 Warhol made a series of large silkscreens on Plexiglas derived from his early films (plate 3.4). The first of these structures, called *Large Sleep* (1965), contains images stacked one on top of another made from two inverted consecutive frames from the 1963 film *Sleep*, a five-hour-plus film made up of multiple fixed-camera shots of Warhol's then lover, the poet John Giorno, asleep. The second, *Large Kiss* (1965), is identical in structure to *Large Sleep* and a similar size. It features two frames from the film *Kiss* featuring Rufus Collins, a friend of Warhol's since the 1950s, and Naomi Levine, described by Warhol as 'my first female superstar.'[33]

The images on clear grounds resemble the acetates, or 'screens', used in the production of silkscreen paintings. George Frei and Neil Printz catalogue similar free standing structures produced from frames of *Eat*, *Kiss*, *Empire* and *Henry Geldzahler*, all films made between 1963 and 1964. The *Catalogue Raisonné* also describes six existing Plexiglas sculptures derived from *Sleep*, including some smaller ones, which were part of an unsuccessful venture to make editions for enthusiasts of the early films.[34] These small Plexiglas pieces assert their status as mementos by showing more features of the medium of film than their larger cousins: there are more than two frames and the sprocket holes are visible. While the smaller versions are only about 30cm tall, the *Large* works are much bigger, *Large Sleep*, for example, measures 153cm tall by 122.9cm wide and it stands on metal supports which equip it for display on the floor of an exhibition space. The *Large* works are still suggestive of the film-reel format from which the images were taken but aspects such as the sprocket holes and the manufacturer's name, present in the smaller works, are absent.

Even more than *Silver Clouds*, this series of works should be vital, at least symbolically, in connecting the two important strands of Warhol's early practice: they 'project' the content of two key early films into the gallery through a design derived from his painting. However, art history does not seem to agree. There is no extensive discussion of *Large Sleep* in the literature on Warhol, although it is referred to in passing. For example, two years after Warhol's death, Marco Livingstone wrote: 'Warhol produced several works in which he screened onto Plexiglas enlargements from his early films [...] acknowledging the common ground of form and technique in his paintings and film'. However, little is said about this 'common ground'.[35] Likewise, Stephen Koch has suggested elusively:

> Almost every one of [Warhol's] early works is marked by a very strong—not to mention rather stable—pictorial composition; all immediately suggest Warhol's earlier choice of photographs for his silk-screens. In fact, he made some very fine silk-screens from the characteristic style from frames of *Eat, Sleep* and *Kiss*.[36]

The image in Koch's book also presents the work as a painting, the stand is not visible and a plain background disguises the transparency of the Plexiglas. However, *Large Sleep* and *Large Kiss*, literally 'standing' between silkscreen painting and film, are emphatically also sculpture: one can move around them, see them backwards, see the surrounding space *through* their clear plastic. This is also a function of Marcel Duchamp's *The Bride Stripped Bare by Her Bachelors, Even*, otherwise known as the *Large Glass* (1915–23) which *Large Sleep* and *Kiss* imitate both in terms of their structure, their title and, as I will argue, their content.[37] Around this time, another Pop artist, Richard Hamilton, was also making his homage to the *Large Glass*, commissioned in 1966 for a Duchamp exhibition at the Tate Gallery. All three artists met at Duchamp's 1963 Pasadena retrospective and I do not doubt that Warhol made these works with Hamilton's project in mind.

Like *Silver Clouds*, Warhol's *Large* works therefore have a three-way categorical ambiguity, with modalities of sculpture, painting and film layered on top of one another. Film is made the subject of sculpture but equally, with films such as *Empire*, of the Empire State Building, and those in which the human subjects were, or were trying to be, still (still like statues, one might say), there is also something sculptural about the subject of Warhol's films. Because of the works' translucence the sculpture reflects a 'loop' of film projected onto the gallery space as if it were a giant film acetate and one were looking back through a cinema screen towards the audience on the other side. A studio portrait taken by Jerry Schatzberg in 1966 goes some way to confirming that the intended function of the *Large* works was to project their images out into the surrounding space, as if the gallery floors and walls were cinema screens. In the background of the photograph, an

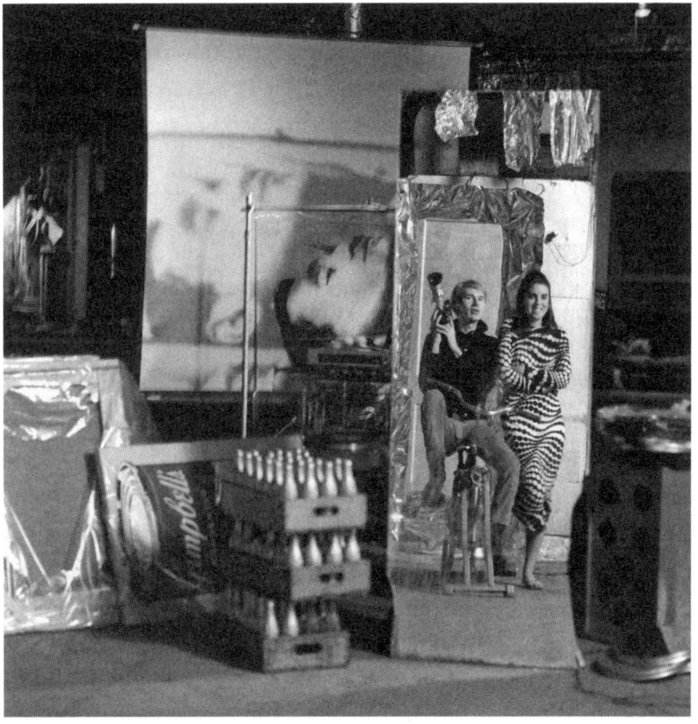

Fig. 3.3 Jerry Schatzberg, Andy Warhol, 'Factory', 1966. Courtesy of Trunk Archive and Jerry Schatzberg.

acetate of the image used for *Large Sleep* is projected onto the Factory's movie projector screen (fig. 3.3.). This is another instance, then, in which Warhol's sculpture, following in the wake of his painting career, attempted to transform the artworld of objects into atmospheres; immersive environments suited to a mode of distracted attention that allowed for a greater focus on social interaction. Warhol's claim that he was going to 'devote his life to the cinema' from this time makes the Plexiglas work a mission statement as well as a sculptural adieu.[38] Thus the Plexiglas works share with the *Silver Cloud* 'paintings' the status of 'retirement' pieces: both are reflective, and both are lenses of retrospection through which one might literally 'look back' at other examples of Warhol's work in the gallery space. Much later, Warhol's *Reversals* and *Retrospectives* series of paintings from 1979 repeat this action of looking back in painting form.

Large Sleep and *Large Kiss* are reflective, self-referential components of Warhol's own body of work as it shifted from painting to film and art-world to underground. As calculated and timely responses to Duchamp's *Large Glass*, these works also reflect on the work of an art historical figure of huge importance for that moment. But, perhaps most importantly, the works should be read as *both* these things. These works were made to reflect the new situation Warhol had fostered around himself at the Factory at this time via Duchamp's conceptual format that rendered vision a sexual practice. In Warhol's version, however, desire does not seem to go anywhere. Warhol, watching Giorno, does not have his gaze returned; Giorno's own image returns on itself. Both men are left with their own thoughts/dreams: the introverted doubling and self-reflection echoing the self-referential and reflexive status of the series more generally.[39] The identical images of Giorno in *Large Sleep* (which I lean my analysis towards here) create a void, the visual content is not 'generative' in the same way that Duchamp's system of hetero-courtship is (which seems to imply a narrative outcome). Instead, *Large Sleep* is both singular and endlessly divisible, it dissolves into the cinematic atmosphere, its main job to cast shadows. This sense of lack and absence can also signify death, 'the big sleep'. Branden W. Joseph has considered the erotics of death imagery as linking the film *Sleep* with an early drawing by Warhol of the dead James Dean.[40] In doing so, he combined a discussion of American culture's 'appropriation and transfiguration of a socially abjected and pathologized image of gay male sexuality' with an analysis of the pulsing, fractal and self-negating mechanisms of pornographic looking.[41]

Both *Large Sleep* and *Large Kiss* are reversible; they resemble windows and they act as lenses; they project outward as much as they echo the cinema screens and canvases that Warhol projected images onto and which the work is formally part-way between. One sees through the characters in *Large Sleep* and *Large Kiss*, doubles of themselves, into the reverse world on the other side where everything, in one way or another, is 'backwards'. All the eyes are closed in these works but each face is two-sided as well as doubled, allowing multiple views and viewing positions. This situation again suggests that while Warhol's visual world was both other to and at the same time made compatible with the normative aesthetic sphere of the gallery, its otherness was constituted by an identity that could not be acknowledged. This is precisely the significance of doubling that Richard Meyer has applied to more famous examples of Warhol's work, such as in his study of Warhol's 'clones'. Of the 1960 image of the gun-wielding Elvis Presley that Warhol used in his 1963 paintings, Meyer writes:

> When a movie still of Elvis Presley seeks itself through Warholian repetition, it discovers a homoeroticism which its original Hollywood context could not acknowledge. In *Double Elvis* Warhol recovers the intrinsic queer appeal of a mass-cultural representation which would otherwise disavow the presence of its (admiring) gay male audience.[42]

In Meyer's analysis the double Elvises find an erotic point of contact, clasping their hands around the gun wielded by the star dressed as a cowboy. In repeating this doubling across media, the *Large* works are important not just because of what they do in bridging the artwork and the films but because they remind us of key theoretical interpretations of Warhol's practice as a whole. In another, Annette Michelson's essay on Warhol's factory and the romantic theme of the *Gesamtkunstwerk*, doubling again enables a metaphysically reorganised world. Echoing *Large Sleep*, Michelson states this is a world 'seen in reverse,' and which, as in Meyer's reading, accommodates difference.[43] She imagines the door to Warhol's Factory as resembling Duchamp's door in *Onze, rue Larrey* (1927)—a 'double door', always both open and closed, revealing:

> the din and clutter, the revelry and theatrics of Bakhtinian carnival. The old Factory, the site of Warhol's recasting of the *Gesamtkunstwerk*, solicits analysis in terms of Bakhtin's master category.[44]

With their focus on doubling, Meyer and Michelson both suggest that the Warholian subject is one to be considered in terms of masquerade: Meyer with figures such as the famous Castro Street clone; Michelson implied through the category of carnival. Yet these are different forms of masquerade and reflect the different approaches the authors take. While Meyer addresses Warhol's subversion of the norms which spectacle promoted, Michelson considers the rewiring of aesthetic and social order from which this work emerged at the Factory. She writes:

> It was Warhol's strength to have revised the notion of the *Gesamtkunstwerk*, displacing it, redefining it as site of production, and recasting it in the mode of carnival, thereby generating for our time the most trenchant articulation of relation between cultures, high and low.[45]

The two theoretical frameworks through which Michelson and Meyer address the different aspects of Warhol's practice—spectacle and carnival—would traditionally be considered antithetical and incompatible. For Bakhtin, 'Carnival is not spectacle seen by the people; they live in it […] While carnival lasts, there is no other life outside it.'[46] Far from being opposed, however, one suggestion that is contained within Michelson's analysis is that, in this case, spectacle and carnival have become embedded within one another: while the site of production was one of disorder as Michelson describes, its articulation was nonetheless broadcast to the cinema audience within the orderly framework of spectacle. And I want to suggest this proximity between spectacle and carnival might be brought to bear on our understanding of the *Large* works. Indeed, my contention here is that another level of masquerade is at play; that, at this moment, Warhol was involved in transforming the experience of spectacle in such a way that it came close to being enveloped by its opposite category of carnival; wherein the one came to be presented in the mask of the other. If so, nowhere else were these two theoretical categories brought into greater proximity, and to greater effect, than at Warhol's multimedia extravaganzas. These, collected under the moniker *Exploding Plastic Inevitable*, were described in an article from the time as 'the strongest and most developed example of intermedia art.'[47] Take, for example, Ronnie Cutrone's recollection of a late EPI performance:

> The last time we played as the *EPI* (without Nico, who had returned to Ibiza) was in May 1967 at Steve Paul's Scene where Tiny Tim used to hang out and Jim Morrison played. Before this people came to watch the *EPI* dance and play, they were entertained, and got a show. But when we played at the Scene I remember Gerard, Mary and I were dancing and the audience came on stage with us and totally took over… Everybody became part of the *EPI*. It was a bit sad, because we couldn't keep our glory on stage, but we were happy because what the *EPI* intended to do had worked—everybody was liberated to be

> as sick as we were acting! All of a sudden there were no dancers, there was no show; the music had just taken everybody at that point. That was the last time I danced, and I think the last time Mary and Gerard danced. I mean maybe they tried futilely after that, but it didn't work.[48]

Between Cutrone's 'glory'—determined by his separation from the audience—and the consequential effect of the *EPI* on that audience, there is a shift that perfectly illustrates the distinction between spectacle and carnival. The intention of the *EPI*, as Cutrone says, was the production of carnival *out of spectacle*; out of the multimedia bombardment that Warhol orchestrated at these events with the help of Danny Williams, who designed its ground breaking light show, and the music of The Velvet Underground. Branden W. Joseph has described in more detail how the *EPI* seized new technologies to engender a situation that brought about the frenzied carnivalesque situation Cutrone describes above:

> At the height of its development, the *Exploding Plastic Inevitable* included three to five film projectors, often showing different reels of the same film simultaneously; a similar number of slide projectors, movable by hand so that their images swept the auditorium; four variable-speed strobe lights; three moving spots with an assortment of colored gels; several pistol lights; a mirror ball hung from the ceiling and another on the floor; as many as three loudspeakers blaring different pop records at once; one to two sets by the Velvet Underground and Nico; and the dancing of Gerard Malanga and Mary Woronov or Ingrid Superstar, complete with props and lights that projected their shadows high onto the wall.[49]

Stephen Koch describes this environment as one 'capable of shattering the senses'. One in which the 1960s message of intersubjective harmony and sexual freedom had, in its gestation in the Factory, gone seriously awry. Recalling Warhol's multimedia onslaught, Koch continues:

> Seeing it made me realise for the first time how deeply the then all-admired theories attacking the 'ego' as the root of all evil and unhappiness had become for the avant-garde the grounds for a deeply engaged metaphor of sexual sadism, for 'blowing the mind', assaulting the senses; it came home to me how

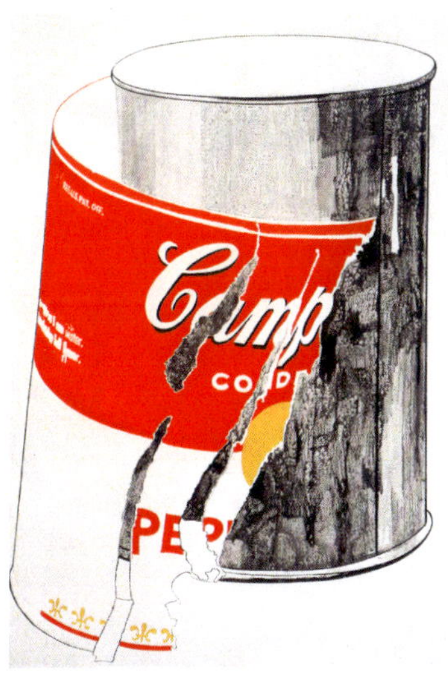

Plate 1.1   Andy Warhol, *Big Torn Campbell's Soup Can (Pepper Pot)*, 1962. Collection of The Andy Warhol Museum, Pittsburgh.

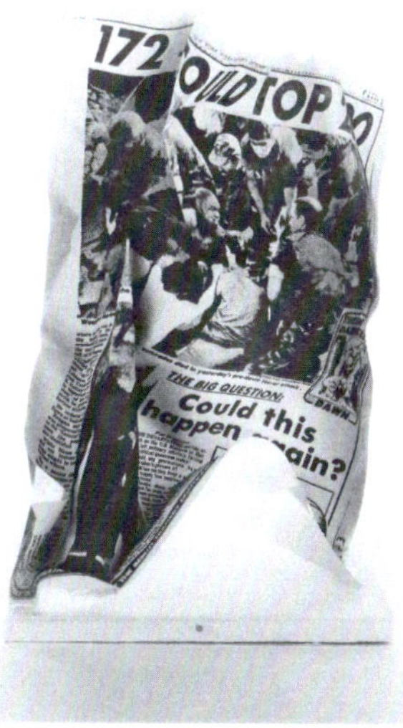

Plate 1.2   Andy Warhol, *Abstract Sculpture*, 1983, Screenprint on crumpled Mylar, 45.7 x 24.8cm, framed 50.8 x 30.48 x 27.94 cm. Collection Christopher Makos. The Andy Warhol Foundation for the Visual Arts, Inc. Photograph Takao Ikejiri.

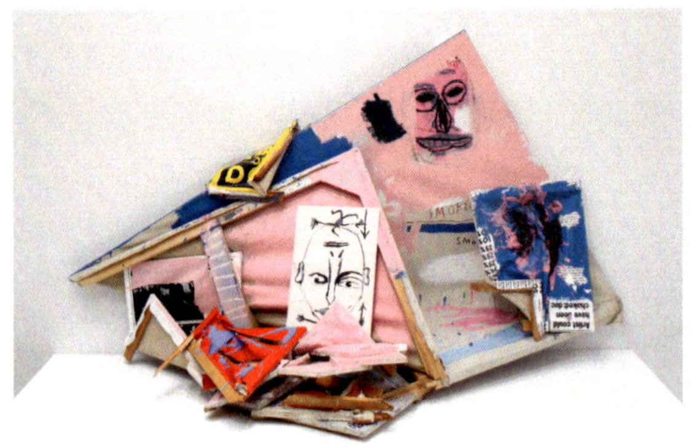

Plate 1.3 Andy Warhol, Jean-Michel Basquiat, Francesco Clemente, *Collaboration (Abstract Sculpture), ca.* 1984. Collection of The Andy Warhol Museum, Pittsburgh.

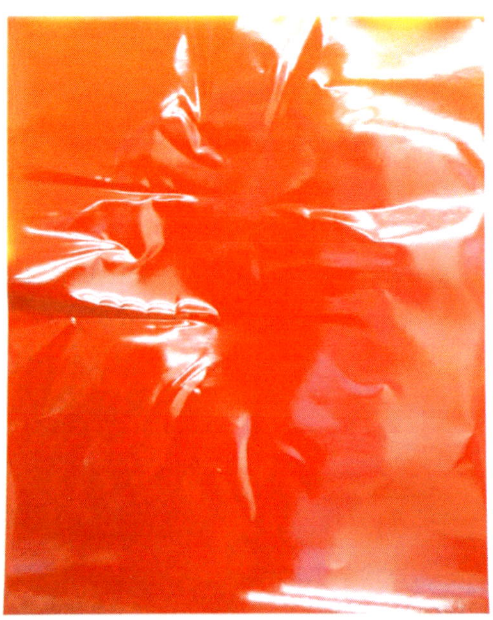

Plate 1.4 Wolfgang Tillmans, *Lighter 84*, unique c-type print in Plexiglas hood, 64 x 54 cm, 2010. Courtesy of the artist and Maureen Paley Gallery.

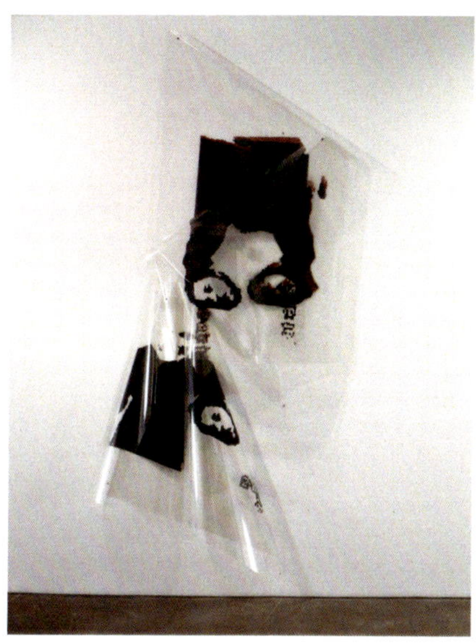

Plate 1.5 Seth Price, Hostage *Video Still with Time Stamp*, 2005, Road-sign inks screen-printed on polyester film, grommets. Courtesy of the artist.

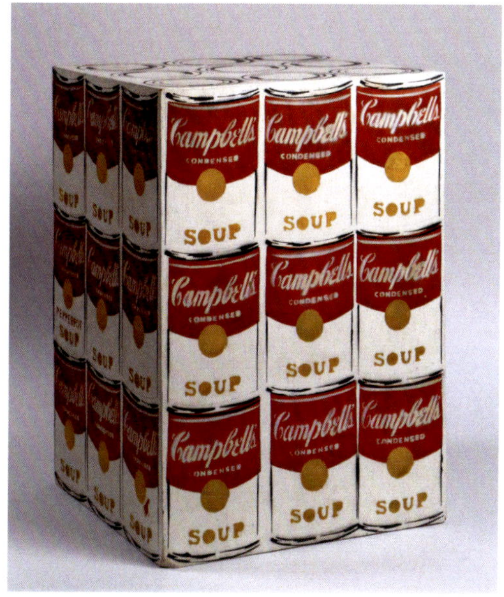

Plate 2.1 Andy Warhol, *Campbell's Soup Box*, 1962. Collection of The Andy Warhol Museum, Pittsburgh.

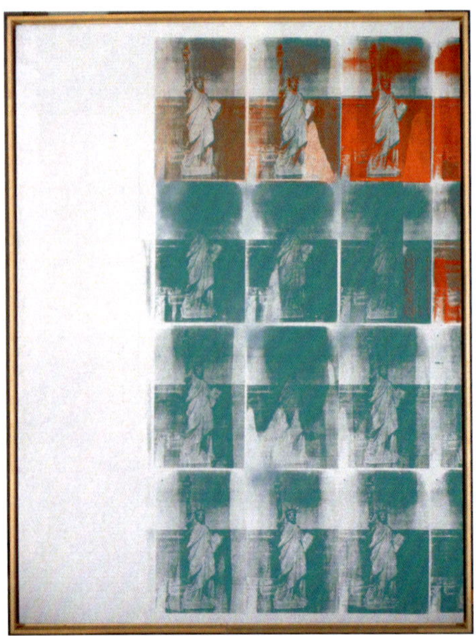

Plate 2.2 Andy Warhol, *Statue of Liberty*, 1962. Collection of The Andy Warhol Museum, Pittsburgh.

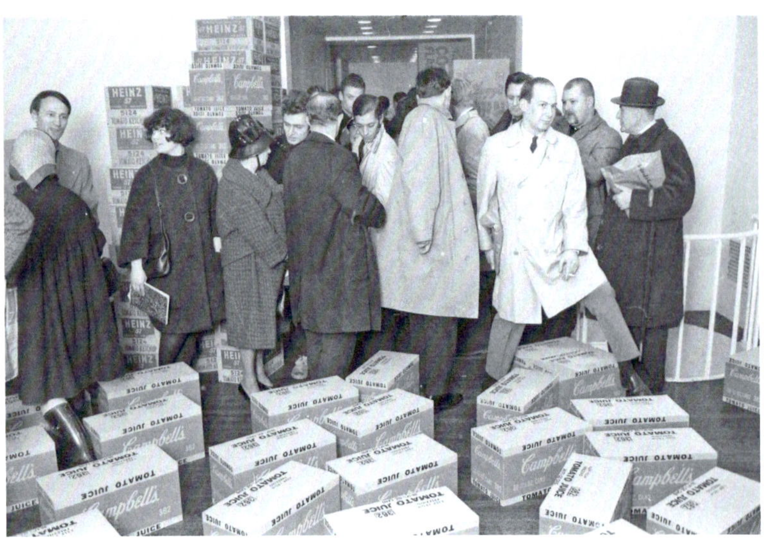

Plate 2.3 Ken Heyman, *Stable Gallery*, 1964. Courtesy of Ken Heyman.

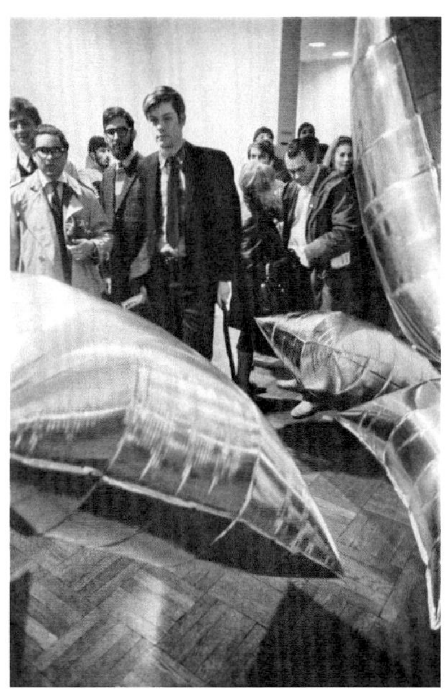

Plate 3.1 Andy Warhol, *Silver Clouds*, 1966. © Nat Finkelstein.

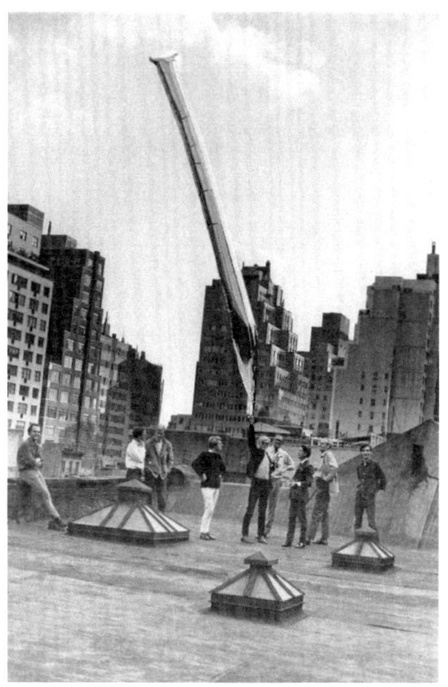

Plate 3.2 Billy Name, *Photograph of Andy Warhol with Infinite Sculpture on roof of the Factory*, 1965. Courtesy of Billy Name.

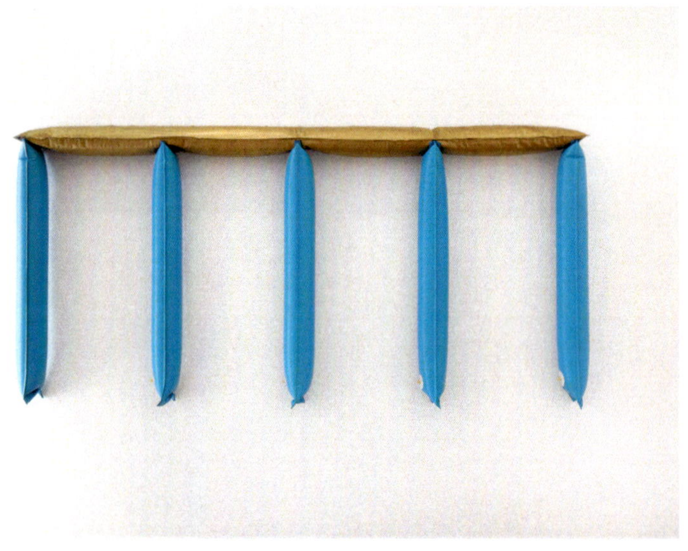

Plate 3.3 IT, *Pneumatic Judd*, 1965. Exhibition view at Raven Row, London, 2013. Photograph by Marcus J. Leith. Courtesy of the artist and TrépanierBaer Gallery.

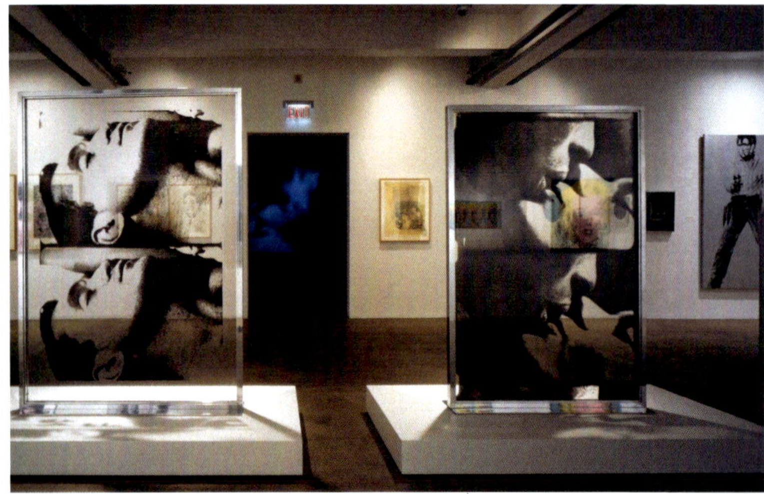

Plate 3.4 Installation of Andy Warhol's *Large Sleep* and *Large Kiss* sculptures at The Andy Warhol Museum, 1994. Collection of The Andy Warhol Museum, Pittsburgh.

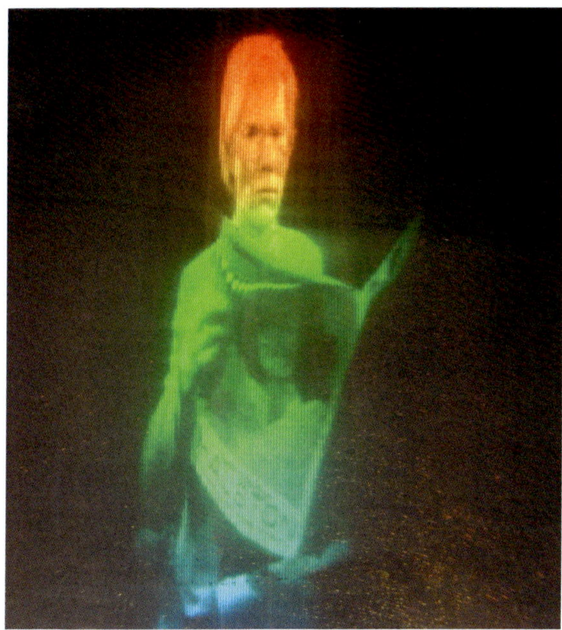

Plate 3.5 Jason Sapan, *Portrait of Andy Warhol*, 1977. Hologram, Plexiglas, light. Courtesy of Jason Sapan.

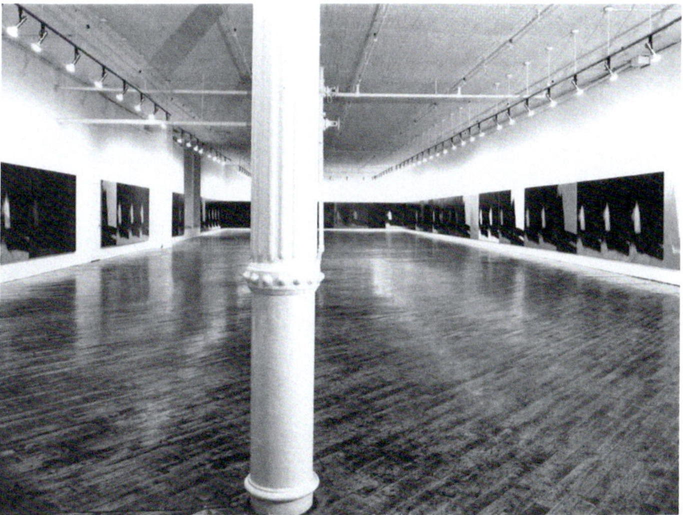

Plate 4.1 Andy Warhol, Installation view, *Shadows*, 1978–79, Heiner Friedrich Gallery, 393 West Broadway, New York City. Courtesy of the Dia Art Foundation, New York.

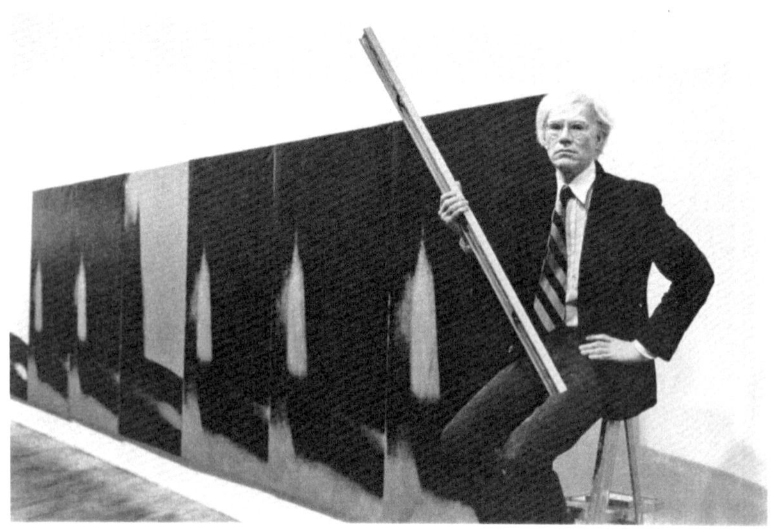

Plate 4.2 Andy Warhol in the installation of *Shadows*, 1978–79, Heiner Friedrich Gallery, 393 West Broadway, New York City. Photo: Arthur Tress. Courtesy of the Dia Art Foundation, New York.

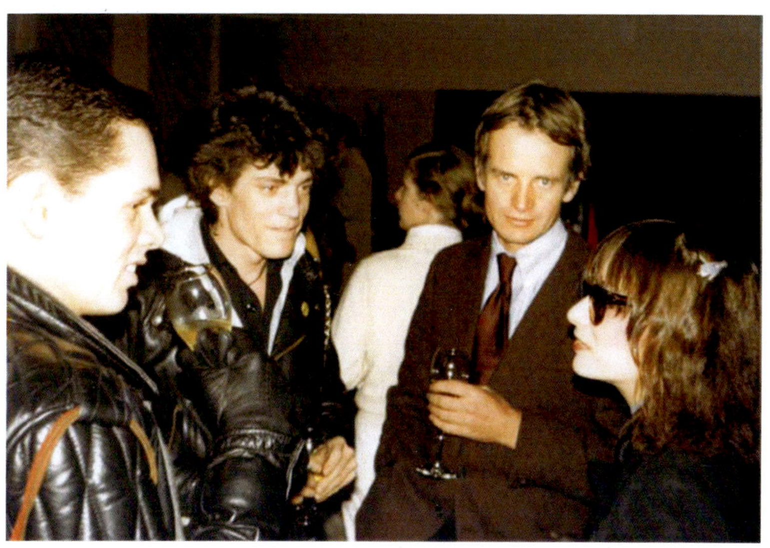

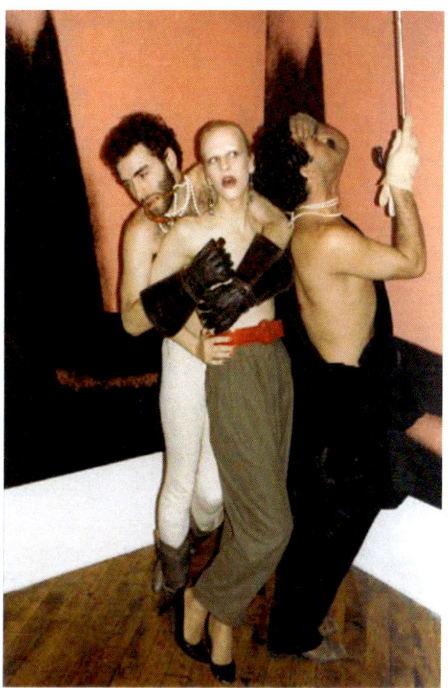

Plates 4.3 and 4.4 *Guests to the Shadows 1979 exhibition*. Courtesy of the Dia Art Foundation.

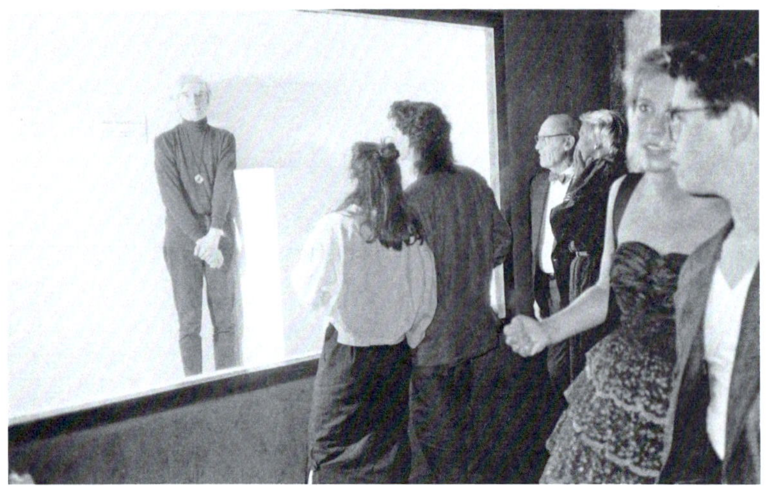

Plate 4.5 *View of Andy Warhol, Invisible Sculpture at Area*, 1985. Photograph by Paige Powell copyright (LOC) 1985.

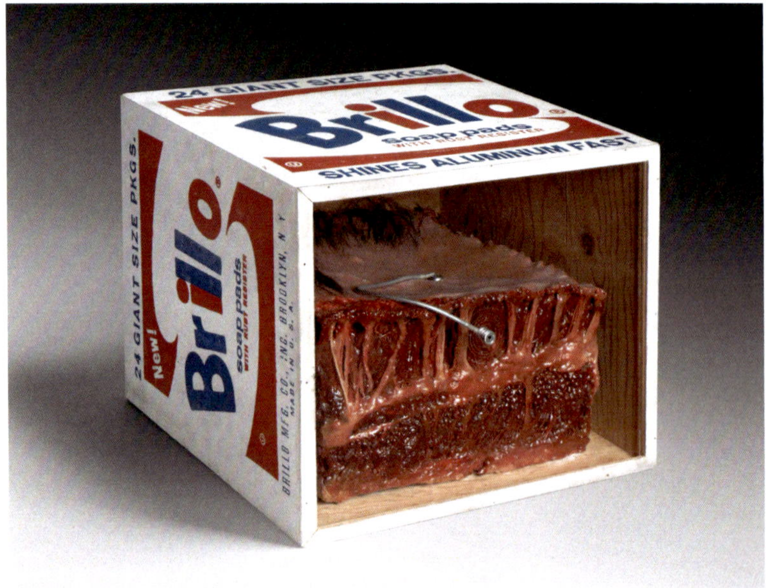

Plate 4.6 Paul Thek, *Meat Piece with Warhol Brillo Box*, 1965. Beeswax, painted wood and Plexiglass. 35.6 x 43.2 x 43.2 cm. Philadelphia Museum of Art: Purchased with funds contributed by the Daniel W. Dietrich Foundation, 1990 © The Estate of George Paul Thek. Courtesy of Alexander and Bonin, New York.

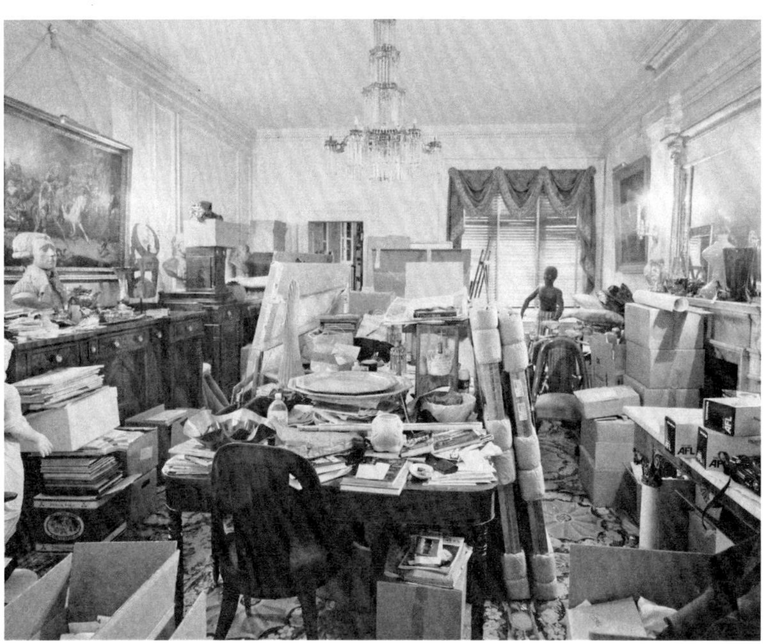

Plate 5.1 Evelyn Hofer, *Andy Warhol Dining Room, N.Y. 1987*, Estate of Evelyn Hofer.

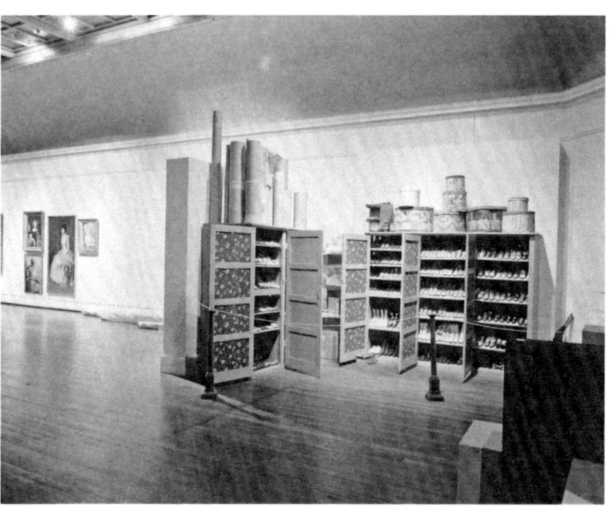

Plate 5.2 *Installation view of Raid the Icebox I with Andy Warhol*, Museum of Art, Rhode Island School of Design, 23 April-30 June, 1970. Courtesy of the Museum of Art, Rhode Island School of Design, Providence.

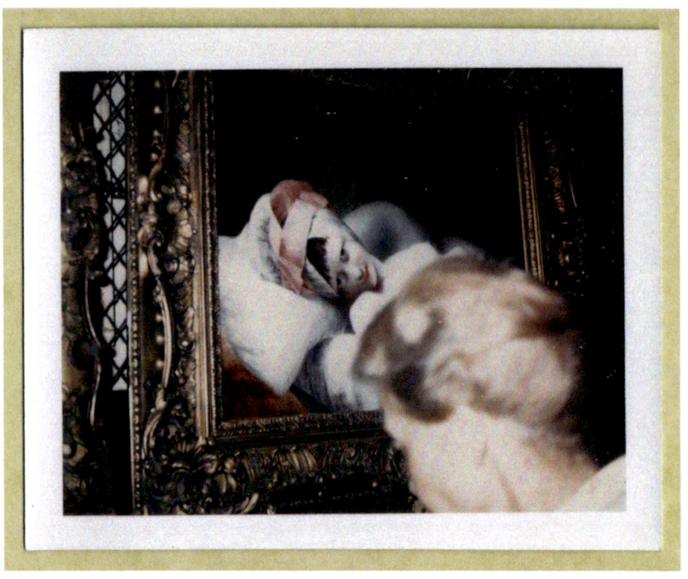

Plate 5.3 Andy Warhol, *Dominique de Menil in front of "Portrait of Lydia" by Rev. Matthew William Peters, from "Little Red Book No. 172"*, 1969. Collection of The Andy Warhol Museum, Pittsburgh.

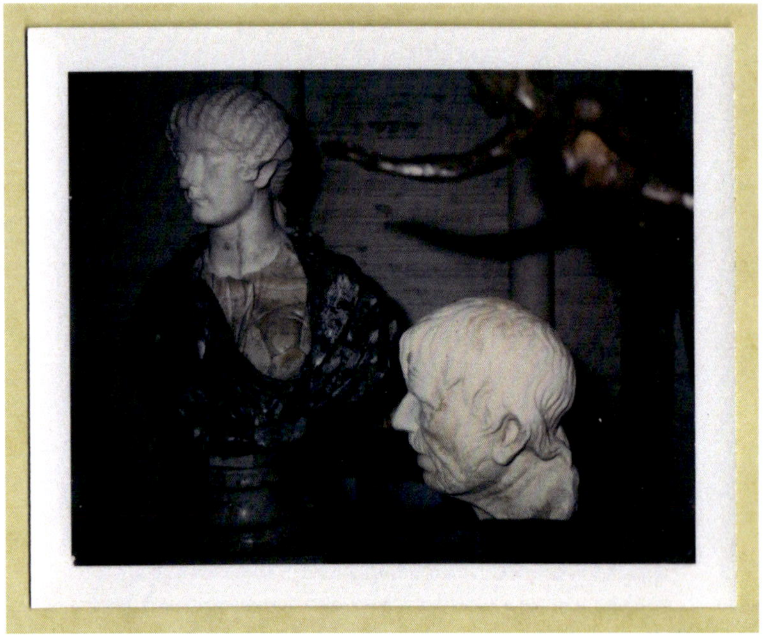

Plate 5.4 Andy Warhol, *Sculpture, from "Little Red Book No. 172"*, 1969. Collection of The Andy Warhol Museum, Pittsburgh.

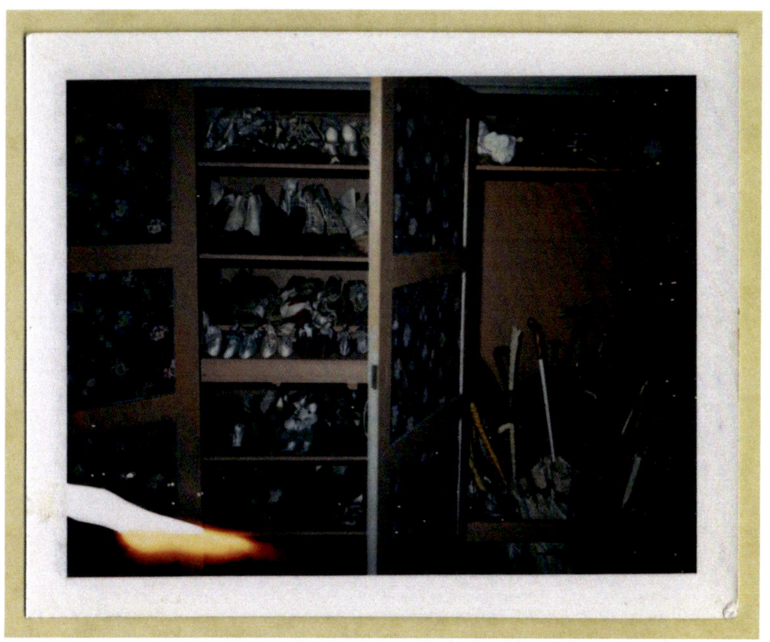

Plate 5.5 Andy Warhol, *Objects, from "Little Red Book No. 172"*, 1969. Collection of The Andy Warhol Museum, Pittsburgh.

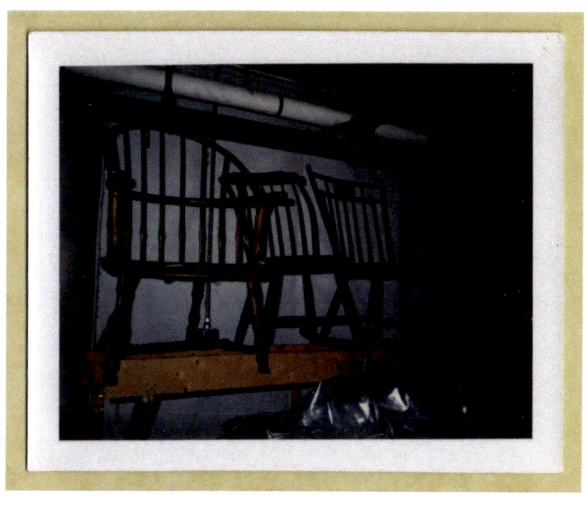

Plate 5.6 Andy Warhol, *Chairs, from "Little Red Book No. 172"*, 1969. Collection of The Andy Warhol Museum, Pittsburgh.

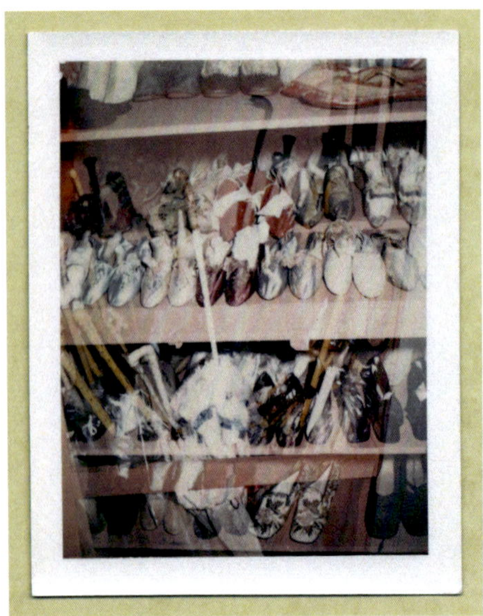

Plate 5.7 Andy Warhol, *Double exposure, historical footwear and antique parasols, from "Little Red Book No. 172"*, 1969. Collection of The Andy Warhol Museum, Pittsburgh.

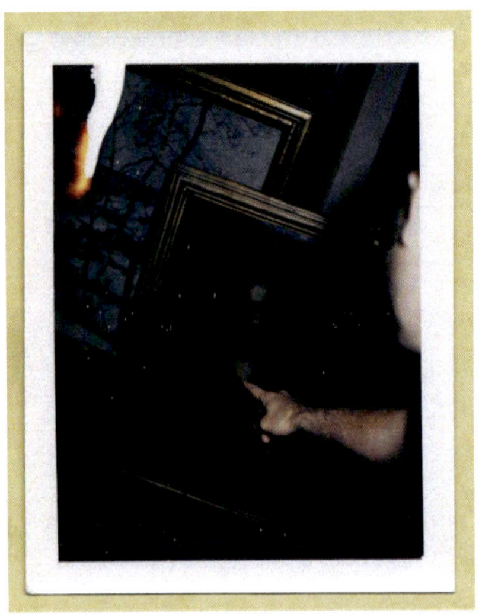

Plate 5.8 Andy Warhol, *Person pointing to a copy of Leonardo's "Mona Lisa", from "Little Red Book No. 172"*, 1969. Collection of The Andy Warhol Museum, Pittsburgh.

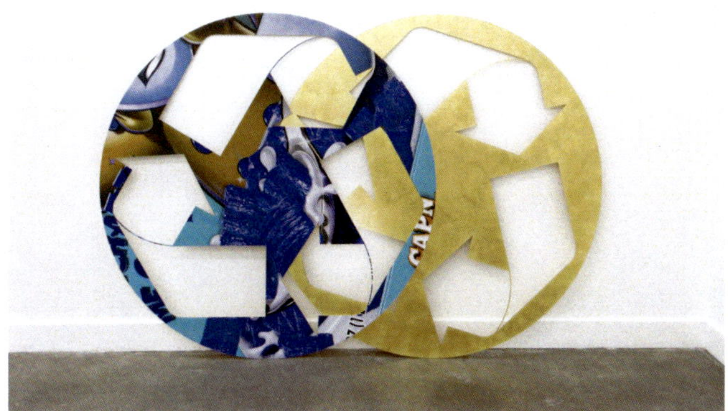

Plate 5.9 Kelley Walker, *Untitled +180 or -180 hue and Untitled*, 2007. 146.1 diameter x .3 cm. Installation shot: Le Magisin-Centre National d'Art Contemporain, Grenoble, France (10/7/07-1/6/08). © Kelley Walker. Courtesy of the Paula Cooper Gallery, New York.

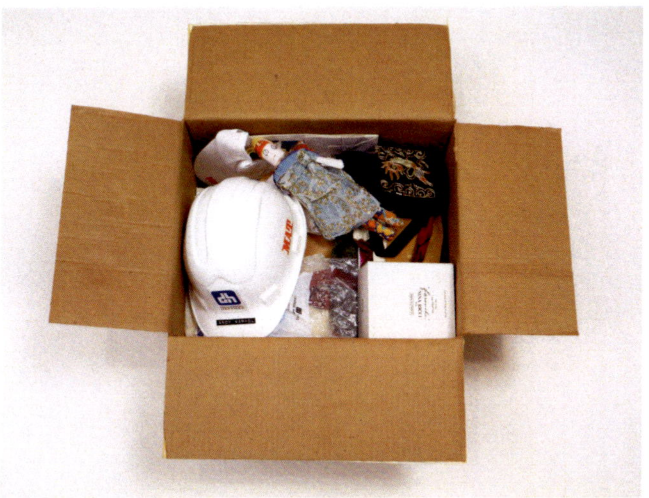

Plate 5.10 Andy Warhol, *Time Capsule -11*, 1977. Collection of The Andy Warhol Museum, Pittsburgh.

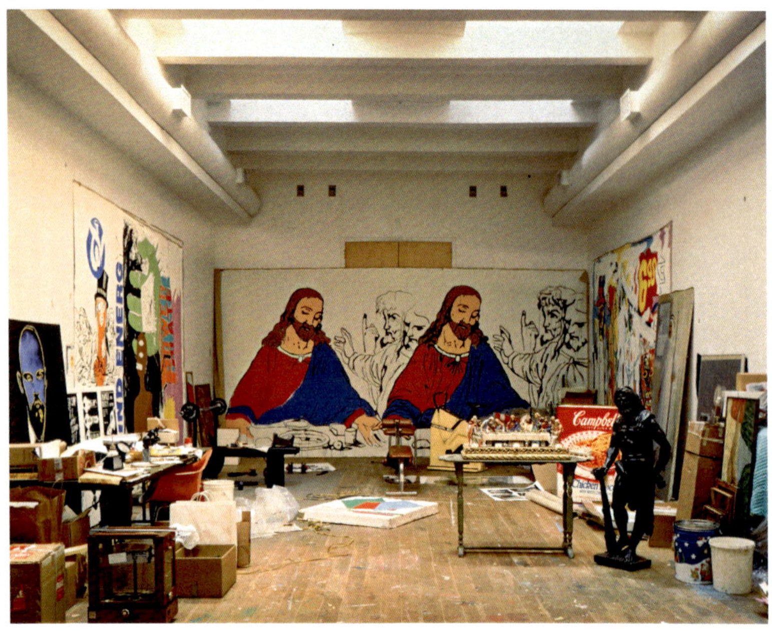

Plate 6.1 Evelyn Hofer, *Warhol's Studio with Last Supper, N.Y. 1987*. Estate of Evelyn Hofer.

the 'obliteration' of the ego was not the act of liberation it was
advertised to be [...] Liberation was turning out to be humilia-
tion; peace was turning itself into rage.[50]

The *EPI* premiered during the same month as the *Silver Clouds* exhibition
opened and can also, as I have argued of *Silver Clouds* and *Large Sleep*, be
seen as an extension of Factory aesthetics into a public space. With *Silver
Clouds* hovering over above, perhaps *Large Kiss* and *Large Sleep*, in the gallery, speak of the borderline between the two different states that Warhol's
underground world shifted between at this moment, with masquerade and
'acting' on one side and full-blown submersion into the world of carnival
on the other. They represent, through their doubling and their projection
out into spectator space, Warhol's deployment of cinema as a nebulous
extension of carnival's atmosphere, yet one that operates according to the
logic of spectacle. A dual consciousness is implied therefore: one spectates
and yet, as a spectator, seen from the other side of the screen, one is also a
carnival-goer in a reverse world where spectatorship itself has become an
arena of carnival. In this way, Cutrone's audience at the *EPI*, driven wild,
turn him into a spectator of his own show. Perhaps themselves masquerad-
ing, as art objects, the atmospheric, cinematic *Large* works trespass on the
space of the artworld and its object at a time when notions of representation were particularly at stake. Yet both works, in standing for Warhol's
Factory, stand for a world in which there can be no trespass, apart from the
trespass of order into chaos, and it is in this that the real transgression lies.

Whether during an *EPI* event, or in the gallery, Warhol's gaze, as both
spectator and participant, disseminates into the audience space. It becomes
climatic, as well as climactic, in the same way the *Clouds* relied on climatic
conditions which stood in for the forms of cinematic and sexualised looking
that occurred in Warhol's underground. The audience become part of a carnival scene, in some way other to who they were when they arrived. To return
to Jerry Schatzberg's photograph of the Factory, the acetate image of John
Giorno, used in *Large Sleep*, projects a huge figure overlooking where Warhol
poses in a mirror reflection—recalling Velázquez's *Las Meninas*—while sitting on an exercise bike, Edie Sedgwick in a hip Op designer dress standing alongside him. In the photograph the image from *Sleep* acts as a banner
under which all activities at the Factory take place. The projection of Giorno

haunts the scene; the large, slightly off-centre image competes with the photographer's intended focus on the figure of Warhol in the foreground. This is the function of these portal-like sculptures which steal away the image and the subject with it into a subversive second life. In the case of the Plexiglas sculptures, as in the *EPI*, the sensual dis-coordination, the loss of any narrative structure, secure viewing position or framing means that the spectator cannot keep the image at arm's length. In the carnival of Warhol's translucent extended film space, the viewer takes part behind the *mask* of spectacle's subject. There is a collapsing of the two orders, which is made possible through an emptying-out of spectatorial roles — as defined by definite objects in definite structures. But Warhol, as ever, does not offer us anything redemptive about spectacle or spectatorship. Instead, he reflects the bleak abandon of the situation of spectacle in a subversive way, and maybe that is all we can hope for. If capitalism's forms of mass media are based on an *illusion* of the carnivalesque, of entering and taking part in a 'second life' *where in fact we remain powerless and detached*, Warhol reverses this model. In his work, we play out spectatorship in the manner of the carnivalesque; we put on the mask of the spectator and act out our role. In this way the dangers of spectacle and the carnivalesque—that the subject is passively detached in the former, and unconscious of the space of carnival in the latter—are overcome. Here by 'playing' the spectator one enters the Bakhtinian fray.

Rain Machine

Fifteenth-century accounts of carnivals include descriptions of mistaken identity that had lasting and brutal consequences. Such things are a measure, indeed, of the carnival's apparent 'realness'. By 1968, the scene at the Factory had got out of control and Warhol Enterprises moved to the smarter location of 33 Union Square, in part to escape the craziness. After the move only a few of the early hangers-on remained, yet the moral confusion might be said to have followed Warhol (himself still in costume as the 'prince of Pop') in the form of Valerie Solanas who gunned Warhol down on 3 June that year. Warhol nearly died of his injuries and when he returned to work after the attack he was a much frailer, more vulnerable creature, while his subsequent work did not include much painting. Instead, with

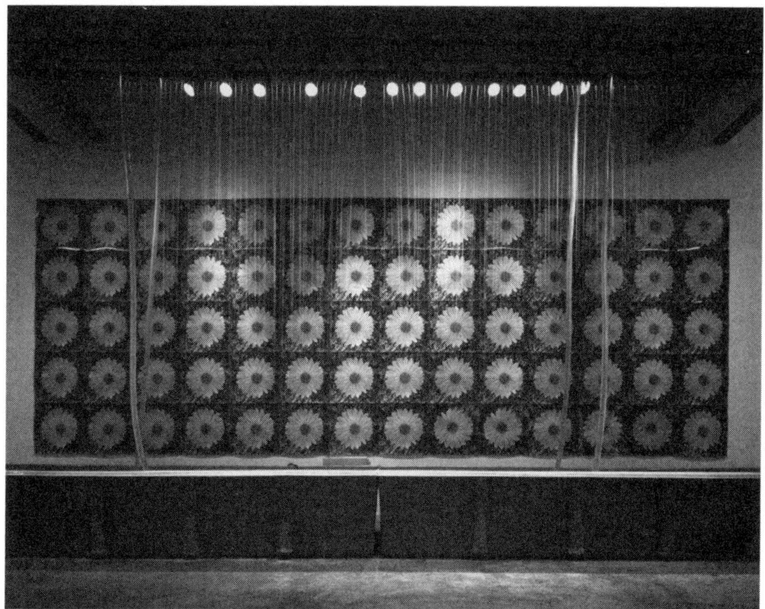

Fig. 3.4. Andy Warhol, *Daisy Waterfall (Rain Machine)*, 1971. Collection of The Andy Warhol Museum, Pittsburgh.

Paul Morrissey as his director, he ramped up his film ventures. At this time of upheaval, however, Warhol was developing a sculpture work, one that speaks to the many themes that distinguish the works already considered in this chapter.[51]

Rain Machine (Daisy Waterfall) of *c*.1970, consisted of a large shower of water in front of a wall of 3D lenticular prints of daisies (fig. 3.4). This work had two manifestations: the first shown at Expo '70 in Osaka, the second exhibited at the 1971 Art and Technology (A&T) exhibition organised by Maurice Tuchman for the Los Angeles County Museum of Art, the home of the A&T programme. A&T assigned artists to industrial manufacturers and, with the technologies these manufacturers offered at their disposal, the artists were then supposed to make novel artworks. Warhol's *Rain Machine* was made in conjunction with Cowles Communications for the images, and Today's Displays for the display and mechanical elements. Tuchman also oversaw the work's installation and, in this capacity, he made important decisions about layout which Warhol had left open, much in the same way as he had in 1963 when he merely sent a roll of *Elvises* to the Ferus Gallery for installation.

Today's Displays, who made shop displays, constructed the 'machine' part of the work. This consisted of a pump and sprinkler system on a metal frame with a reservoir beneath. While their use of technology was not the focus of the collaboration, the inclusion of the company reminds us of an earlier period in which Warhol's artistic development was very much entwined with this industry. The overall effect of the work as a 'display' is not so far from the work Warhol did as a window dresser for Bonwit Teller in 1955, where Robert Rauschenberg, Jasper Johns and, later, James Rosenquist were also employed, and where Warhol worked again in 1961 when Gene Moore showed Warhol's early paintings in the shop window.[52]

Cowles produced visual panographics, rectilinear, ridged, plastic images which give a slight 3D effect and which are sometimes still seen on postcards. Warhol had been initially earmarked to work with a company capable of making holograms but in the event did not because, as a report from the programme says, 'by the time Warhol was really committed to the project, the only contracted corporation able or prepared to execute an elaborate holographic display — Hewlett-Packard — was already engaged in collaboration with Rockne Krebs.'[53] A poor second to holography, the panographic images did not work as Warhol hoped: the images only move at all if you are less than ten feet away, which was not much considering that *Rain Machine* is 20 feet across and the screen apparatus stands nearly six feet out from the wall. The work proceeded through a constant series of compromising adjustments as Warhol's expectations about the production were disappointed. Jane Livingstone, writing for A&T, recalls Warhol's comments at the time:

> It occurred to Warhol at this time that he liked the idea of simply displaying the rain producing mechanism forthrightly, rather than encasing the pipes and trough in a wooden struc-ture, as he had in his earlier small model.
>
> One of the artist's reasons for this decision had to do with his attitude about the 3D printed images as such. He had said to MT, 'You know, this 3D process isn't all that glamor-ous or new or exciting.' He wanted, therefore, to present the

images in conjunction with a naked, unembellished and inelegant structure so that they would *reveal themselves*—maybe perversely—in their rather vulgar and certainly imperfect quality. His original idea for the holograms, to be seen hazily through water, or snowflakes, or vibrating and out of focus, held over in his approach to the 3D printed images: he had wanted, in his word, a 'ghostly' effect. However, the reality of the situation by the time the daisy pictures and rain machine were visualized together, fell short of this vision of ghostliness. Warhol thus adapted his approach to a changed aesthetic.[54]

According to Livingston, Warhol had 'thought vaguely about imagery such as a sphere or cube'.[55] The choice of flowers had not been part of Warhol's earliest plan, but was put forward by one of the corporation's people when Warhol canvassed for ideas at a meeting. Another suggestion, that the images be presented in series, meant that the work became a return to, even a parody of, both the style of formal arrangement and the subject matter that, at the time, Warhol was most famous for – now all arranged by a committee of industry men. Such a relationship was very much how Warhol had once worked as an advertising illustrator: the scenario of going before a board, and of having one's creations tampered with and returned, was one to which he was no stranger. His culling of ideas from colleagues was not novel either and such stories constitute an important part of Warhol's mythologisation. The board's attempts to make a safe suggestion and repeat the success of Warhol's *Flowers* (though a new image, this time of a daisy, was chosen) lends the work, if accidentally, the same 'reflective' quality that I have argued is a feature of *Silver Clouds* and the *Large* works. The pastoral theme of *Rain Machine* is itself also an indicator of a quality of wistfulness, which again echoes *Flowers,* as well as *Silver Clouds* and *Cow Wallpaper* from the period surrounding Warhol's 'retirement' and time of self-reflection.

Most vitally, the work restages, through sculpture, an aesthetic encounter that is characteristic of the cinema and in doing so transposes it into an artistic context. As with *Large Sleep* and its deathly image of Giorno, and with the *Clouds* that 'finish off painting' and yet remain, Warhol's 'ghostly' restaging in *Rain Machine* is imagined as a haunting (see quote above). In the final production, the rain, which descends in two parallel bands or screens, is lit downwards, but originally the plan was to light it side-on. Coupled with the cinema-screen proportions of the arrangement of the flower prints, the work clearly indicates a cinematic encounter. If more effective side-lighting had been available, the design would have caused the falling droplets to 'flicker', replicating the flicker of film cascading over a cinema projector's lamp. This was an important feature of Warhol's early single subject films and *Screen Tests* where the effect had been exaggerated through the use of a slowed-down projection speed of 16fps.

The A&T had parallels with EAT, the organisation Experiments in Art and Technology with which Warhol had already been associated. Both encouraged artists to make use of technologies used by and developed within industry. However, Tuchman's enterprise took quite a different form from that of EAT with A&T having a far more corporate orientation. Rauschenberg, who worked with A&T but for whom, as a co-founder, EAT was of greater importance, was very insistent that the two organisations' approaches were distinct for ideological reasons:

> I don't see that A & T and E.A.T. are in competition… [EAT] was an idea before its time, even though it was a little late. It still didn't come from any vogue. You started from the idea of art […] we had to do just the opposite and say that we are not involved in aesthetics.
>
> We are not censors, we are not talent scouts […] You started from the other end, and because of your endorsement and the fact that you provided the possibility of a guarantee of a showing, it meant that if [artists] committed themselves, then they would have to do it well, which we couldn't do. All of our things begin at one end and either die before they get to the other end or the work is finished. You started at the art end […] In E.A.T. we say, we can get something started but we can't promise you anything.[56]

Rauschenberg hints that, over and above the differences of their approaches, since EAT (actually inaugurated before A&T) came 'a little late', by the time the results of the A&T commissions (beginning in 1968) were shown in 1969–70, A&T was significantly out of touch. Rather than this be a question of trends, however, the timing of the project was crucial to the way it stood in relation to politics. By this time, the beginning of a long period of Republican rule, industry's problematic relation to the American war machine, in overdrive during the excesses of the Vietnam War, had significantly soured the appeal of partnership for artists.[57] The social and industrial shifts at this time, reflected in what Rauschenberg observes as the bankruptcy of the A&T's endeavour, return as one point of focus in the next chapter. But it is worth observing that just when the industries that A&T ostensibly promoted were headed toward crisis, the model of corporate self-promotion through art and artists, something it could be said the A&T did pioneer, helped define new ideas about corporate identity.[58]

The distinction that Rauschenberg makes between what was made for EAT and that made for A&T is also applicable to Warhol's work: between that made in conjunction with Klüver and later with A&T. While *Silver Clouds* are a refusal of traditional aesthetic relations and a breach of genuinely new territory facilitated by new technology, the *Rain Machine* can be seen as a return to a motif from Warhol's oeuvre that, as I have argued, was already loaded with the associations of kitsch. This statement of disdain for artworld aesthetics was then recycled, minus any irony, by the panel Warhol consulted and adapted for the technology—and industry—on offer. That said, the *Rain Machine* idea nevertheless seems an appropriate follow-up to an installation of bionic *Silver Clouds*. We know very little about Warhol's original concept, which was for a series of 'weather machines', primarily because the models that he had made have not survived.[59] However, we do know that the project was originally intended to comprise three machines, rain, snow and wind, each with a three-dimensional image accompanied by 'real' sculptural sets with simulated elements. While Warhol had envisioned a holographic image floating behind a screen of weather for the *Rain Machine*, in the case of the snow and wind machines, the image was designed to be within, or surrounded by, the snow and vibrating wind.[60] *Rain Machine's* 3D images are seen through a screen of rain so that the meteorological drama is both the figure against the background and a screen through which to see the image.

Warhol was disappointed with the effect of the rectilinear display of *Rain Machine* when he had originally wanted to do a hologram work—as had been suggested to him at the point of his first contact with A&T. He also knew of Bruce Nauman's experiments with holograms, which he saw in Nauman's solo exhibition *Holograms, Videotapes and Other Works* in 1969, and which he had been impressed by. Nauman had been in contact with A&T before Warhol, but had secured collaboration with manufacturers of holograms who were not part of the A&T program. While Warhol's own '3D' prints were of limited effect, the potential to make mechanically reproducible, photographic images in 3D that holographic technology offered was something that stayed with Warhol. In *The Philosophy of Andy Warhol*, the idea obviously still has currency five years later:

> Holograms are going to be exciting, I think. You can really, finally, with holograms, pick your own atmosphere. They'll be televising a party, and you want to be there, and with holograms, you will be there. You'll be able to have this 3D party in your house, you'll be able to pretend you're there and walk in with the people. You can even rent a party. You can have anybody famous that you want sitting right next to you.[61]

The Philosophy was written in 1975 although it riffs on a persona that Warhol had constructed and cultivated in public during the 1960s. As I have already said, much of *The Philosophy's* content was generated by Warhol's co-workers, in particular Bob Colacello and Pat Hackett, doing their best Andy Warhol impressions. However, this passage may well have been initiated by Warhol himself. The beginning of this section, at least, stands out: the tone changes, it is more tentative and one wonders if the subject matter—not something of immediate concern to those at the Factory at this moment—would have figured without Warhol voicing his own preoccupation with the medium. Warhol's eagerness to collaborate with a company capable of manufacturing holograms for the A&T might have been because, in a moment after tiring with painting, and during his shift to film production rather than direction, the hologram, which was quite new in 1969, might have looked like a urgent and exciting direction to take. Warhol was always open to exploring the possibilities of new technologies, as the recent discovery of a series of works produced with the Amiga 1000 computer testifies.[62]

Though the opportunity might therefore have arrived somewhat late, in 1977 Warhol, at last, worked with holograms. That summer, Warhol sat for a portrait at 245 Seventh Avenue, then studio of 'Dr Laser', Jason Sapan. Sapan had begun work on holography in 1968, like Billy Klüver, in the employment of Bell Laboratories. And again, like Klüver, Sapan's work was pioneering. In 1968 the company ran an exhibition called *A Science Tune In* at the Time-Life Building where Sapan worked, demonstrating holography to the public for the first time in America. Sapan's portrait, this '3D Warhol', measures ten inches tall by 20 inches across (plate 3.5). The hologram is displayed behind a clear curved Plexiglas screen in front of a black Plexiglas background, causing it to appear to 'float'.[63] It is what is known as an internal hologram, which means that not only is the image visible in three dimensions but, as you move past, the subject—in this case Warhol—moves, turning the page of the copy of *Interview* he is holding, and thoughtfully, rather sternly, looking up at the camera as he does so.[64] The total piece represents about 15 seconds of recorded time but appears still from a fixed point of view. After the shoot, Sapan twice visited the Factory, then at 860 Broadway: once to install his portrait and once more to pay Warhol a visit. While at the Factory he noticed that the hologram 'was one of the few signed pieces of art he kept in his personal office there.'[65] These comments come from correspondence with Sapan in which he confirms that 'Andy was very interested in the hologram.' Sapan continues:

> Andy was very quick to understand exactly what it was I was going for and was incredible at following direction. He made the shoot a breeze. The result was perfect. I found him to be quite easy to talk with and very much into cooperating on the creative process. It was one of my favourite experiences [...]. I think the hologram itself is one of my best pieces as well.[66]

Like the previous endeavours—approximating holographic effects for A&T, and imagining the potential of holograms for a book of *Philosophy*—this work was also undertaken in collaboration. But it can be said that this time it finds Warhol pursuing a genuine interest in a non-ambivalent way, outside commercial commission or money making endeavours, and working in a concerted and committed partnership. In Sapan's account of their collaboration there are no traces of the affectations that sometimes characterise Warhol's approach to work such as the off-hand gesture, deferring decision making to a panel and de-skilled production. Instead, the Warhol hologram portrait collaboration, as part of the history of Warhol's work and working, is neither off-hand nor throwaway.

Rather, the image actually portrays Warhol's strained relationship to his viewer in the artworld. Sapan describes the look Warhol gives the camera as 'indifferent.'

In many ways, the hologram embodies what the work in this chapter attempted to achieve, and which was imagined in his *Philosophy*: 'atmospheric' moving images that could provide the platform for, as well as the content of, action. Through these works, Warhol imagined a virtual world, facilitated by a new medium which combined the possibilities of TV and film and, at the same time, exceeded the self-important objecthood of the artworld, the 'little squares hanging on the wall'. Indeed, the earlier *Large* works actually approximate some of the formal, technological components that constitute the hologram. Both are rendered on free standing Plexiglas 'screens', yet the image of both, in each case comprised of multiple images taken in temporal sequence, extends into empty space. With *Large Sleep* and the other Plexiglas works, it could be said that Warhol imagined holographic display, with all its possibilities and potential, before it was available to him. In doing so, and in common with *Silver Clouds* and *Rain Machine*, Warhol continued to develop new possibilities for sculpture. It is the category of sculpture that, according to Jason Sapan, is crucial to understanding the hologram:

> I would state unequivocally that the hologram is in fact a sculpture in light. It is there but it is not there. Although it might not be a solid material, it is still a visually solid dimensional piece of contemporary art.[67]

4

The Artwork Across the Street

Shadows

In the previous chapter, I argued that through such sculptures as *Silver Clouds* (1966), *Large Sleep* (1965) and *Rain Machine* (*c.*1970) a cinematic space — container of the aesthetic and social space of Warhol's underground — came to be transported into the artworld and the gallery's space of encounter. In these works, as in much of the work in this book, sculpture intervenes with the gallery's function of protecting social order. At the same time, they represent an impediment to the forms of reproduction — sexual, machinic and visual — which can be assimilated by capital. Whereas Duchamp's *Large Glass* figures looking as symbiotic with insemination, a symbiosis which Hollywood harnesses on an industrial scale, Warhol's couplings present negations that hover in stasis. This is sculpture recast, as I suggested in the first chapter, as 'out-cast' of these systems of reproduction, coming into being only on exit from relays of images. I have argued too that this is still a condition of the sculptural object today: this state of sculpture as shadow of an image-world of multiple, simultaneous formats and far-reaching and immediate transmission.

If the sculptural has come to represent that which exists in the shadows, antithetical to ideological motives connecting visibility with production and objecthood, then the aesthetics that supported those motives between 1964 and 1966 was the kind of realism on which the positions held by both Arthur Danto and Donald Judd relied. The luminous clarity, specificity and positivism of this form of realism, I have argued, flattens out the contours that define class boundaries. *Silver Clouds* responds to this way in which social difference was being neutralised by the rational order of 'object specificity,' by casting the indistinct atmosphere of the Factory's permanent night-time over the territory of the artworld. As 'moving images' and momentos of his movie making, the works also suggest an invasion by the Factory's 'sub-culture' that had been made famous in Warhol's films. The work therefore repeats, in another register, the affront of the *Personality of the Artist* exhibition in 1964: bringing the low into the space of what was high. In what will be the focus of this chapter, many of the same operations were repeated: Warhol's *Shadows*, exhibited in 1979, re-ground spectatorship in the social upheavals of their time.

In the latter half of this chapter, a series of smaller works will be considered that replay this trespass upon protected order and its hierarchies by an unwanted social reality. These works give us a feel for the sensibility that informs the high profile installation works. They show how aware Warhol was of interpersonal space and how thoughtful he was about his status as a coveted society figure whose presence in social space could be commodified. Warhol's negotiation of these complications, by means of both 'presenting' himself as empty or absent and by giving 'presents' to others that were 'empty', is explored in this section. At the same time, the mark of friendship—or more—was often the invitation to step into, or on, Warhol's personal space.

Rather than a trespass or an act of subversion, however, *Shadows* is more often understood as in accord with its institutional surroundings and, in so being, reflective of the priorities of Heiner Friedrich and Phillipa de Menil who commissioned the work following the establishment, in 1974, of what is now the Dia Art Foundation, previously the Lone Star Foundation. Indeed the installation was tailored to the space where it was first displayed at the Heiner Friedrich Gallery in 1979. It contained 83 large (76 × 52 inch) coloured canvases, part of a series numbering 108 of which The Lone Star Foundation had bought 102 (plate 4.1). On these lay silkscreened, largely black images transferred from photographs of a shadow interspersed with canvases bearing the negative of that image. In total, seven or eight different screens were used to make the images.[1] Before screening, Warhol covered the surface of each canvas with paint using a sponge mop: set against the black inks, the 17 different colours he used are not the plain, solid mattes of the American brand that appeared in his earlier work, but suggest opulence, sometimes seediness. They are night-time, neon colours applied unevenly: chartreuse, midnight blue, aubergine, skin tones; an almost luminous yellow like street signage. The canvases were lined up so that they touched each other on the walls of the gallery's two rooms following its circumference continuously, enveloping the viewer in a pulsing, glamourous, environment.

Since its inception, the Foundation had been associated with Minimalist artists such as Dan Flavin and Donald Judd, and *Shadows* continues to be interpreted in terms of Minimalism's devices by the curators at Dia : Beacon where the work is on view today. Lynne Cooke describes *Shadows* in terms that echo Minimalism's orientation around the outward, visible exterior of the object, its undifferentiated relation to the architectural framework of the gallery space, and the spectator's willingness to take these elements as 'given', as Judd has said.[2] Yasmil Raymond, meanwhile, describes *Shadows* with something of the flavour of Judd's prose: 'Far from replicas', she writes, 'each *Shadow* corresponds to a form that reveals, with precision and self-awareness, its space, directing the spectator's gaze to light, the central subject of the series.'[3] In both cases *Shadows* sets in chain a series of assertions of positive presence: the *Shadow*, the form, the space, the light. Yet, far from neutral, I will argue that these positive relations extend to relations of value in the gallery and on to the viewer. Through claims about real space, the value of the art object can be equated directly with the viewer and his or her entitlement to that space.

In the original exhibition, the number of paintings displayed was defined by the available wall space. It was intended that the canvases would also touch the floor but, in the end, they were hung with just enough of a gap to prevent their getting kicked. When Warhol had shown his *Hammer and Sickle* paintings in Paris, in May 1977, there had been a riot at the gallery.[4] In the case of *Shadows*, the work had already been bought, so property had to be protected. However, positioning the work on the floor would have allowed it to fully assert a dual purpose—crucial, as I will argue, for its understanding—as both the object of spectacle whilst at the same time part of the container and ground for it. The fact that this was not achievable might go some way to explaining why *Shadows* is not generally considered as the critical intervention I hold it to be.

This dual modality of the work and, indeed, its relation to spectacle in general as a condition of imaging and representation, highlights an aspect that the statements by the Dia curators do not stress. As much as *Shadows* might suggest the groundedness of an object in the real conditions in which one beholds it, they also suggest indeterminacy, imprecision and non-specificity and of course, *Shadows* are images. Raymond intimates this herself when she describes *Shadows* 'correspondence' with a form, and we might wonder if this form is Minimalism's 'specific object'. But, if so, it is one that has been rendered in darkness and negative space: it is in stark opposition to the description of the work in terms of the literalism, clarity and positivism of Minimalist anti-illusionism.[5] In the following analysis, my argument will hinge around this play of positive and negative and *Shadows'* ability to both intimate and subvert the aesthetic of Minimal Art. It is through an act of subversive complicity that we must understand the work and, in so doing, the critical position that it takes.

Mark Francis's essay, '*Horror Vacui*: Andy Warhol's Installations', is one reading that has considered Warhol's *Shadows* in terms of a subversive engagement with institutional space. This understanding of Warhol's work as negational contrasts, of course, with Minimalism's positivism. For Francis, Warhol's installations, throughout his career, highlighted an equivalence between the hollowness of American existence and the 'pristine vacuity of a conventional modern gallery space': between two nothings not considered to be equivalent; two vacuums set apart by the class barrier of the white cube's elite culture.[6] Francis argues that Warhol attempted to overcome this inequality with installations that 'reconnected the museum with its repressed or forgotten siblings, the department store, the supermarket, the dance club, the attic, and the basement.'[7] Although the importance of the last two items in this list will only become apparent in the final chapter on collections and collecting, Francis' point—that these repressed spaces emerge in Warhol's installations—is key to understanding the

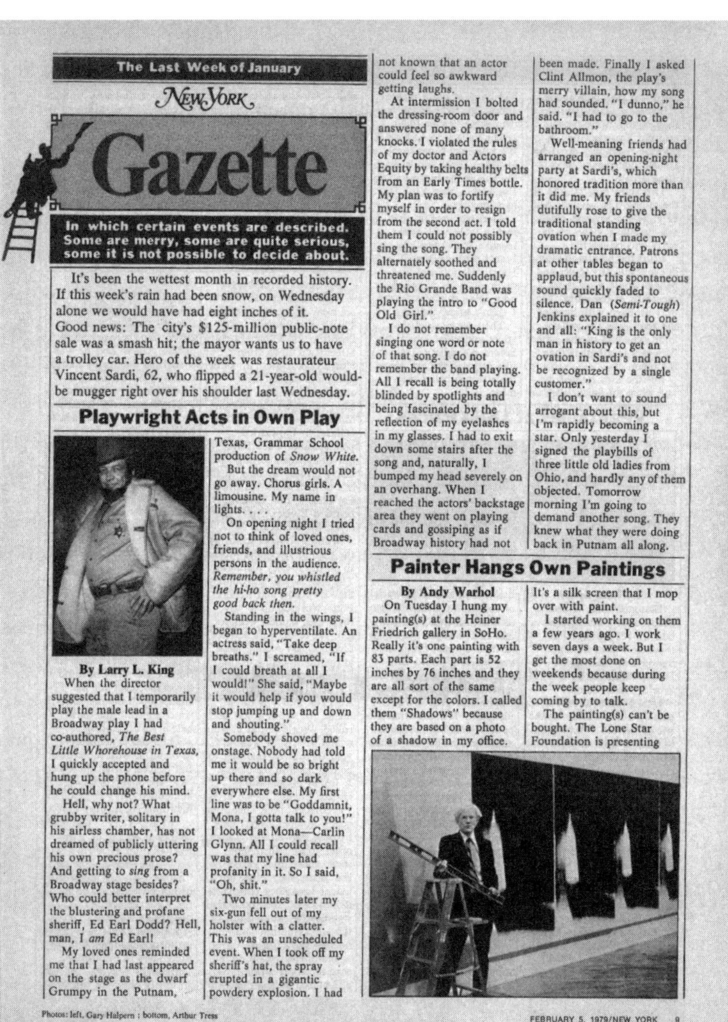

The Last Week of January

NEW YORK

Gazette

In which certain events are described. Some are merry, some are quite serious, some it is not possible to decide about.

It's been the wettest month in recorded history. If this week's rain had been snow, on Wednesday alone we would have had eight inches of it. Good news: The city's $125-million public-note sale was a smash hit; the mayor wants us to have a trolley car. Hero of the week was restaurateur Vincent Sardi, 62, who flipped a 21-year-old would-be mugger right over his shoulder last Wednesday.

Playwright Acts in Own Play

By Larry L. King

When the director suggested that I temporarily play the male lead in a Broadway play I had co-authored, *The Best Little Whorehouse in Texas,* I quickly accepted and hung up the phone before he could change his mind.

Hell, why not? What grubby writer, solitary in his airless chamber, has not dreamed of publicly uttering his own precious prose? And getting to *sing* from a Broadway stage besides? Who could better interpret the blustering and profane sheriff, Ed Earl Dodd? Hell, man, I *am* Ed Earl!

My loved ones reminded me that I had last appeared on the stage as the dwarf Grumpy in the Putnam, Texas, Grammar School production of *Snow White.*

But the dream would not go away. Chorus girls. A limousine. My name in lights. . . .

On opening night I tried not to think of loved ones, friends, and illustrious persons in the audience. *Remember, you whistled the hi-ho song pretty good back then.*

Standing in the wings, I began to hyperventilate. An actress said, "Take deep breaths." I screamed, "If I could breath at all I would!" She said, "Maybe it would help if you would stop jumping up and down and shouting."

Somebody shoved me onstage. Nobody had told me it would be so bright up there and so dark everywhere else. My first line was to be "Goddamnit, Mona, I gotta talk to you!" I looked at Mona—Carlin Glynn. All I could recall was that my line had profanity in it. So I said, "Oh, shit."

Two minutes later my six-gun fell out of my holster with a clatter. This was an unscheduled event. When I took off my sheriff's hat, the spray erupted in a gigantic powdery explosion. I had not known that an actor could feel so awkward getting laughs.

At intermission I bolted the dressing-room door and answered none of many knocks. I violated the rules of my doctor and Actors Equity by taking healthy belts from an Early Times bottle. My plan was to fortify myself in order to resign from the second act. I told them I could not possibly sing the song. They alternately soothed and threatened me. Suddenly the Rio Grande Band was playing the intro to "Good Old Girl."

I do not remember singing one word or note of that song. I do not remember the band playing. All I recall is being totally blinded by spotlights and being fascinated by the reflection of my eyelashes in my glasses. I had to exit down some stairs after the song and, naturally, I bumped my head severely on an overhang. When I reached the actors' backstage area they went on playing cards and gossiping as if Broadway history had not been made. Finally I asked Clint Allmon, the play's merry villain, how my song had sounded. "I dunno," he said. "I had to go to the bathroom."

Well-meaning friends had arranged an opening-night party at Sardi's, which honored tradition more than it did me. My friends dutifully rose to give the traditional standing ovation when I made my dramatic entrance. Patrons at other tables began to applaud, but this spontaneous sound quickly faded to silence. Dan (*Semi-Tough*) Jenkins explained it to one and all: "King is the only man in history to get an ovation in Sardi's and not be recognized by a single customer."

I don't want to sound arrogant about this, but I'm rapidly becoming a star. Only yesterday I signed the playbills of three little old ladies from Ohio, and hardly any of them objected. Tomorrow morning I'm going to demand another song. They knew what they were doing back in Putnam all along.

Painter Hangs Own Paintings

By Andy Warhol

On Tuesday I hung my painting(s) at the Heiner Friedrich gallery in SoHo. Really it's one painting with 83 parts. Each part is 52 inches by 76 inches and they are all sort of the same except for the colors. I called them "Shadows" because they are based on a photo of a shadow in my office. It's a silk screen that I mop over with paint.

I started working on them a few years ago. I work seven days a week. But I get the most done on weekends because during the week people keep coming by to talk.

The painting(s) can't be bought. The Lone Star Foundation is presenting

Photos: left, Gary Halpern ; bottom, Arthur Tress

Fig. 4.1 Arthur Tress, 'Painter Hangs Own Paintings', *New York Magazine,* 5 February, 1979, p. 9.

acts of trespass that *Shadows* commits. And, following Francis, I would suggest that in order to appreciate the critical statement this work makes, an equivalence between the specific spaces that *Shadows* invokes and the particularity of the gallery it was shown in is a crucial consideration.

Many of the best clues that *Shadows* was not fundamentally an endorsement of house policy are to be found in the publicity and press for the exhibition (fig. 4.1). In the publicity photos by Arthur Tress, Warhol sends up the self- aggrandisement of the Minimalist and post-Minimalist artist. Warhol poses in front of his installation by a stepladder holding, indeed wielding, an extra-large spirit level (see also plate 4.2). In these pictures he appears more confident than usual. In one image he stands contrapposto, brandishing the spirit level across his hips. In another, he perches on the ladder with the spirit level erect in his lap, rather explicitly suggesting the relationship between potency and the technical mastery of the space of the gallery. Perhaps what these photographs illustrate is the artist empowered by precision, a power that protests to be no more than an objective concern for what is 'given' and the measurable conditions in which it is given in. We might consider Warhol's patriarchal posturing as a parody of the self-image associated with the Heiner Friedrich Gallery. One of these publicity photographs (the one in which Warhol stands rather than sits) was published in *New York Magazine* a month after the show opened and accompanied a short statement by Warhol called 'Painter Hangs Own Paintings'.[8] There are two passages in Warhol's short, very deliberate text on which I want to place special emphasis, and these both give substance to *Shadows*' critique. In what follows, I first want to consider the allusion Warhol makes to the 'art across the street'; and second I want to deal with his reference to the work as 'disco décor'. These two passages occur, respectively, at the end of the text and in the middle:

> On Tuesday I hung my painting(s) at the Heiner Friedrich gallery in SoHo. Really it's one painting with 83 parts. Each part is 52 inches by 76 inches and they are all sort of the same except for the colors. I called them 'Shadows' because they are based on a photo of a shadow in my office. It's a silk screen that I mop over with paint.
>
> I started working on them a few years ago. I work seven days a week. But I get the most done on weekends because during the week people keep coming by to talk.
>
> The painting(s) can't be bought. The Lone Star Foundation is presenting them and they own them.
>
> Someone asked me if they were art and I said no. You see, the opening party had disco. I guess that makes them disco décor.

This show will be like all the others. The review will be bad – my reviews always are. But the reviews of the party will be terrific.

I had the painting(s) hung at eye level. Any lower and people would kick them, especially at the party. The only problem with hanging the show was the gallery floor. One end of the gallery is a foot higher than the other.

But the kids helped me, and when we finished we all had lunch. I ate a pickle and drank some Evian and then some Perrier Jouet.

The gallery looked great. It's a simple, clean space. My Mao show was bigger, but this is the biggest show I've had in New York City in a long time.

After we were finished, I took a walk with some friends. We stopped at Ivan Karp's gallery, O. K. Harris. He told me that there are a lot of people now doing shadows in art. I didn't know that. Then we crossed the street and went into Holly Solomon's gallery. I always like to see if the art across the street is better than mine.[9]

If the Heiner Friedrich Gallery was, by the late 1970s, associated with Minimalist artists, there were also galleries that presented alternatives and, curiously enough, two of the most important of these appear here. The work at the Holly Solomon Gallery, to which Warhol refers, was a show of Pattern and Decoration art, by either Robert Kushner or Valerie Jaudon. And, at the O.K. Harris Gallery, Warhol saw either Jack Mendenhall, Jack Radetsky, Davis Cone or Larry Brown, all Photorealists who were on exhibition over this period.[10] Unlike Minimalism, both Pattern and Decoration and Photorealism were predominantly painting movements, and both considered themselves as developing on forms of the American vernacular and, therefore, as representational. Unlike Minimalism's monolithic anti-anthropomorphism, for both of these movements there was a tendency towards seduction and to seeing the viewer as part of a larger public reflected in the work.[11] In the case of Pattern and Decoration, some of the founding members of the group were allied to feminist politics, consciousness raising and the elevation of the status of work traditionally performed by women. Claims for the importance of craft, in both movements, sat alongside the representation of a modern, highly mediated experience.

Again, we can see this as being in contrast to Minimalism's by then nostalgic evocation of industrial fabrication in the midst of the collapse of American industry during this period. Dieter Roelstraete has observed of Photorealism's relation to Minimalist art:

> It obliquely reflects (no pun intended!) both the central economic event of the era—the triumph, incarnated by the glass-sheet office tower, of the service (*and* culture) industries over more traditional, ageing industries from the secondary sector (such as steel and coal), whose Spartan work ethic and macho machine-aesthetic still informed, in a melancholy kind of way, the Minimalism of Donald Judd and Carl Andre—as well as, more literally, the actual conditions of labour (i.e. glass-encased office work) in this new regime of consumption rather than production.[12]

Though Warhol typically feigns naivety in 'Painter Hangs Own Paintings', *Shadows* does seem rather carefully poised between these two artistic trends across the street from one of Minimal Art's places of pilgrimage. The Photorealists, as Warhol relates from his conversation with Ivan Karp, used shadow in their work to point to the medium of photography. In the case of Pattern and Decoration, comparison is less oblique since the repeating images in *Shadows* produce a pattern, and the work is explicitly described by Warhol as decoration. Indeed, the exhibition was used as a backdrop for a fashion shoot for the April 1979 edition of Warhol's magazine *Interview*, restaging Cecil Beaton's famous 1951 *Vogue* shoot in front of work by Jackson Pollock at the Betty Parsons Gallery (fig. 4.2). At the same time, the work's formal likeness to that of figures like Clifford Still and Mark Rothko is undeniable and in this way *Shadows* travesties this earlier movement—which Warhol's Pop work had helped supersede in 1962–3—by producing 'gestural abstraction' with a photographic image and a sponge mop.[13] Like the *Cow Wallpaper* (1966) and *Mao Wallpaper* (1974) before it, as décor the *Shadows* might be seen as wantonly neglecting Harold Rosenberg's warning to Abstract Expressionist artists against 'apocalyptic wallpaper'.[14]

Warhol's remarks about decoration in the press were also, no doubt, written with critic René Ricard in mind. Ricard had dismissed *Shadows* as, to quote Warhol's *Diaries*, 'just "decorative"' at the show's preview. In the 1960s, Warhol had often described work, such as the installations of *Flowers*, as decoration and he had, of course, long experimented with wall-papering gallery spaces.[15] However, it seems the case that here Warhol was attempting, for his largest installation and largest commission in a long time, to say something more particular, and this has to do with the context in which the work was displayed. In the press release, Warhol appropriates the highly loaded term decoration to reframe the work as 'disco décor' rather than as art. This occurs in the text following the sentence in which he names the Lone Star Foundation as the owner of the paintings, a conjunction of statements that acts to devalue some of the Foundation's investment. As 'disco décor', *Shadows* refers, of course, to a very particular cultural moment. The film *Saturday Night Fever* had made disco an overnight global phenomenon the year before Warhol began work on the series.[16] Warhol himself had been on the scene at Studio 54 since the mid-1970s and for years his work, as well as social schedule, had revolved around late nights spent in Studio's VIP basement (though this did not mean that he didn't also keep his eye on other movements of the time, such as punk and New Wave). The fashion shoot staged at the gallery further ties the work to disco since one of the models, Janis Savitt, wears an all-white Yves Saint Laurent trouser suit, styled very much like that worn by John Travolta in *Saturday Night Fever* (fig. 4.2). It is notable also that the shoot used the whole exhibition as a backdrop, rather than a single painting as in Cecil Beaton's Pollock shoot, emphasising the whole space of the exhibition and suggesting its new role as a dancefloor.[17] As a floor piece that delineated the perimeters of the space of the gallery and, by doing so, reframed that space as a disco, this was a work that turned the entire gallery space, apart from the representational space within each canvas, into a dance floor.

The invasion of the gallery by a disco, of course, represents a direct challenge to its agenda (plates 4.3 and 4). In her work on wallpaper and contemporary art, Elisa Auther has described the dual affront that the symbolism of *Shadows* presented, both as 'decoration', that scourge of high art, and as an implicit 'queering' of the gallery space through the association with disco.[18] In addition to *Shadows'* formal and thematic ties to the art 'across the street', some of which had an overt feminist agenda, we might add that the set of associations between the decorative arts and femininity, and disco and homosexuality, which are condensed in

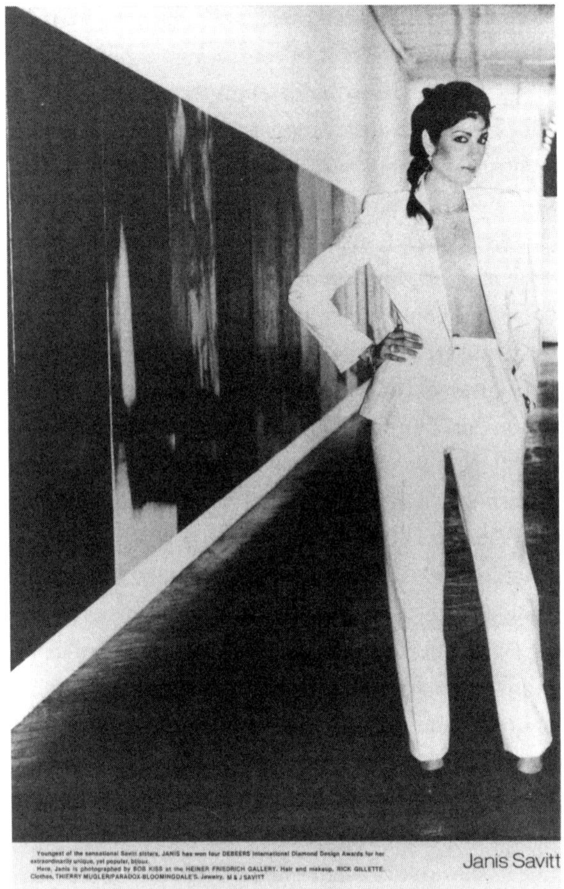

Fig. 4.2. Originally published in *Interview* magazine, April 1979. Courtesy of BMP Media Holdings, LLC.

Shadows, would have only been put in greater relief in contrast with the Minimal Art that was native to the Heiner Friedrich Gallery. This could be seen as reflective of the white, straight, rock and roll crowd—a 'heavy metal' crowd—which was opposed to disco, and whose music superseded it in the mainstream.

Again, as I considered in my discussion of Warhol's *Brillo Boxes*, Minimalism's iconography has been subject to critique, most notably in Anna C. Chave's analysis of Minimal Art's 'rhetoric of power'.[19] However, again, what I want to suggest does not so much revolve around the alternative iconography that disco offers but its alternative model of aesthetic reception. I want to read *Shadows* as undoing the co-constitution of value in the relationship between the institution and its participant that was typical of Minimalism. In order to do so, Warhol's strategy here, as it was in the case of *Personality of the Artist* and *Silver Clouds*, was one of aesthetic recoding, rather than disavowal. Despite not being at floor level as intended, *Shadows* suggested an integration with the gallery's architectural structure of floor and wall, and also set up a relationship to an 'object' within this space, intimated by the shadow image.[20] And like its Minimal counterpart, *Shadows* still suggested that relations between the object, the space and the person were on one even plane. But in doing so, the work ultimately reversed how these relationships establish the status and importance of the object by instead making its arena, the gallery floor, a dancefloor: a collective space that had had radical social implications during the years of disco. I want to read this new order as a reversal of the constitution of value at the Heiner Friedrich Gallery, whereby the outside space of the disco displaces Minimalism's object presence, demoting it to the image of its shadow in the paintings. In his description of the aesthetic relationships constitutive of disco, Tim Lawrence describes a situation that we might read as the exact opposite of that described of Minimal Art:

> as the guests acclimatize to their new surroundings bodies begin to sway, arms start to stretch, legs limber up, and feet unconsciously flicker. Note by note, beat by beat, the music becomes more intense and rhythmic until everyone and everything is drawn into a dizzying display of movement. The source of the music, however, remains a mystery: party host David Mancuso is placing records on his AR turntables but his inspiration comes from the dancers, who in turn are inspired by the music. The messages are untraceably complex—no physicist could hope to calculate the unfolding relations of energy, force, and motion—but the communication is unmistakable.[21]

In the dance club, the recursive relationship between the work and the audience reaches towards collectivity, rather than individual experience. Unlike Minimalism's environment, which defines the register through which the spectator must engage, disco reflects the will of its audience and is defined in accordance with it. The selections of records by the DJ changes with the dancers' increasing participation, while they come together in response to create the expressive, fantasy environment for which disco is both famed and derided. Visually, *Shadows* replicates this experience. In their singularity, they respond only as images of shadows, reflecting merely an obscure version of an implied object in the room. As décor, however, *Shadows* pulses, marking a beat, and like disco records, all variations on the same formula, they are slotted into place where it makes sense. They define collective space and give it shape, and respond as a backdrop for the imaging environment of those in the room collected together, posing, dancing, invading the gallery. The gallery is now orientated around the people in the space, now a disco, where it had once centred around the Minimal object. There is a suggestion that it is Minimalism's gaze, the concern for the conditions of light in the gallery, that casts the shadows, and that these signify the missing presence of the Minimal floor piece that has been annexed by the disco. The Minimal object becomes a shadow cast by the *détournement* of its own ideology.

In this condensed series of allusions and associations we might think of the artworld spectator, displaced along with high art values by the repurposing of the institution. If the object had once reflected the constructed value of the spectator as part of an enveloping perceptual 'reality', then, as a shadow-image, it does the reverse, exposing the inter-dependencies of imaging with perception. In a final irony there is one more substitution that adds to the critique, and here we must bring iconography back in. The disco, of course, is no less a fantasy environment than the art gallery. While Minimal Art came to represent institutional power dressed in the overalls of manual labour, in *Saturday Night Fever*, disco anointed John Travolta's Tony Manero as its king. A shop boy at a hardware store in Brooklyn, Tony's dead-end job encapsulates the situation in the late 1970s wherein working America had had to face the demise

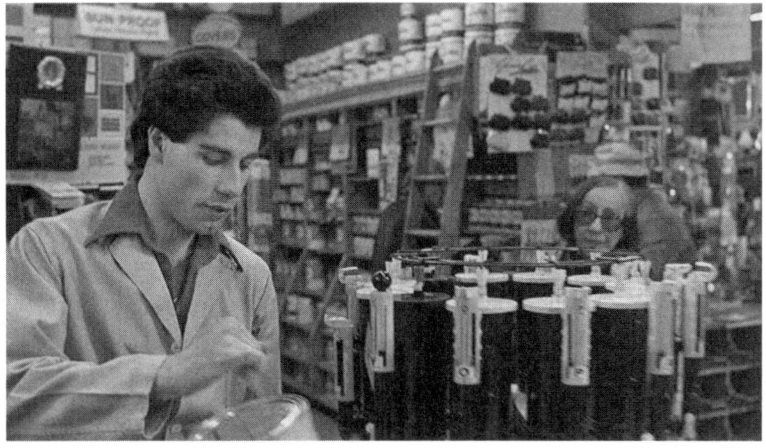

Fig. 4.3 *Saturday Night Fever* (film still, hardware store). Dir. John Badham, Paramount Pictures, 1977.

of traditional American industry and the shift in emphasis towards consumer driven, service economics; something not represented in Minimalism's heroic iconography (fig. 4.3.). When Dan Graham gave Minimalism a 'homecoming' in his 1966 magazine piece *Homes for America*, it was precisely with images of products in hardware stores that recalled the stacked and serial arrangements of Minimalist work. By reversing the subject-object encounter as I have described, viewers who continue to look to the art object for an image of their own self-worth are now dressed in the overalls of Minimalism's inferred industrial iconography.

If *Shadows* ranks amongst the greatest critical interventions of all Warhol's works, and the idea of the spectator as trespassing on the gallery space put social class once again at the core of the work's message, other largely forgotten works make explicit how precisely Warhol's critical sense was tuned to the dynamics of identification on which *Shadows* relies as a critique. In 1985, Warhol made another piece of disco art, this time a performance with props titled *Invisible Sculpture*, installed at the nightclub Area in New York. This work consisted of a bare plinth installed in a vitrine-like structure built into the club which made a name for itself with elaborate and ambitious themed nights: Faith, War, Elements, Retrospective and so on. Here Warhol posed in the glass-fronted booth standing between an empty plinth and a label for the work mounted on the wall behind the plinth (rather than on it) that reads 'ANDY WARHOL, USA, INVISIBLE SCULPTURE, mixed media, 1985' (plate 4.5). Warhol stood stock still, while club-goers stared through the glass. Hal Foster recalls being at this event and noticing Jean Baudrillard staring at Warhol, who was staring back at him. Foster comments that he thought this meeting of key post-modernist minds would cause some kind of visceral effect, 'an explosion'.[22] When Warhol left the space, the implication was that the space he had vacated had become an 'invisible sculpture'. In Paige Powell's photograph of the event, Warhol appears very much his public self: stiff, intimidated—wearing a crystal pendant to ward off harm—and in a raking light that casts an elongated profile shadow on the wall, very much like the print self-portrait, titled *The Shadow*, that he had made four years before.

In an interview with Benjamin Buchloh around the same time, the discussion of the work at Area is framed by references to the period in which he showed *Shadows*. Warhol also mentions working on invisible painting as well as invisible sculpture.[23] He may have meant his 1980 *Portrait of Linda Cossey with a Camera*, which used black-light ink that became invisible in normal light.

> **Warhol:** But the thing I was really trying to work on was the invisible painting, the invisible sculpture that I was working on. Did you go see the show at Area?
>
> **Buchloh:** No, not yet.
>
> **Warhol:** Disco Art? You haven't done Disco Art yet? Really good art—you should see it. It's going to be over soon. A lot of work by about thirty artists; it's really interesting.
>
> **Buchloh:** What did you do at Area?
>
> **Warhol:** The invisible sculpture, but it's not really the way I had planned it. I've been working on it with the electronic things that make noises go off when you go into an area. But this one down here, it's just something or

> nothing on a pedestal. But Arman has a beautiful bicycle piece down there at Area. It filled one whole window, one whole window filled with bicycles. It's really beautiful. I think he's such a great artist.[24]

Arman's work is not dissimilar in effect to the stacks of *Brillo Boxes* that are both the subject of viewership and obstruct it, and the artists regarded each other highly. The installation at Area clearly demarcates an 'artspace', using a glass wall to separate the club area from the room in which Warhol posed with a label and plinth. Perhaps we might see this as the reverse of *Shadows'* act of invasion, placing the art space in the disco, rather than the disco in the art space. Yet here, Warhol's self-presentation as trapped by the mini-artworld around him, and as absurdly standing by the 'emperor's new clothes' gesture of the empty plinth, corrects any sense that in doing so he is reversing the political message of the earlier work. Warhol is on hand to guide the viewer towards the 'something or nothing on a pedestal', perhaps a comment on the dematerialised work, associated with the period 1966–72, whose continued relevance was challenged in the late 1970s by artists Warhol championed and who featured alongside him at Area.

But if Warhol's comments ground *Invisible Sculpture* in the moment, five years earlier, of *Shadows* and of the experiments with invisible painting, this was also the period that he first experimented with the idea of invisible sculptures, producing a different installation called *Invisible Sculpture* and a series of smaller related works, from which the later work evolved. This first *Invisible Sculpture* was installed in Warhol's studio around 1980.[25] Ronnie Cutrone, Warhol's assistant at the time, recalls:

> Andy wanted to make *The Invisible Sculpture* [...] So again we got out the Yellow Pages and found burglar alarms, different systems. Some with sound, some with light beams. They were all different looking because they had different shapes and different systems. We mounted these burglar alarms on brackets all around the perimeter of the big room in the middle of the Factory, which was by then referred to not as the Factory but as Andy Warhol Studios. And we aimed them all at the centre of the room where nothing existed.

> If you walked into the room and you hit this centre point, all of these alarms would go off. You'd have every different kind of sound; chirping, booming, buzzing. It was funny.
>
> The Invisible Sculpture stayed up for a long time, but it was experimental really. We only had it activated for maybe a month. It used to drive Fred crazy; it was almost like a practical joke. Andy and I would drag someone in and say, "This is the new art; go stand in the middle of the room." And they would, and all the sirens would go off. Then Fred would come and say, "Andy, I'm *on the phone*." Or Brigid would yell. Everybody would yell because Andy and I were constantly having people walk into this imaginary space.[26]

This anecdote highlights the fine line between the work of art and the work of making art in the strained, very 'real' world in which Warhol lived and at a time when Warhol's workspace was progressively becoming more professional. In 1973, still affected by the shooting and concerned by breaches of security, Warhol relocated again from where he had been at 33 Union Square West to 860 Broadway at the north end of Union Square. These security-enhanced headquarters, now 'studios' rather than a 'factory', were where what became known as Warhol Enterprises came to be based. As Cutrone makes clear, however, the *Invisible Sculpture* actually disrupted the work of Warhol Enterprises, stalling attempts at slick moneymaking operations. This leads to an odd paradox: unlike the society portraits, sales from *Interview* and large gallery works—which all 'brought home the bacon', as Warhol would say of his commercial endeavours—the alarm works, which were non-commercial and retained the experimental and chaotic feel of old 'Factory life', mirror that which, in the real world, absolutely encapsulated the evolution of Warhol's work and public status. Namely, as an alarm work, it defended privatisation and the consolidation of value.[27]

Eventually, the work was taken down because of the disruption it caused. Matt Wrbican comments:

> Warhol wanted it to be installed in a gallery space. Had that actually happened, visitors to the gallery most likely would have been very much put-off by the noise, avoiding entering the gallery, and spreading the word to stay away from Warhol's show. He was convinced not to exhibit the work, no doubt by most of

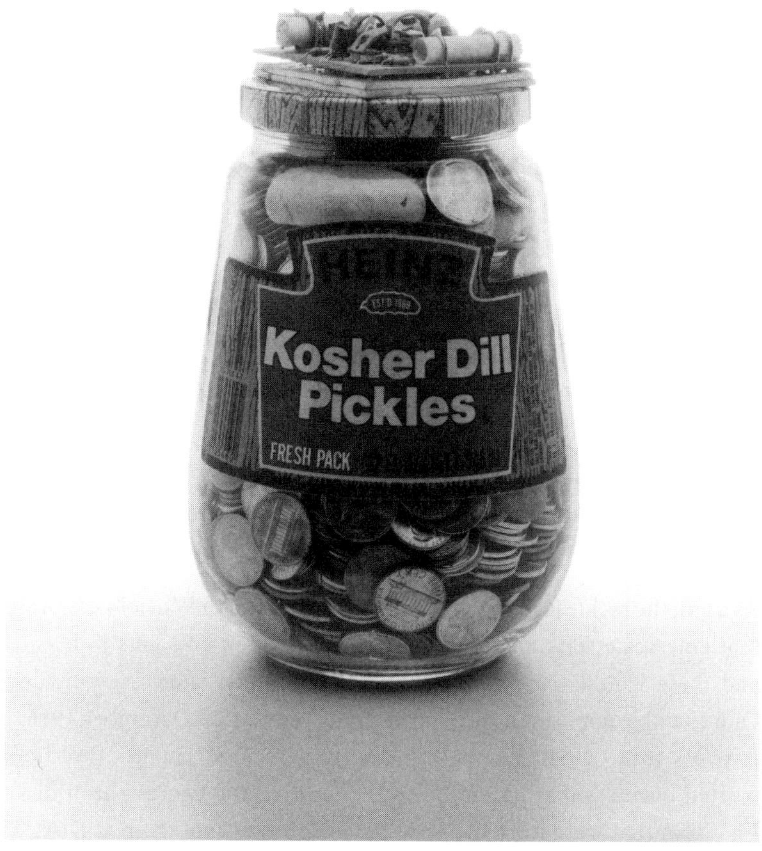

Fig. 4.4. Andy Warhol, *Pickle Jar with Alarm*, *c.*1983, Mixed media, 15.24 x 10.16 x 10.16cm, photograph Takao Ikejiri.

> his staff, business colleagues, clients, and friends; when it was installed and operating in the Factory, everyone who walked through the space was constantly setting it off, disrupting all work and thought.[28]

The smaller works belonging to the same series of experiments as the early *Invisible Sculpture* consisted of pickle jars and other containers fitted with alarms, and were given as jokey gifts filled with coins or paper money (fig. 4.4). One such occasion is reported on April Fools' Day 1979 in the *Diaries*. Here, Warhol gave Victor Hugo 'a Money painting for his birthday and money in the kosher pickle jar that makes a burglar-alarm noise when you open it'.[29] In 1978, a similar jar was also put on show filled with $104,000-worth of gemstones on loan from a dealer.[30] The *Ellensburg Daily Record* for 23 March that year reports the stir this caused in, of all places, the Soviet periodical *Literaturnaya Gazeta,* which commented that it was symptomatic of a culture in which money rather than people was the measure of everything.

Warhol may well have got the idea for such alarm works from Jean Tinguely, who had showed alongside him at the first Pop group exhibition at the Sidney Janis Gallery in New York in 1962. Tinguely's work is described in Victor Bockris's biography of Warhol:

> Tinguely showed an icebox that had been stolen from an alley outside Marcel Duchamp's secret studio. When you opened it, a very noisy siren went off and red lights flashed. It set the noise and tone that was to continue all the way through the sixties.[31]

As a gift, the pickle jar work picks up another strand in Warhol's sculpture that emerges at this moment. Warhol would often give gifts to friends and these would very often be sculptural objects, often ready-mades. One example appears in the *Diaries* from Tuesday 23 December 1986.[32] It refers to a Christmas present Warhol gave Fred Hughes (Warhol's trusted business partner and friend): 'he loved the two cast iron disks I got him that were from the West Side Highway. I got them at Doyle's.' Another example is the present Warhol made for Jean-Michel Basquiat in 1985: 'I brought him a present, one of my own hairpieces. He was shocked. One of my old ones. Framed. I put "83" on it but I don't know when it was from. It's one of my Paul Bochicchio wigs. It was a "Paul Original." '[33] The crumpled newspaper print *Abstract Sculpture* referred to in the first chapter was also a gift, given to Warhol's friend and assistant Christopher Makos, who was a key influence on developing Warhol's photography practice over the 1970s and 1980s. Another work, which was also a gift to Makos, further cements the idea of the sculptural object as the apt medium for gifts. 'Cement' is literally the word here, as Makos's present evolved from experiments Warhol had made with cement boxes (fig. 4.5):

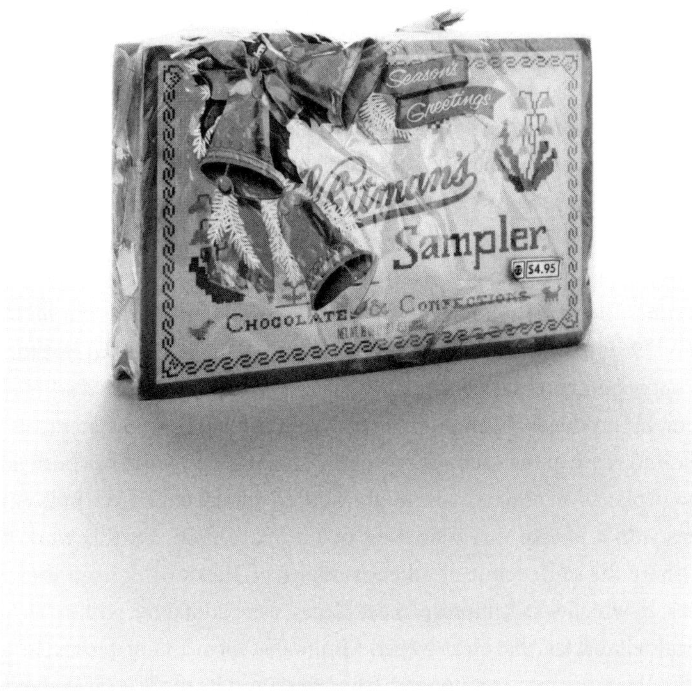

Fig. 4.5. Andy Warhol, *Whitman's Sampler*, c.1984. Cement filled candy box with cellophane wrapper, 17.78 x 25.4cm, photograph Takao Ikejiri.

> Now *my* gift is a tiny little version that's four inches by about three inches by about two inches tall. And it's a Whitman's box of chocolates that's been emptied of its chocolate and filled with cement. The punch line is that, even though it's filled with cement, it's very, very lightweight. It fulfils the original idea of cement. It's very nihilistic. It doesn't mean anything. I think he signed it on the inside. Sealed the box up. Resealed it in the cellophane wrap. And that's it. No one knows what's in the box. I know it's a little bit heavy.[34]

All these works have connotations of trash and hollowness; they are self-consciously bad gifts. But they are also bad in the sense that they attack their recipients in one way or another. Like the alarm works, the chocolate box is a gift with a sting in its tail. Warhol was paranoid about hangers-on using him, and perhaps these self-defeating or sabotaged gifts were tests in which, as the saying goes, all that remained to be counted was the thought.

A final, earlier gift reintroduces many of the different elements of this chapter. The work incorporates a *Brillo Box*, was made shortly after these were exhibited at the Stable Gallery and develops the critique they make of the detachment of the artworld from the real world at the time of the rise of Minimalism. Like the *Personality of the Artist*, it anticipates the erroneous claims to realism associated with Minimalist aesthetics that were nascent at this time. The work in question is Paul Thek's *Meat Piece with Warhol Brillo Box* of 1965, for which Warhol himself donated to Thek a *Brillo Box* for the accomplishment of the work (plate 4.6). Thek's mobilisation of Warhol's iconography produces a complicated and carefully positioned statement. His profound sense of the vacuousness of the New York artworld has been taken as an explanation as to why he might want to 'fill up' one of Warhol's empty boxes with a lifelike wax rendering of a hunk of flesh. Yet this work does not share the same tenor of other examples of Thek's work from the same series, in which wax sculpture 'meat pieces' were contained within 'technological reliquaries' that clearly aped Minimalist form and materials. In such works, what the two components (the 'meat' and its display case) stand for are clearly diametrically opposed and set against one another. They constitute a dirty protest against works, which, as Thek has commented, were out of touch with a world that was 'falling apart': that were not 'real'.[35] The *Meat Pieces* subvert Minimalism's coolness and refinement expressed by materials that evoked erudition and sophistication. In these works, Thek puts the abject and carnal in the formally affirmative heart of the modern object, making it act as a lens for horror, but also provides a space vacant for occupation (because of the repellent flesh) by a nomadic homosexual gaze.

In Thek's *Meat Pieces*, the dynamic between the use of advanced 'cool' materials in geometric, rational order and the severed, splintered and mutilated gore is part of the same preoccupation with disaster found in Warhol's *Death and Disaster* series. Here, the industrial advances that stood so much for progress at this time became perpetrators of an abstract-seeming violence in the images of automobile and aeronautic disasters, the space race and the threat of nuclear war in the backdrop. Thek's works act as capsule deconstructions of this super-tech super-violence and are equally 'alarm' pieces warning against the confidence and entitlement of the social elite.

Thus, Thek's *Meat Pieces*, housed in their slick, minimal containers and later given the name *Technological Reliquaries* are sympathetic to the awareness, also present in Warhol's painting, of the dangers, as well as the glamour, of the modern world. So it would seem odd for the *Brillo Box* version of *Meat Piece* to function in accordance with the same critical position that Thek takes towards what he sees as the dangerous fantasy of early Minimalism's aesthetic. By way of an explanation for the work, Thek is reported to have said to Warhol: 'all that your *Brillo Boxes* need is a piece of flesh inside.'[36] In this statement there is the suggestion that Thek, who was no stranger amongst Warhol's coterie, sees his addition to the *Brillo Box* as complementary to Warhol's work, not as hostile to it in the way that his transgression of Minimalist aesthetics was. Thek makes Warhol's object whole, at the same time exposing the original as hollow, like all Warhol's gifts, by taking away the blank bottom face and replacing it with glass after the addition of the wax work. Yet I would suggest that the intrusion is still a trespass of sorts, a consensual violation: it still contains a friction, one with homoerotic overtones, that prevents the work falling into the realm of collaboration. It is still literally an upending and, on the part of the *Brillo Box*, it is still guilty, as was its maker, of the superficial nonchalance that characterised much of the 'cool' work grouped together at a time when Minimalism, as a term, had yet to be generally recognised. Collapsed in the gift are ideas of critical 'reception' and interpersonal politics, of sexual practice even: of being a 'giver' and a 'taker'. To return to the broader theme of this book, the reception of these sculptural works brings to light an awareness of one's complicity with a structure of value in which nothing is cost-free. Receiving is as much a self-authored statement about one's sense of self-worth as it is a state imparted by another's giving. Within this, however, Warhol contrives a space in which clever, sensitive people might engage in a meta-exchange of the symbolic awareness *of this fact*: a gift of trust that says, 'I know, and I know you know too.'

These gift-works are therefore related to the idea of trespass. The gifts signal that a certain amount of trespass into Warhol's fiercely protected space is allowable: that is the gift, rather than the 'empty nothings' of the physical things—no head under the hair, no chocolate in the box. Warhol's giving was an indication that one was allowed to take; it was an acknowledgement of someone's entitlement to his resources. As gifts between understanding friends, and as non-commercial exceptions to Warhol Enterprises, these works make the critical statement of works like the *Brillo Boxes* and *Shadows* explicit (albeit as jokes). Warhol's work highlighted how the artworld acted towards those members of the social class whose values and value it reflected: its gifts and 'gifted' people are also empty. Warhol re-set the alarm so that inhabitants became intruders, and he did this in varying degrees in everything from major, epoch defining exhibitions, to small areas of the Warhol office he had decided to command. In these works, the sculptural encounter is constituted by the carelessness of those who fail to acknowledge whose toes they are stepping on. Again, the works make a spectacle out of what is invisible in that place of greatest visibility, class, and the most concentrated target of this statement became the reconstitution of the viewer-subject in the gallery space after Minimalism. This reconstitution relied on the viewer's compliance with the works' circumscription of the spectatorial experience. At the same time, this new order also dissolved the visibility of entrance into this territory by emphasising the equivalence between the space inside and outside the white cube. Warhol's works satirise the idea of any fluency, however. The objects become sentinels of missteps and breaches of territory, registered by the kicking of the facsimiles of Campbell's Tomato Juice boxes, for example, and by visitors stepping into the alarm-activated area.

Where one, as a viewer, put one's feet was crucial in the negotiation (both and at once deliberate and careless) of the space around the boxes at the Stable Gallery. But footprints of careful as well as careless feet are also important features of Warhol's visual vocabulary. For example, the theme of footsteps is found in the *Dance Diagram* paintings, the images for which were taken from a popular instructional book of dance steps that provided a crucial point of entrance into American society at the time. Further, in 1961, Warhol tried out a Cageian strategy, leaving a section of canvas on the pavement to accumulate footprints. According to Ronnie Cutrone, at the same time as the *Brillo Boxes* were being prepared, Warhol had also made a footprint canvas using the blue and red paint that featured on the boxes themselves.[37]

This sensitivity to being stepped on, and the aesthetic sensibility that it highlighted, remained with Warhol and, in their work at least, became something that he shared with Jean-Michel Basquiat. This is evidenced by their collaborative series of paintings *Dollar Sign, Don't Tread on Me,*

1984–5. In this work's association of the two symbols of American nation-hood and ideology, the Gadsden Flag and the sign of the US currency, Basquiat has painted the snake pointing downwards in one instance, and hung by its tongue in another. In the studio, Basquiat's footprints, amongst others, found their way into Warhol's work, as their collaborations, which were frequently produced on the floor, would get trodden on. This was also the case with the *Oxidation Paintings* of around 1977–8. Multiple times in the *Diaries* Warhol considers it significant to relate the clumsy trespasses of those who tread on the canvases that were laid out on the floor of the studio. One episode involves Brigid Berlin's pug dog, caught walking over a still-wet canvas in Warhol's studio: a photo of which appears in Warhol's *America*.[38] Another, more telling, example is from 1980, when Prince Michael of Kent visited Warhol in the studio with *Vogue* editor Diana Vreeland and stepped on a canvas laid out on the floor: 'Prince Michael walked right on it, he thought it was a floor covering. So Fred asked him to autograph it. And he just signed it "Michael," he doesn't use "Prince." '[39] En-title-ment is the theme of this episode, inimically combined with spatial awareness in the clash of artworld and real world: one can imagine Prince Michael setting off an alarm in Warhol's head.

However, the foot and its print were not markers of oafishness per se. They were also, as might have been suggested by their association with the *Oxidation* or *Piss Paintings*, and following that, perhaps even the *Dance Diagrams*, the source of excitement and erotic charge. Thus, although the footprint is an index of trespass, it could also become part of a sexual exchange or the mark of some other rarefied encounter. So, for example, in the transcripts of David Bourdon's conversations with Warhol at the start of the 1970s, Warhol mentions going to see the footprints, rather than the handprints, of film stars set in concrete at Grauman's Chinese Theatre.[40]

Warhol's foot fetish is also the subject of significant attention in the literature.[41] In the following extract, from an interview conducted by Robert Reilly for the Yale student magazine in 1966, it is difficult not to imagine the scene between the impressionable young man, slightly out of his depth, and the mischievous Warhol.

> **Old Owl:** Why else do you wear boots? Besides to be taller?
> **Warhol:** […] Well, I'm a sadist.

O O: What do boots have to do with being sadistic?
Andy: Ah, well, you can step on people.
O O: Oh, really?
Andy: Have you ever been stepped on? It's fascinating.
O O: I'll have to try it sometime.
Andy: Oh, your boots are so big. They're very steppable.[42]

In a whole array of works that followed the analysis of *Shadows* in this chapter, trespassing footsteps show, more broadly, how Warhol interacted with his environment and those within it. And these works are linked to Warhol's equally curious gift pieces through the theme of entitlement. Throughout this book, Warhol's strained relationship to objects and the entitlements that, both in the artworld and outside, they could reflect inspired great work. In the case of *Shadows*, Warhol reversed the recursive, inter-affirming constellation of engagements between individual viewer, object and gallery space, to provide a space for forms of collective and anti-elitist identities. *Shadows* suggested a trespass on the territory of the artworld and, like much of the work before it, this was based on the displacement of institutional space in favour of the spaces of common culture. He haunted the institutions of art, its gallery space and its pervasive sense of reification, with something more unassuming, refusing the art object's authority over the viewer.

5

A Waste of Space

> There should be supermarkets that sell things and supermarkets that buy things back, and until that equalizes, there'll be more waste than there should be. Everybody would always have something to sell back, so everybody would have money, because everybody would have something to sell. We all have something, but most of what we have isn't saleable, there's such a preference today for brand new things. People should be able to sell their old cans, their old chicken bones, their old shampoo bottles, their old magazines. We have to get more organized.[1]

The condition of Warhol's sculpture has often been described in my analysis as negative, as that which is cast off. It stands for missing bodies, as much as it is a 'body of work' that is missing from our understanding of Warhol. In Warhol's sculpture we often find him shying away from the demand, seemingly made by an object-world, that he should fill space. In the major exhibitions on which I have focussed, the sense is that Warhol is making his absence, rather than his presence, felt; hence the irony of the title of the *Brillo Box* exhibition, *The Personality of the Artist*. Instead, there is an equivalence between the objects in these exhibitions and the people who fill them as spectators: the boxes left scattered become indexes of the spectators. As a hindrance to access, the work contested the viewers'

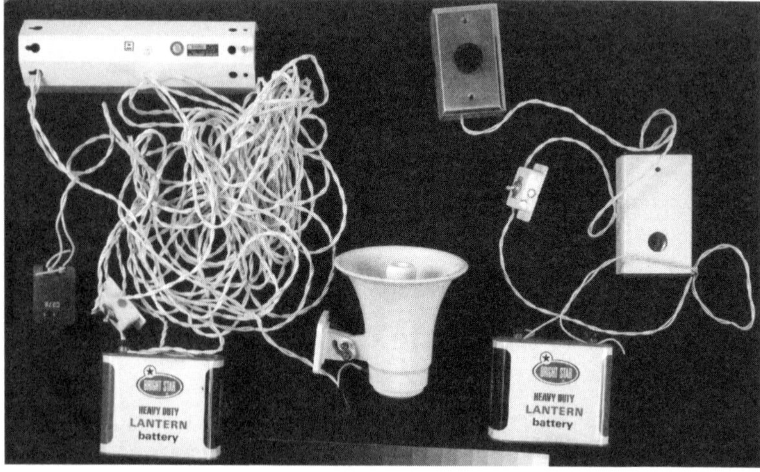

Fig. 5.1 Materials for abandoned version of *Invisible Sculpture, ca.* 1979. Collection of The Andy Warhol Museum, Pittsburgh.

sense of entitlement and belonging, provoking their jostling the boxes in order to re-secure their space in the gallery. The work highlighted a mis-identification, or perhaps a struggle for identification, between artworld and real world brought about by the blurring the installation produced. If, for Rainer Crone and Hal Foster, the critical punch of Warhol's images of this period came from their being walked past (either in the gallery or in relation to the oblivious 'passer-by' in *White Burning Car III* (1963) on whom Foster dwells), the boxes create the same effect by being walked into. As we have seen, *The Personality of the Artist* works by doing exactly what Arthur Danto said it did not: it created, in parallel to the gallery space, an illusory 'ghost' environment that gestured outside the gallery and the artworld and towards the stockroom—or, in the case of the exhibitions of *Shadows* and *Silver Clouds*, towards the disco or underground cinema space. In *Invisible Sculpture*, twenty years later, the empty plinth is a social platform but one that spectacularises the very absence of spectacle, putting a question mark over the status of spectatorship. As Neil Printz writes, Warhol 're-zoned' empty space as sculpture and, in doing so, Warhol made the empty space of the gallery *also* a real world 'elsewhere', requiring different forms of interaction.[2] And it was primarily sculpture that enabled these operations in Warhol's work. The clash of registers, played out on the level of installation and social position and placement, created obstacles of the self; the spectator is always, as Warhol remarked of himself in *The Philosophy*, the wrong thing in the right place.[3]

Although his sculpture often included painting in its composition, throughout his career Warhol attempted a more direct translation of his painting practice into a three-dimensional format, experimenting with holographics, projected film images and 3D paintings. The promise of these technologies was that they seemed to extend the photomechanically produced image into three-dimensional space. However, despite the holographic portrait made with Jason Sapan in 1977, Warhol's lasting ambition to make his own perfect 3D images was forever out of his reach. His final attempts came in the 1980s. In the book *Thank You Andy Warhol*, Stuart Pivar, 'scientist, entrepreneur, collector and art patron', describes how Warhol, in the years before his death, enlisted his help to source the technology for making what Pivar calls 'sculpture portraits' from camera images. Pivar describes something very much like today's 3D printing machinery, whereby lasers cut into or bond material in accordance with designs or images from 3D imaging technologies. This technology, which today is increasingly commonplace, was too expensive for Warhol to access and so, according to Pivar, he instead resorted to plan B, making life casts enlarged by a third and painted.[4] Pivar was Warhol's first subject, but the series never took off. Instead, what remained in the aftermath of the abandoned project were pedestals. Pivar recounts that, following these investigations into 3D portraiture, Warhol claimed that it 'was harder to find a good pedestal than make a good piece of sculpture',[5] and so planned an exhibition of them: 'wood pedestals, marble pedestals, alabaster pedestals, wood pedestals painted to look like marble and alabaster'.[6] The plan for this exhibition of Warhol's hard-won collection of these things replaced the out-of-reach project for mechanical portrait busts. The idea harks back to the empty pedestal alongside which Warhol exhibited himself.

In turn, *Invisible Sculpture*'s earlier incarnation—the burglar-alarmed space in Warhol's studio—left a box, now in the Andy Warhol Museum Archive, full of dismantled motion-sensitive burglar alarms (fig. 5.1). Packaging boxes also reappeared in two later works, both made during Warhol's experimentation with cement in the early 1980s.[7] The first, *Concrete Block* of 1982 (fig. 5.2), was a plain cardboard box, filled with

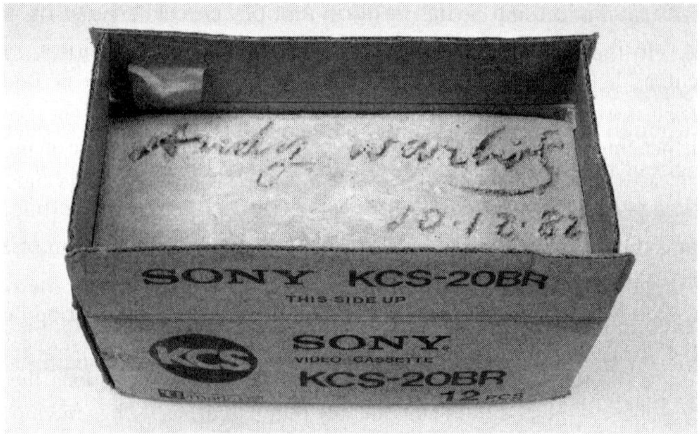

Fig. 5.2. Andy Warhol, *Concrete Block*, 1982. Collection of The Andy Warhol Museum, Pittsburgh.

cement; the second is *Whitman's Sampler* (c.1984), the cement-filled candy box with a cellophane wrapper. Both works are signed on the inside of the boxes, gestures that, again, hint at an equivalence between art and emptiness. Everywhere it is as if there is material piling up. Everywhere there is junk left behind by Warhol's attempts to erase, to do without subjects and objects, and make art out of atmosphere and emptiness. It is this material that today fills the empty space left by Warhol's life, but it had begun doing so long before he died. The consideration of this material, as it mediates between social, personal and artistic values, is the subject of this chapter.

From Leftovers to Recycling to a Critique of the Category of Appropriation

Warhol complains in *The Philosophy of Andy Warhol* that 'what I've always wanted, [is] not to have anything—to be able to get rid of all my junk—maybe put everything on microfilm or holographic wafers—and just move into one room.'[8] By condemning his own possessions to the status of 'junk', Warhol expresses a sense of feeling burdened by objects. The statement is reminiscent of the mantra 'one less object', which ten years earlier had provided the rationale for *Silver Clouds* and the hope that they would float out of the Castelli Gallery window. As objects symbolic of Warhol's painting, *Silver Clouds* did more than self-negate: they took with them not just the paintings they represented, but an entire aspect of Warhol's identity as Warhol-the-painter amid Castelli Gallery cohorts such as Jasper Johns and Roy Lichtenstein. Warhol wanted to spring clean and start out fresh. Yet the familiar Warholian fantasy of substituting the object with the three-dimensional image, and taking the image beyond the constriction of two-dimensional illusionistic space, is also expressed by this work. We find a similar idea in the above quotation from *The Philosophy* about the holographic wafers in the desire to retain a kind of access to the things he wishes would disappear. Objects and empty spaces; art seems to have the potential both to become junk and to clear junk space. Warhol gives empty space the status, as well as the kind of commodity value, that is reserved for only very distinguished objects. In contrast to space's irrefutable worth, the value of the object becomes questionable. His 'stark' and 'no comment' early work is a painterly equivalent to this emptiness, one given an ironic twist in the case of *The Personality of the Artist*, as Brillo and Campbell's box facsimiles filled up the actual space of the gallery.[9]

In 1988, 13 years after the publication of *The Philosophy*, Sotheby's posthumous auction of Warhol's possessions included over 10,000 objects in collections of 3,436 lots, and raised $30 million (with an average price per item of $3,000). Warhol clearly never achieved his ambition of getting rid of his valuable junk. One might see the auction as a final bid to create his idea of a perfect sculpture: an empty room seen through a peephole from the other side.[10] We get a sense of the breadth and depth of Warhol's collecting from a description in the catalogue of his collection of Americana and folk art shown in the 1977 exhibition *Folk and Funk*:

> Andy Warhol, the consummate collector, is passionate about all forms of folk art—cigar store Indians, carousel figures, ships' figureheads, weathervanes, whirligigs, decoys, primitive paintings, shop signs, quilts, coverlets, hooked rugs, painted furniture, and pottery. He also collects jewellery from the 1940s and 50s and good signed pieces and mass produced plastic jewellery from the 1930s; great Art Deco furniture by master French ébénistes like Jacques Emile Ruhlmann; tapes of conversations with celebrities; American Indian artefacts; contemporary and

historical paintings by artists such as Roy Lichtenstein and Maxwell Parrish; junk mail; American Empire furniture; gold coins; thousands of carats of mineral stones; books of all kinds; and 'Americana'—architectural ornaments, amusement park appurtenances, nickelodeons, pinball machines, cookie jars, toys, copper molds for manufacturing dolls and toys, Fiesta Ware, Westinghouse refrigerator ware, 1939 World's Fair souvenirs; *no* Andy Warhols.[11]

But Warhol's collection also included many things that did not make the list above, so another account is required. Bob Colacello, in his book *Holy Terror*, recounts a conversation with Brigid Berlin in the immediate aftermath of Warhol's death in which she gives what we might consider as an alternative inventory to that in the *Folk and Funk* catalogue. She describes a visit to his home, a place which Warhol kept private from his friends and colleagues during his lifetime:

> It was unbelievable. I wanted to puke. You couldn't get in the dining room, there were so many shopping bags and boxes and statues. It was disgusting. Sad. The only thing I could think was 'Has Jed seen this?' And then I went upstairs to Jon Gould's room and when Jon left Andy didn't move one thing. Andy's Valentine's Day cards to Jon were still in the drawer. And the *whole house* was filled with shopping bags filled with Andy's collections […] it was all consumption and possession and just that, just having things to have them, not to make the house look good or anything.[12]

Warhol's collecting overlapped with personal difficulties with hoarding and letting things go, something Evelyn Hofer's photograph of Warhol's dining room clearly shows (plate 5.1). In interviews with survivors of Warhol Enterprises, he is repeatedly described as a 'pack rat.'[13] The difference between the accounts given by Berlin and the exhibition catalogue is a question of framework, of public and private space. But the Americana, which Warhol first bought as junk in the 1950s, could only be seen as having a value at that time (regardless of the value it was to take on later) if imagined within the latter, pathological context; one that considered all things, all kinds of junk, as worth retaining. The sickening, overbearing immensity of the junk that Warhol left behind should be redeemed as a vital, though problematic, corollary of that which was skimmed off the top and taken to Sotheby's.

When Warhol began going to junk shops and flea markets in the 1950s, there was no established collectors' market for folk art and Americana, certainly not for the kind of Americana that Warhol predominantly collected which would have then been described with the very loaded term 'kitsch'. Sold as junk, the objects, however, later took on significant value as a market emerged.[14] Although this market was flourishing when his collection was displayed to the public as the exhibition *Folk and Funk*, curated by Elissa Cullman and Sandra Brant for the Museum of American Folk Art in 1977, Warhol was apparently discouraged from further pursuit of his collection and he expressed regrets about the display of his objects. Importantly, Warhol's collection of Americana and folk art began in tandem with the development of early work, such as the series of *Campbell's Soup Cans*. This is significant, and not just for the shared subject matter of American identities. As we have already seen in relation to the work of Anthony E. Grudin, as symbols of aspiration, working class people consumed 'all-American' products like Campbell's because they promised a gateway into a culture that was otherwise intolerant of, and unwilling to represent, their kind of social difference.[15] If, following Grudin, the subjects of the early paintings might represent a modern America, and the rites of belonging to it through belongings, then the collected objects from times gone by represented what was hokey and had been replaced.

However, perhaps the situation is not quite so dichotomised. A considerable portion of the subjects of Warhol's early work was what had been leftover, left out or even killed off by the American machine. For example, in the *Death and Disaster* series, participation is revealed as fraught with danger (something made especially apparent by *Tuna Fish Disaster* of 1963). The cycles of production and consumption, undertaken by Warhol at this time, picture, in turn, the cyclical nature of the culture that he observed. Such an ethos was also expressed elsewhere in the work of the artists that Warhol most admired: in the reuse of items found on the street in the work of Robert Rauschenberg and Jasper Johns, as well as through the influence of Emile de Antonio who had fostered and supported Warhol's artistic development. Writing on the aesthetic of overspill that he shared with Warhol, de Antonio stated that 'my long history with John Cage and Robert Rauschenberg enlightened me about the uses of junk, the detritus of modern industrial society as a source for the materials of art'.[16] De Antonio's own breakthrough work, *Point of Order* (1963), re-edited the used kinescope footage of the Army-McCarthy hearings which, according to Branden W. Joseph, de Antonio 'found languishing in an old CBS warehouse'.[17] This work was conceived by de Antonio as a critique of the machinery of American political power:

> My movie is against the whole Establishment [...] the film is not an attack on McCarthy. The film is an attack on the American government. My feeling is that if you look at the film carefully, Welch comes off as badly as McCarthy. He comes off as a rather brilliant, sinister, clever lawyer who used McCarthy's techniques to destroy McCarthy... I wanted the whole system exposed.[18]

To repeat an observation made in Chapter 3, in both of their works Warhol and de Antonio present the American spectacle as the means through which people are ostensibly offered access to identity, culture and public discourse, but are, at the same time, inhibited from political agency. Without commentary, their work merely repeats the spectacle in a new context, re-presenting the visual material—perhaps the only viable strategy of critical framing when it is 'the whole system' that is considered to be problematic. It is an engagement with ideology that is, in a direct way, also an aesthetic position defined by an un-slanted, depthless perspective on that culture. This is something made literal in Warhol's early paintings, a challenge both to ideas of critical distance and to elevated bourgeois tastes for depth.

Like de Antonio, Warhol orientated his aesthetic around both the source material and the attitudes left over from the boom era of the 1950s. It has been noted that many of Warhol's early subjects are rooted in this same era, even if they are also stimulated by an immediate present. The *Marilyn* series begun in August 1962, for example, is a response to the film star's death on the 5th of that month, but the image that Warhol uses is from a publicity photograph for the film *Niagara* (1953), taken right at the moment when Monroe became a star.[19] This might also be said of Warhol's production technique, which is usually considered in terms of the technicised Fordist factory line, and hence as being modern. But, like the Hollywood era to which Monroe belonged, by the early 1960s the heyday of the American factory was over, and postwar economic prosperity had come to an end with the advent of unsettled socio-economic times and an economic crisis that began in 1957 and lasted until 1961. When it came to making his own films, Warhol also used leftovers. His radical, unedited approach blurred the line between what was waste and what would make the cut, but it was the performers themselves whom he explicitly identified in terms of leftovers. In a passage from *POPism* he recalled:

> The people I loved were the ones like Freddy, the leftovers of show business, turned down at auditions all over town. They couldn't do something more than once, but their one time was better than anyone else's. They had star quality but no star ego—they didn't know how to push themselves.[20]

The leftover refers to something overarching and essential about Pop: how Warhol dealt with and related to the material he used, and how that material occupied space. Leftovers are an important theme in both *The Philosophy* and *POPism* that, more than any other, makes it possible to read *The Philosophy* as something serious and coherent, a real philosophy emerging above the montage of voices simply imitating Warhol that it is often taken to be. With leftovers, Warhol gives us an explanation of his Pop strategy and process:

> At the end of my time, when I die, I don't want to leave any leftovers. And I don't want to be a leftover […] I always like to work on left overs, doing the leftover things. Things that were discarded, that everybody knew were funny. It was like recycling work. I always thought there was a lot of humor in leftovers […] I'm not saying that popular taste is bad so that what's left over from the bad taste is good: I'm saying that what's left over is probably bad, but if you can take it and make it good or at least interesting, then you're not wasting as much as you would otherwise. You're recycling work and you're recycling people, and you're running your business as a by-product of other businesses. Of other *directly competitive* businesses, as a matter of fact.[21]

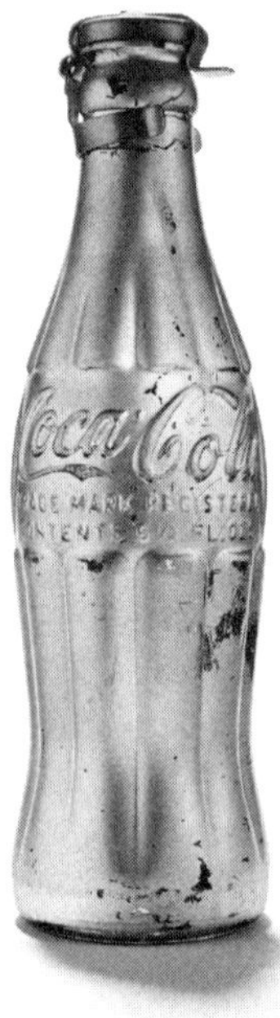

Fig. 5.3. Andy Warhol, *You're In,* 1967. Silver aerosol paint on bottle of Coca-Cola, 20.3 × 6.4 cm. Photograph Takao Ikejiri.

If Pop's material is leftovers, its process is that of recycling. Warhol describes his vision of Pop as a form of recycling: how Pop *Art* is not just a reflection of popular *culture* but a means for the interrelationship between the two through recycling.

Warhol's retaining of the leftover might be more hoarding, more pathology, but this is legitimised by an economy of reintegration, as well as a war on waste. Pop re-represented an American populace whose aspiration it was to consume, it deepened the penetration and visibility of the things that high culture overlooked, and put high culture itself to work in doing so. Yet, as Warhol himself makes clear, the leftover maintains a direct correlation with the commercial entity from which it is derived, one that threatens to trespass both on the artworld and also the commercial space from which it originated. One early example that did this rather too well is the 1967 work *You're In/ L'eau d'Andy*, which had been evolving as an idea since 1964 (fig. 5.3). Warhol remanufactured 100 Coca-Cola bottles, painting them silver and giving them new tops, and then filled them with perfume. Unlike his soup can paintings, which were considered 'art' productions, producing a consumable—such as perfume — fell into the category of 'directly competitive business' in the eyes of the Coca-Cola company, which subsequently issued a cease-and-desist letter. This provocation must also have had something to do with the work being a series of sculptural objects, an actual series of things to sell. The pun in the title of the work emphasises recycling's practice of taking what is leftover and making something desirable out of it. In *The Philosophy* Warhol remarks on recycling faeces as food, and this is almost that idea in practice: Andy's waste water re-consumed as perfume from a container originally intended for a beverage.[22] The whole work riffs on Warhol's celebrity status, and the condition of being 'in'. Of course, today many celebrities have released at least one fragrance for sale. *You* might also become 'in' by consuming the aura of the *Zeitgeist*-capturing Warhol, whose celebrity originated in the recycling of that which was considered a waste product of culture.[23] Little has been made of these ideas of Warhol's, in the terms he set out, yet his use of reuse overlaps with, and is considered as vital to, the history of another concept that is today ubiquitous in art history and criticism: appropriation.

Appropriation's critical bite is given to lie in its relationship to theft. This, for example, is something highlighted in Rosalind Krauss's important discussion of the term in relation to the work of Sherrie Levine.[24] In the famous examples of appropriation art in art history, by Richard Prince and Sherrie Levine, what is appropriated represents dearly held values (not least originality) and with their appropriation there is an immediate implied challenge to them: it follows that you would only want to steal something of value. Yet the Marlboro advert, or the Brillo Box, or indeed the folio plates re-photographed by Levine, are also ubiquitous and, in some way, vacuous, at a distance from the discerning gaze of high culture. With their translation and transubstantiation, the images can take on other values given to them, and so a territory is redefined. Though it is the case that the term recycling sometimes features in conjunction with appropriation in writing on art (for example, in Nancy Spector's catalogue essay for a 2007 Richard Prince exhibition at the Guggenheim, the terms 'recycling' and 'appropriation' are used both by the author and in quotations from the artist), only 'appropriation' is used in passages of elevated consequence, or where the work is placed in the larger context of art history.[25] Instead of theft, therefore, I want to suggest that appropriation might be seen as enabling the expansion of elite culture into the territory of that which is common. This suggests that, when we talk of appropriation in art history, we are confronting something that is reactionary and territorialising about our discipline — in its relationship with the wider world — as much as we are dealing with its capacity to critique.

In cultural studies, Andrew Ross and Evan Watkins have latched onto the passages in *The Philosophy* in which Warhol describes his 'philosophy of leftovers'.[26] They both see Warhol's recycling as perverting the heavily determined ground of cultural production, its target the culture of omission and distinction (precisely the condition of elite cultural discourse) that leads to neglect and waste. Watkins observes how good taste is constituted through an academic or academic-like culture that holds the high in check with the low, posturing as both anti-elitist and yet also as rightful custodian of the avant-garde. Recycling blurs these distinctions on which values, local to art and good taste, rely.[27] That these studies do not take place in art history perhaps suggests a residual distaste for models of production that threaten the bourgeois currency of good taste. Today, the use of the term appropriation 'automatically' gives work left-political kudos: yet, as the term itself becomes endlessly recycled in art history, we are not fully mindful of how loaded it is.

It is important that during both the moments to which the art I have referred to belonged, the early 1960s, and the late 1970s and early 1980s, the perceived autonomy of elite culture was considered to be under threat. Pop, for many, seemed to collapse the distance between high and low. Pictures generation appropriation artists competed in the 'culture wars' with artists who embraced a new proximity to markets and commercial demand. The most vilified of these latter artists were targeted for their 'bad' appropriation, their pluralism, yet perhaps we might see recycling in some of their work today and give it new consideration. Warhol was caught in these culture wars, adored by the Neo-Expressionists while his early work became newly appreciated as proto-conceptual and proto-appropriation by the academy. Warhol's work is pivotal in this history then, but I would suggest with de Antonio that recycling owes its origins to Robert Rauschenberg. A telling feature of the initial reception of Rauschenberg's *Combines* (approx. 1954–64) was that their inclusion of everyday objects was criticised for not being properly integrated into a coherent artistic form. The work was compared unfavourably to Dada which, despite its emphasis on sociological forms of fragmentation, was considered to do this. Rauschenberg had failed to make the things he used 'his own' in this work. Yet, this sense that the everyday object retains some autonomy is important to the aesthetics of recycling; re-use is not totally transformative, but originates in the Cagean idea of letting things speak on their own. The independence of the recycled object means that its value lies in something independent or distinguishable from the overall body of the work: a singularity, even a functionality, that survives transition into the context of 'art'. Of course, Warhol's mechanised procedures of production put pressure on this model, but what is crucial here is the displacement of the pre-existing values of the artworld by the everyday commodity brought into the gallery. As Warhol states (and it bears repeating): 'You're recycling work and you're recycling people, and you're running your business as a by-product of other businesses. Of other *directly competitive* businesses, as a matter of fact.'[28] Instead of models of reproduction and multiplication, what I am proposing with the model of recycling is that value always has a location, and a loss of value is always implied with relocation of that value elsewhere. The example that again comes to mind is *Invisible Sculpture*, where Warhol draws to our attention the contingency of his presence, making an artwork, a sculpture no less, out of the absence he leaves behind. This understanding of Warhol's work problematizes the all too easy assumption that it is seamlessly compatible with the modern conditions of duplication and mechanical reproduction belonging to his famous subject matter of media imagery. What follows is an account of two of Warhol's largest recycling projects, *Raid the Icebox I* (1969–70) and *Time Capsules* (1974–), and an analysis of how these works confront and upset the values art history sustains through relations of space (proximity, distance, territory and trespass) that are central to the aesthetic judgements for and against work, like in the examples above, in which the material of the work is sourced directly from sites otherwise considered valueless.

Mental Space: Warhol's *Raid the Icebox I*

In 1969, Warhol was invited to curate an exhibition based on articles chosen from the backrooms and stores of the Museum of the Rhode Island School of Design. He was the first of what was hoped would be a series of artists to guest curate in this way, hence the work's title: *Raid the Icebox I*. During the summer of 1969, he and a small entourage, including the writer David Bourdon and Warhol's business manager, Fred Hughes, visited the museum storerooms with the museum's curatorial staff including Daniel Robbins, the director of the museum until 1971. Both Bourdon and Robbins wrote essays for the exhibition's catalogue while Warhol himself documented the proceedings with a Polaroid camera and tape recorder. In his lively catalogue essay for *Raid the Icebox I*, Robbins wrote of the effect Warhol's intervention had: 'our conception of our jobs as curators is rather sweetly altered.'[29]

The exhibition opened in Rice University Institute for the Arts in Houston (opening 20 October 1969); and travelled to the Isaac Delgado Museum in New Orleans (opening 17 January 1970); and finally, Rhode Island School of Design's Museum of Art in Providence (opening 23 April 1970). At each location, the objects were displayed in curious arrangements, quite unlike traditional museological presentation. The collection of objects retained the sense of having risen from the shadows of the stores as understudies of the stars of the museum's collection. But by replacing objects that exemplified the best that historical periods, cultures and tastes had to offer, with objects that eschewed this kind of representation entirely, the work, as I will argue, fashioned a highly suggestive approach to thinking about the political stakes of the museum display. With *Raid the Icebox I* Warhol took the Pop strategy of recycling the leftover to the institution and extended sculpture's ground into institutional and architectural space. Lisa Graziose Corrin, a curator who, in the 1990s, did much to establish the place of 'artist in the museum' works as a key form of critical intervention, writes that *Raid the Icebox I* was 'not an exhibition, it was a fully conceived installation artwork in which even the seemingly random choice and placement of the objects was consequential'.[30]

In the course of his visits to the Museum of Art at the Rhode Island School of Design, Warhol directed the removal and transportation of nearly 400 objects from the museum stores to the floor spaces of the museums to which the show would travel (fig. 5.4 and plate 5.2). His arrangement of the items preserved much of their appearance as he had encountered them in the stores. Collections of objects, sometimes simply piled up, crowded areas, abandoning the disciplines and practicalities of display. The objects chosen

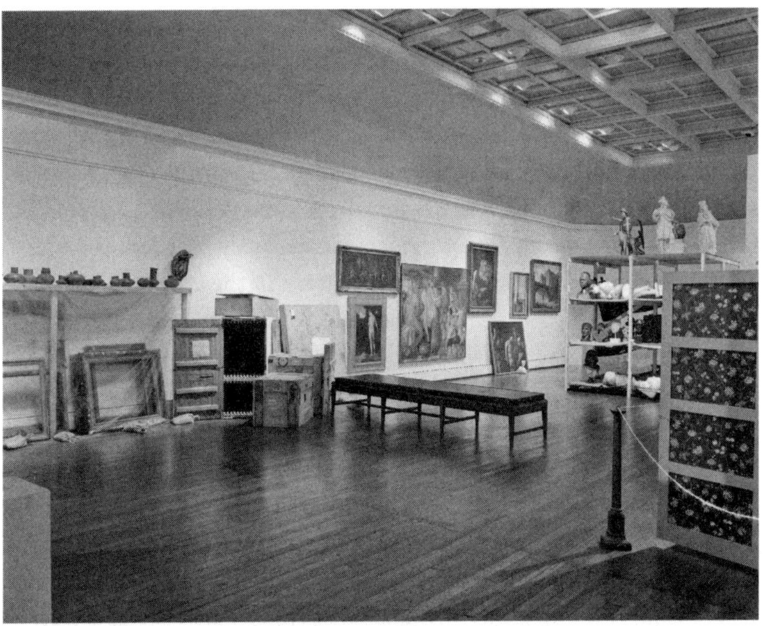

Fig. 5.4. Installation view of *Raid the Icebox I* with Andy Warhol, Museum of Art, Rhode Island School of Design, April 23-June 30, 1970. Courtesy of the Museum of Art, Rhode Island School of Design, Providence.

were often specimens that were in some way less than exemplary, and the way in which Warhol displayed these works in rafts made the discrimination of 'good' and 'bad' examples more or less impossible. It was a commentary on cultural values, one that sought to redress hierarchies through a display that disrupted the order of things in the museum. Warhol's rehang subverted an American ideology of distinction: advanced, yet absorbent of European traditions, master of historical narratives, and, within the museum, supported by a culture of originality, strict discernment, striation of value and quality of example. The rehang revealed American elite culture as one among many, with varying examples, varying values, and no less adrift in the swim of history.

Turning the museum inside out, Warhol displayed whole racks of objects from the stores as they had been found: shoes, some odd, some duplicates, were massed together in cupboards six shelves deep, with stacks of decorative hat boxes sitting on top, and piles of magazines and assorted publications tied with string on the floor. There were art objects on display too, including paintings, though some were torn and either waiting for or beyond repair. Fakes were included, as were real works by members of the Western canon: Velazquez, Cézanne and Degas, for example. Much of what was exhibited could be described as junk, but Warhol insisted that each object be meticulously labelled and classified. As a result, by far the largest inventory in the catalogue, which is arranged primarily between 'single objects and objects in series', pertains to the footwear that featured.

This organisational scheme rather camouflaged, however, the huge range of Native American pieces that Warhol chose. Robbins writes that, when showing Warhol around, the objects that he (Robbins) thought noteworthy, such as fine Oriental vases, notable pieces from antiquity, 'the most extravagant laces, the richest Ecclesiastical vestments' — in other words, those objects which reflected the values of the museum—'did not elicit a flicker' from Warhol and that, instead, Native American work was frequently chosen.[31] The inventory of items in the catalogue supports this perception of things, but only to an extent.[32] Warhol did choose more Native American work than might have been representative compared to the whole array of the store's holdings, and he certainly passed over major examples from other collections.[33] But, despite this interest, works by Native American peoples did not constitute anything close to a majority of the work in the exhibition overall. Further, in the catalogue they were organised according to the same order as everything else: not 'other', as Robbins' commentary suggests we should understand them, but featuring under the anonymous subheading 'Baskets, Ceramics and Textiles'. Although Warhol's actions during his visits certainly made it seem to Robbins that he was privileging Native American work for display in the catalogue the work is both equal and invisible within the museum's hierarchy of objects. Robbins' account seems not to be troubled by what this curatorial decision to pit the Native and colonial against each other might have meant, and that silence has continued in later discussions. Nonetheless, determined identity correction and overt politics is certainly one way of looking at Warhol's approach here. The period of the exhibition overlapped with the Red Power occupation of Alcatraz Island and anticipated the time, three years later, when

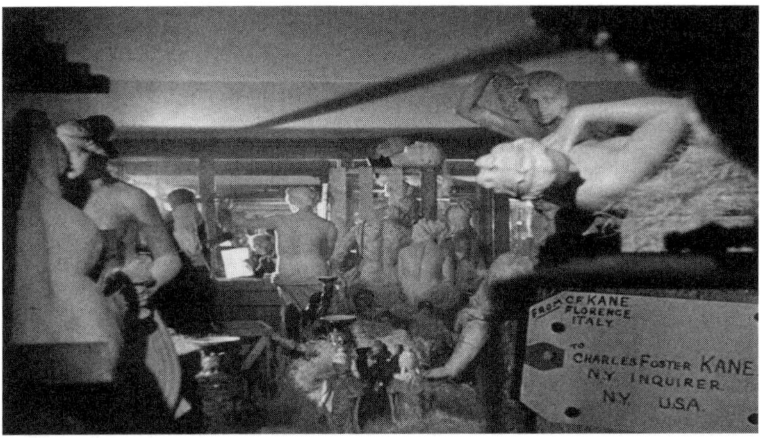

Fig. 5.5. *Citizen Kane* [Film still, Kane's office]. Dir. Orson Welles. RKO Radio Pictures, 1941.

Marlon Brando, due to receive an Oscar for *The Godfather*, boycotted the award ceremony and caused a public scandal by sending human rights activist Sacheen Littlefeather in his place.[34] The fact that *Raid the Icebox I* so resembles the sets of some iconic American films, particularly *Citizen Kane*'s Xanadu and, even more so, Big Daddy's cellar in *Cat on a Hot Tin Roof*, emphasises this sense of colonial or imperial misadventure in a typically Warholian way through reference to Hollywood's golden age (fig. 5.5 and 6). With *Raid the Icebox I* Warhol was, perhaps, recreating the pathetic final scenes of these movies in the museum. These portrayed the American Dream with nowhere to go, disappearing amid epic piles of priceless yet unwanted and unvalued antiques, plied from Europe and the colonies with the huge wealth of American industrial empires. Warhol thus figured the institution, and America, as another Kane or Big Daddy—or indeed, as it would turn out, another Warhol.[35]

Comparisons of the installation of *Raid the Icebox I* with views of the stores themselves were made in published material at the time and there is no doubt, taking the catalogue into account, that the space to which these broken, undesirable objects belonged was also on display. The objects themselves were anti-objects that transferred the dark of the museum stores to the space of the gallery in the same way *Silver*

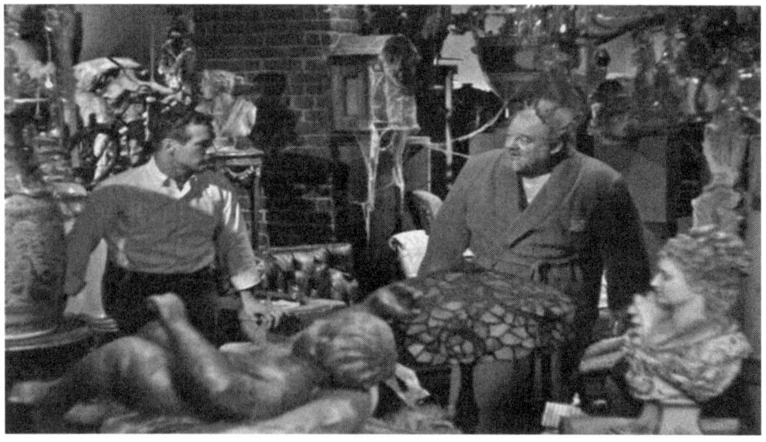

Fig. 5.6. *Cat on a Hot Tin Roof* [Film still, Big Daddy's basement], Dir. Richard Brooks, Metro-Goldwyn-Mayer, 1958.

Clouds had brought the underground to the institutional surface three years earlier. One of the most dramatic features of the exhibition was the hoard of Windsor chairs, many broken but kept for spare parts to use to maintain the museum's finer examples (fig. 5.7). These were exhibited all in one room, on the floor in crushed rows and mounted, as if hovering, on the wall, a hanging electric light casting shadows in all directions.[36] Elsewhere a group of large gilt-framed paintings, of a variety of traditional scenes, were stacked together. Bourdon describes them:

> Some were sideways, some had only their backs showing. Warhol declared he wanted the whole stack, including the miscellaneous sandbags that were strewn around on the floor. And he wanted to exhibit them 'just like that.' 'We'll put the best one on top, show a corner of one, and the back of another.'[37]

One wonders what the status of 'the best' precisely consisted of here for Warhol. Again, Warhol's hostile disregard for these paintings echoes the statements of disregard *for painting* he made at the time of the *Silver Clouds* exhibition. On both occasions, the works were taken from their normal place on the wall and instead entered into a larger, cluttered world. The paintings were the best of the worst perhaps: rejects, donors, unwanted gifts—a carnivalesque parody of connoisseurship that occurred across the installation as a whole. In so being, the category of 'best' becomes, in its ambiguity, also emancipatory: work that did not fit in with fashion or taste, but which was well-made or attractive, could be appreciated alongside the failures that showed up the museum's pretensions.

The inventory for the exhibition also included a ginkgo tree much like the one that Warhol had spotted in the Rhode Island School of Design Museum's sculpture garden. This was displayed at the front of the exhibition. David Bourdon, in his catalogue essay, recorded:

> Returning to the Director's office, Warhol glanced out a window at the enclosed sculpture garden, pointed to a ginkgo, and said: 'I want that tree.'
>
> 'Fine, we'll get a copy. Write that down,' Robbins snapped at his assistant. 'Tree to the right of the bust of Ingres.'
>
> Back in the office, Robbins informed the curator of the costume collection that Warhol wanted to borrow the entire shoe collection. 'Well, you don't want it *all*,' she told Warhol in a rather disciplinarian tone, 'because there's some duplication.'
>
> Warhol raised his eyebrows and blinked.[38]

This episode shows that, as we have seen multiple times in this study, Warhol's dealings with objects were mercilessly levelling: tree, shoes and bust of Ingres. We might think of Émile Bourdelle's bronze cast of Ingres (thought to be the second casting; the first, and more famous, resides in the Musée Bourdelle in Paris) as representative of the category of art. Here it sits awkwardly between the natural one-off and the mass-produced, artistically insignificant multiples. It is reduced to a site marker (both literally, locating the whereabouts of the tree and, metaphorically, as marking the place of culture) in a reconfigured moral order in which the other objects have preference. This suggests that Warhol was interested in natural history, something that the worn shoes and ginkgo cannot hide about themselves, but which is quite distinct from the art

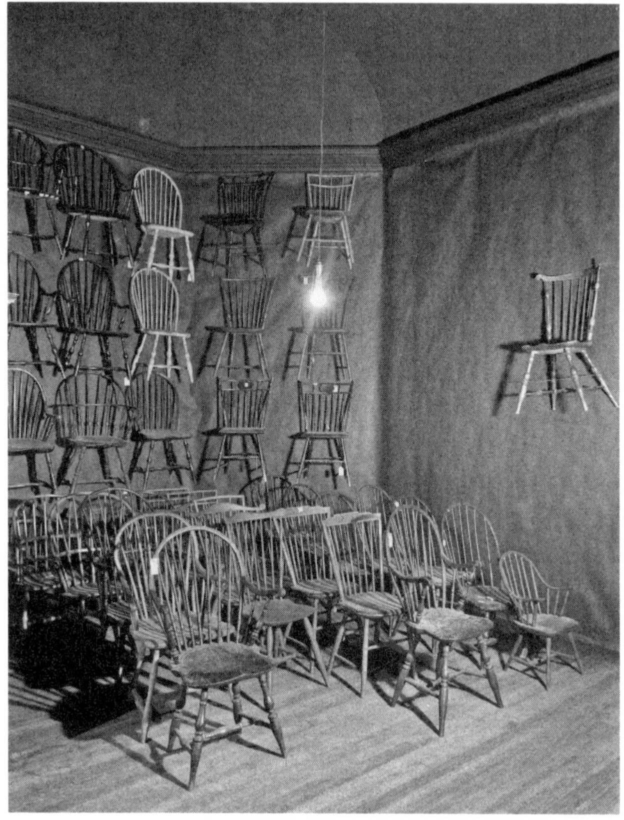

Fig. 5.7. Installation view of *Raid the Icebox I* with Andy Warhol, Museum of Art, Rhode Island School of Design, 23 April- 30 June, 1970. Courtesy of the Museum of Art, Rhode Island School of Design, Providence.

history for which the portrait bust stands. In a piece on Warhol's collecting of Native American artefacts, Tony Berlant, another Warhol associate, tells Ralph T. Coe that Andy 'liked to think how things evolved, how works were used within cultures, and how they passed (in his mind's eye) to myriad owners and cycles of usage'.[39] Things that are part of 'natural history' seem to have something to do with recycling and how Warhol imagined the sculptural too. Of the Navajo textiles he collected he said: 'I like them best when they have holes in them, they're cheaper, and they're more sculptural'.[40] In a way that is akin to my argument in Chapter 1, sculpture here has to do with a sense of something as subject to accidents, duration and the environment, and this is how we might understand the objects above, ironically pitted against the traditional category of sculpture represented by the Bourdelle.[41]

The equivalence Warhol's curatorship suggested between different kinds of objects and different ways of considering them also enabled these objects to speak to one another. Not only did the space of the reject invade the space of the example, but objects impacted on each other, breaching individual spaces of meaning, category and narrative order. From Warhol's Polaroids of *Raid the Icebox I* we get a sense that things have taken a life of their own, autonomous of the space that they previously commanded as certain kinds of visual object (plates 5.3–8). As both these and the exhibition photographs show, Warhol achieved an effect of animation and bizarre anthropomorphism. Walt Disney, of course, was Warhol's favourite 'living' artist (a view he stood by in interviews even a decade after Disney's death).[42] In photographs of Warhol's arrangements, the faces in the paintings and sculptures seem in discourse. All kinds of objects strike up relationships, brought into proximity within the visual framework of both the museum and Warhol's Polaroid camera. A selection of images in the catalogue, which match up with Polaroids of the time found in the Warhol archive, extend this sense further, using this second layer of mediation of the photographs to continue the play. One prominent oil-on-canvas portrait in the exhibition features on the front and again on the back of the catalogue. Both times it is propped up by the same man who we see behind the picture's frame and whose face is now also a portrait. He wears a slightly glazed look, staring into the middle distance. The two individuals, the woman in the portrait and the handler, look as if they might have just had a falling-out: the expression of the woman in the painting looks very disapproving.[43] The photograph brings into another medium the sense of animation that Warhol's handling of the museum objects brought to the exhibition spaces. In the photo, the real person becomes involved in a moment of drama like that occurring between the objects throughout the exhibition. The sense of mischief in Warhol's approach is palpable from the catalogue, with both essays from the time emphasising the 'fresh eyes' with which Warhol approached the material.

Raid the Icebox I has been considered a partner work to *Folk and Funk*, notably in the essay by Michael Lobel on Warhol's combined 'closeting' and 'collecting', published in *Art Journal* in 1996, and in the essay by Lisa Corrin, published in 1995 for a special issue of *Rhode Island School of Design Museum Notes* which followed the death of Daniel Robbins. Deborah Bright, in a later essay, provides summaries of these two articles:

> In Lobel's [essay], *Raid the Icebox I* and *Folk and Funk* both offered the artist an occasion to recontextualize objects from high culture, folk culture and popular culture, investing them with new value. Lobel likens this activity to the way the closet allows the gay subject to take the heterogeneous elements of his life and create an erotics of simultaneous display and secrecy that preserves access to, and mobility in, straight society while mirroring back a coherent image of an idealized and eroticized self.
>
> Lisa Graziose Corrin contributed an essay on the importance of *Raid the Icebox I* in developing a genealogy for 1990s museum interventions by conceptual artists such as Fred Wilson, Joseph Kosuth, Andrea Fraser, Louise Lawler, Christian Boltanski and James Luna. Though unique as an activity in Warhol's oeuvre, Corrin viewed *Raid the Icebox I* as entirely consistent with Warhol's aesthetic in its blurring of the boundaries among categories of taste, its refusal of judgement and selection, its preoccupation with series, its parallels to Warhol's own acquisitive passions and the artist's reconnecting of the nineteenth-century museum to its mass-market twin, the department store.[44]

Both authors consider *Raid the Icebox I* as overlapping with the shopping, collecting, curating and hoarding that went on in Warhol's personal life. However, Lobel's reading of the haphazard arrangement of objects in *Raid the Icebox I* and *Folk and Funk* is contrasted in his essay with the presentation of objects at the Sotheby's auction which, he says, emphasises the extent to which the image of Warhol's collecting at the latter was 'tidied up'. This point about tidying is central to Lobel's article, which draws out a 'correspondence between the logics of the museum and of the closet [...] by which [...] a seemingly stable and closed sphere of heterosexuality is constituted in relation to a debased sphere of homosexuality.'[45] Warhol's untidiness, his ambiguity, disrupted the outward order maintained by both museum and hetero-normative orders, and thus disrupted the cultural priorities that they represented. This was achieved through the exposure of the closet, which, importantly for social order, mediates public and private spaces. Lobel's suggestion, further, that *Raid the Icebox I* (as well as Warhol's studio and living spaces) was a kind of mental space and also that *Folk and Funk* was an approximation, on the part of its curators, of how Warhol saw his own collecting and its excited, rampant hold on his attention, will be central to the following analysis. The objects in *Folk and Funk* were 'in casual disarray', according to a review, and Lobel sees this as suggestive of the collection 'as a sort of playscape of the artist's mind', while 'both closet and collection provide material or spatial models for thinking the self.'[46]

While *Folk and Funk* might symbolise the 'outing' of the contents of a closet, it is another question whether or not it was representative, in any faithful way, of the subject Andy Warhol. Before *Folk and Funk*, Warhol's collection, dispersed and mostly, though not all, hidden in amongst the expensive junk of closed rooms, arguably resided only in the space of Warhol's imagination.[47] The display of Warhol's collection of Americana and folk art at *Folk and Funk* took the objects away from this mental space into the ordered, buttoned-down space of museological display, despite having been arranged to dimly echo the chaos of *Raid the Icebox I*. Thus, although the exhibition gave some sense of the heterodoxy of Warhol's taste, it was indicative of the process of normalisation that the collection underwent when put on show. Perhaps its bad likeness—the shock, not of outing and exposure, but of misrepresentation—was why Warhol expressed his dissatisfaction at the time over *Folk and Funk*.[48] By comparison, *Raid the Icebox I* might be considered to have been an actualisation and, therefore, faithful representation of the mental space that Warhol's collections inhabited; played out in, and in defiance of, the order of the museum at the Rhode Island School of Design. Yet, despite its symbolism, *Raid the Icebox I* should not necessarily be celebrated as a representation of Warhol's mental space. As we have seen, this could be deeply dysfunctional. The disarrangement of the objects in *Raid the Icebox I* foreshadowed the state in which Warhol's possessions were found in his home after his death, where, according to *Newsweek's* Cathleen McGuigan, 'Jewellery was found in cookie tins; a Picasso was stuck in a closet. Another closet was stuffed to the top with stunning Navajo blankets.'[49]

Lobel's vision of *Raid the Icebox I* as a mental world is echoed in Corrin's essay:

> In *Raid the Icebox I*, Warhol knowingly exhibited the world according to Warhol. Even the exhibit invitations—hot pink object labels from storage combined with a photograph of Warhol in the act of clicking his Instamatic camera—eloquently announced that the subject of *Raid the Icebox I* was Andy Warhol, as Daniel Robbins stated in his catalogue.[50]

We might think back here to *You're In/L'eau d'Andy*, with its reuse of Coca-Cola bottles sprayed silver. This work, like *Raid the Icebox I*, re-orbits an established American identity to instead circle around and reflect Andy Warhol by referring to his 'essence', in this case his urine, and silver, the identifier for his hip status. With *Raid the Icebox I*, Warhol found a way to augment and orchestrate the currencies of the museum, taste and historical and discursive order around himself in the same way as he diverted and recirculated aspects of the commercial world in his earlier art. As Corrin states, the idea, which appears throughout the literature on *Raid the Icebox I*, that Warhol was the true subject of the exhibition, has its origins in Robbins's catalogue essay, the best description of the work from the time. Robbins writes: 'all things become part of the whole and we know that what is being exhibited is Andy Warhol.'[51] Similarly emphasising the playfulness and masquerade of the work, Peter Wollen writes:

> It is as if the label 'Andy Warhol' would signify, not a person, in the sense of a human subject, but storage: boxes, reels, spools, Polaroids, all labelled 'Andy Warhol'. It would be an immense museum of junk (or rather, since it could all be metamorphosed into commodity form, a department store or gigantic thrift shop). At the root of this attitude we find once again many affinities with Cage's aesthetic.[52]

Generally, the literature on *Raid the Icebox I* by Bright, Corrin, Lobel and Wollen, and the essays by Robbins and David Bourdon in the original catalogue, give the reader a sense that Warhol nurtured, even indulged in, a form of solipsism, to the extent of devising an idiom *of solipsism* in his approach to 'artist as curator' and 'artist in the museum' works. However, in this 'in-his-own-world' aesthetic, in what seems to be solipsistic, there is a position of critique that continues the mode of Warhol's earlier work and the influence on it by Emile de Antonio that I have argued for in this chapter. De Antonio also emphasised an art form that presented the idea of a whole system, a complete picture. *Point of Order*, like *Raid the Icebox I*, is entirely constituted by, and conceived in relation to, the leftover, with de Antonio also using material from stores. Yet *Raid the Icebox I*, because of the apparent solipsism, the proximity to Warhol's personhood—seen as 'zany' or somehow not serious—is seen as a refutation rather than instantiation of considered critique.

In Robbins's description of his time with Warhol, showing him around the museum while following his instructions for the exhibition, Warhol is presented as a genius, and at the same time as someone who needed minding. Interestingly, in terms of the overall theme of this book, Corrin proposes that Robbins acted as a 'discrete but sculpting presence', suggesting again that Warhol himself was the subject of the exhibition — as if he too were some kind of artefact. Robbins's assessment of Warhol's work, however, is nothing but respectful, indeed rather awed, and his overall impression of the work is, rightly, that it was radical. Warhol's action causes Robbins to exclaim: 'what violence the idea of spare parts does to our fanatical notion of uniqueness and the state of an object's preservation!'[53] But in stressing the singularity of Warhol's 'innocent' attraction to objects, Robbins rather glosses over the potential criticality of Warhol's specific choices by imagining Warhol as an instinctive, natural, force. Here the idea of Warhol in his own world is partly down to Robbins's lack of appreciation of the social content and substance of what Warhol chose. Warhol's inclusion of Native American work is put down merely to his esotericism. Bourdon also mentions the partiality of Warhol's selections, half-apologising for them on his behalf. This characterisation of Warhol is echoed by Corrin when she describes the *Raid the Icebox I* project as a whole as 'charming in its remarkable lack of self-consciousness.'[54] What Corrin admires in Warhol's work is contrasted against the austere seriousness of the moment in which she is writing. Corrin acted in Robbins's role in 1992 when she worked with Fred

Wilson on the production of *Mining the Museum* at the Maryland Historical Society. This was one of the 1990s' most significant works of institutional critique, in which Wilson drew attention to the museum display's complicity with, yet erasure of, the history of slavery. In her article she writes of her fatigue, four years on, with 'clichéd' artist in the museum projects and laboured discourses of criticality, and she sees *Raid the Icebox I* as the 'pioneering forerunner of the "movement"', and refreshingly devoid of any political agenda.[55] For her, Warhol is a pioneer of the form that later critique would take, rather than of the critique itself. Yet Warhol's inclusion of artefacts that signalled a history of a repressed people, placed in dialogue with the objects of those guilty of that repression, prefigured exactly the strategy Wilson employed in *Mining the Museum*. Where the two works differ is in the forthrightness of Wilson's agenda, which contrasts with the occlusion of Warhol's curatorial decisions, both by the protocols of categorisation ('Baskets, Ceramics and Textiles'), and by Warhol's self-representation as idiosyncratic and incapable of advancing a determined agenda.[56] His provocativeness during the visits, described by Robbins, are put down to his reputation as a mischief-maker.[57]

One way in which Corrin's assessment is like Bright's and Wollen's is the way that Warhol's behaviour—described as distracted, perusing and waiting to be titillated—exposes the museum as the kin of the shopping mall, a point we have seen made already by Mark Francis in relation to Warhol's *Shadows* and *Personality of the Artist* exhibitions.[58] In Bright's account, we find a Warhol even more in character:

> [Warhol] violated the boundaries of masculine seriousness, scholarly detachment and that palpable sense of larger mission that characterizes the curatorial project, giving voice to the spontaneous feminine passion of the impulse shopper [...] Like a shopaholic on speed.[59] It is true that when Warhol came across objects in the museum stores which he wanted to include he gave the cue: 'I'll take them.'[60]

Thus we might agree with Bright and see Warhol as consciously representing a position outside the institution, one of gendered specificity and even 'class sensibility' which he brought to play havoc with the masculine elite order of the museum. Bright characterises Warhol as a scruffy, nutty embodiment of commercialism; his critique as a rather blunt sabotage and subversion informed by an affinity with the cheapness of proletarian and feminine tastes and habits.[61] The distracted, browsing, blue-collar Warhol that Bright describes contains echoes of the ditzy genius described by Robbins. Yet she claims, without evidence, that Warhol was 'ambivalent about the project from the start', and that his assistant, Fred Hughes, had led the way, eager to exploit his connection with the de Menils and to 'feather his own and Andy's nests'.[62]

In Wollen's text, the seemingly arbitrary way in which Warhol made selections for *Raid the Icebox I* is understood in the context of the work of Rauschenberg and Cage, and their uses of found objects and chance procedures: 'At the root of this attitude we find once again many affinities with Cage's aesthetic: the refusal of hierarchy or consequence or narrative.'[63] Indeed, as I have suggested, Warhol's use of leftovers, discussed throughout this chapter, has much in common with Rauschenberg's and Cage's bypassing of traditional modes of authorship and their use of reuse. But, for Wollen, even Cage's influence does not redeem Warhol's contrariness, leaving him to conclude, as we have seen, that the main exhibit in *Raid the Icebox I* was Warhol himself. Wollen's assessment quickly devolves, like those above, into an assessment of personality: in this case that Warhol, 'the childhood reject and misfit', was projecting, surrounding himself with the leftovers with which he identified. Further, in doing so, Wollen says in *Raid the Icebox I* Warhol was commoditising his persona in the art form of those leftover objects he chose for display.[64] This kind of psycho-biography may not deserve extensive focus in its own right, but it is remarkable that in relation to a work of such acknowledged importance all the authors above reach the same diagnosis, which I have characterised as akin to solipsism, each time undermining the status of the work as critique.

The above authors are squeamish, I want to suggest, about the proximity to valuelessness and waste that Warhol's work threatens. They recoil from the dusty and dysfunctional; from the status of underling; from a cheap world, an essentially tasteless world. However, such a proximity is implicit in the process of recycling, during which the valueless and the valuable blur into each other. And the threat of this proximity is psychic: that these objects, usually not considered worthy of display, might actually have a certain power. In his essay, Robbins describes his own encounter with this power:

> Warhol made a specification at this point: he requested that the catalogue entry for each item be as complete as possible [...] each object is obliged to carry its full set of associations, and a weird poetry results; the combination of pedantry and sentiment that can be read in the entries is the serial imagery of history. There are personal overtones of almost unbelievable poignancy in the now-anonymous rubbed kid heels of some fine lady's shoes.[65]

While museum displays formalise the presentation of objects of historical value on behalf of those that history places in positions of authority, a worn shoe catches Robbins off-guard. He makes an identification that recognises the vulnerability of this authority even at the risk of his own investment in it. The 'weird poetry' that Robbins describes might be interpreted in the terms that Jonathan Flatley has used in his more recent work on Warhol's collecting. Flatley takes up Walter Benjamin's concerns with the collector's '"physiognomic" interest' in objects.[66] Benjamin was interested in a form of reception, just as in Robbins' description, whereby leftover fragments can produce vivid historical insights akin to psychoanalytic unearthings. Moments such as these helped Benjamin to imagine an alternative to what he called the 'once-upon-a-time' model of level and homogenous linear history — precisely the territory of the traditional museum display.[67] Flatley suggests that Warhol in Rhode Island, free-associating, mingling amid the leftover oddments of the museum stores, shares something with Benjamin's collector. It is this threat of exposure, what Flatley calls an 'affective openness to the world', that is at the heart of what I have argued has caused others to distance themselves from what they saw as Warhol's solipsism and peculiarity.[68]

In Benjamin's thoughts on collecting, published as 'On Unpacking My Library: A Talk about Book Collecting', there is a suggestion of solipsism: 'To renew the old world—that is the collector's deepest desire.'[69] Taken in the context of the rest of the work's advocacy of second-hand and cast-off books—of the leftover, and the collector's special relationship to it—the expression of this desire provides an image of a revolutionary solipsism of renewed worlds emerging from the world built around the self (a collector's collection always locates the individual at the centre of it). This idea of renewal describes the way in which the old world of the historical past becomes animated through the collector for Benjamin: 'inside her there are spirits, which have seen to it that for a collector, ownership is the most intimate relationship one can have to objects. Not that they come alive in her; it is she who lives in them.'[70] Renewal, an encounter with the new world of the past through a collection, was the radical potential Benjamin saw in the activity of the collector, but one could also become submerged, like the fictional figures of Big Daddy, Kane and Warhol himself, amid ruinous mountains of expensive junk.

Benjamin's and Warhol's use of the leftover is, in both cases, an art of recycling. Indeed, describing his *Arcades Project*, Benjamin was keen to stress that it was reuse, rather than appropriation, that was essential to the way he employed quotations:

> This method of study: literary montage. I have nothing to say. Only to show. I will not appropriate any ingenious formulations, not steal anything valuable. But the rags, the refuse: I will not describe but rather exhibit them.[71]

If Benjamin's radical aesthetics of recycling mirrors the endless revolutions of the production and consumption of the commodity—setting mimesis against mimesis, fetish against fetish—Warhol's Pop work did so with an even greater sense of overlap. In *Raid the Icebox I*, Warhol usurped space that was already attributed to the elevated cultural value of art with his own equally powerful cultural value, allowing the objects he represented (and which could only, otherwise, be interpreted as representing him) to communicate something of their identity and the historical significance of that identity. That is the key to the work's transgression, not so much a trespass but an invasion and an unleashing. But it is also true, of course, that Warhol's Pop recycling mirrored the commercial cycles belonging to the commodity and were ambivalent in a way that de Antonio's and Rauschenberg's use of the leftover were not. Companies such as Campbell's and Coca-Cola quickly took positions on the use of their products in Warhol's art. In some cases, it was seen that Warhol added to the kudos of the brand, and so his recycling came to be appropriated back. Today, this kind of recycling, in which part of production's role becomes the harnessing of consumption

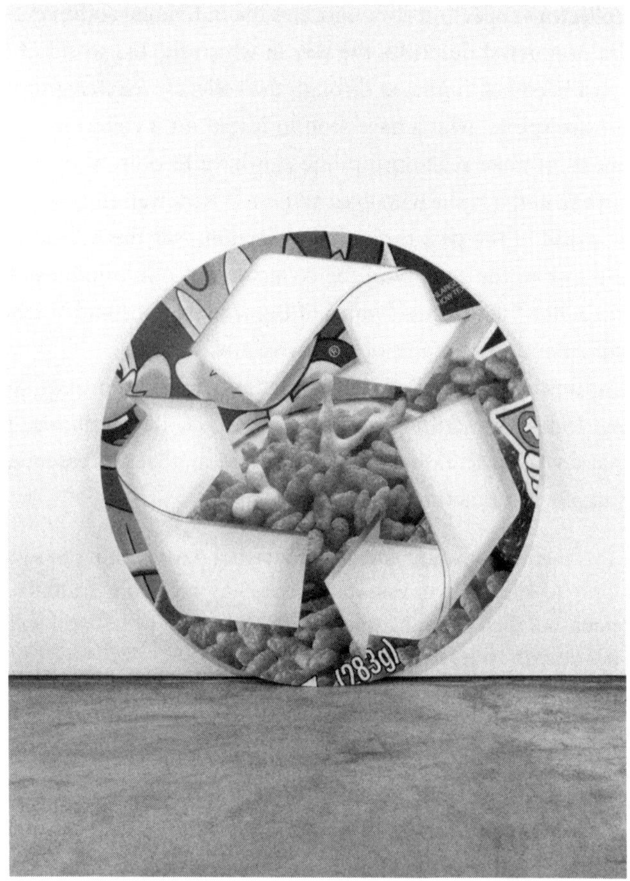

Fig. 5. 8. Kelley Walker, *untitled*, 2006. Laser cut steel, digital image (scanned poster), and gold leaf, 146.1 diameter x .3 cm. © Kelley Walker. Courtesy of the Paula Cooper Gallery, New York.

for the purposes of driving more consumption, is increasingly important. Like Warhol's choice of Campbell's soup, our commodity choices are surveyed and information about our buying habits are sold on to advertisers. Making consumption visible produces a new commodity, as well as promoting more consumption, thus perpetuating value. The model of the 'prosumer' — the collapse of producer and consumer — has been key in recent analyses of art that reflect the introduction of these mechanisms into everyday life, and, of course, the primary example is our use of the Web.

Today's corporate realisation of the potential of making consumption visible is expressed by artists for whom recycling is a key theme. Here, Warhol's precedence and influence is essential, yet is so far under-analysed. For these artists, recycling's corporatisation is an inescapable fact. For Kelley Walker, an artist who has persistently referred to Warhol's oeuvre (recycling it, from the *Death and Disaster* series to the Rorschach paintings of the early 1980s) recycling 'connotes not just reclamation but also the countering never-ending cycle of consumption necessitating recycling'.[72] Walker has used the three-arrowed recycling symbol in sculptures since 2003 (fig. 5.8 and plate 5.9). Then, at his debut at Paula Cooper Gallery in New York, and for a period afterwards, the symbol appeared cut in large steel discs. On one side of the discs are printed digital images of scanned surfaces—such as cereal box packaging—with gold leaf on the other, glowing on the wall against which they are propped.[73]

The situation that Walker describes—whereby recycling is necessitated and structurally incorporated in different ways, simply in order to feed production rather than to reclaim or conserve — is a global-financial reality. It also describes the circulation of images in digital relays. Reflecting the argument of this chapter, this state of recycling is something that Walker, like Benjamin, places in opposition to the art-historical paradigm of appropriation: 'I think appropriation points to or suggests some sort of original — a locatable source that one appropriates and in many ways eclipses.'[74] Thus, confirming what we have seen already, both appropriation and the related act of plagiarism simultaneously demarcate and ascertain value, and are unlike recycling in that they either add to, or threaten to take away, the value of an original, while at the same time changing its significance. In recycling, value is located in the act of exchange—value *as* exchange rather than exchange value — because exchange is a unit of the continuation of the system. Warhol's instinct that recycling could be integrated into commercial models on a wide scale, as demonstrated by the passage at the start of this chapter, was right. Today, the retrieval of different kinds of value has been hardwired into technologies of image distribution. Indeed, the arrow logo itself speaks of something undeniably corporate.[75] Yet in considering recycling as partly 'about reclamation', Walker affirms what de Antonio and Warhol saw in recycling's politics. This is to do with reframing and reclaiming for the subject, perhaps not a public sphere, but at least a space of collective identification that has been taken over by ideology. What we concede is what Warhol demonstrated with Pop: that perhaps you can only do this with the material that increasingly insidious institutions and mechanisms provide — and only in short windows before that identification is fed back into the system.

However, the discussion of online technologies as 'image economies' somewhat misrepresents the imagined and fantastical worlds that they foster. And here, again, *Raid the Icebox I* provides a useful model for thinking through the contemporary moment. We maintain an idea of object-hood in the ways we draw things into relation around ourselves online, even when these 'things' exist on a technological platform that deals exclusively with images. This gets lost in the theory and intellectual culture determined by the image, because the technology through which we both filter our experience of the world—and communicate it to others — is predominantly image-based. While this is apt to represent the extensity and morphism of the modern imagination—and of course determines that imagination so that it becomes compatible—there is a continued object-orientated perversity in the way in which we negotiate the virtual world. Therefore, the spatial metaphors applied to the Web (such as 'navigating', 'surfing' and 'cyberspace'), which have been derided as misleading in critical approaches, in fact have a value as they describe a spatio-temporal, phenomenological engagement. And, although it is certainly misleading to suggest that the Web itself is appropriately described as a space, one's engagement with it is frequently determined by the same mental work of orientation as, for example, collecting, shopping in a supermarket, or rifling through a museum's stores.[76] It is this work of locating and location, locating oneself in relation to what else is out there, that indicates that the Web is negotiated as an object world. Similar orientation work was performed by Warhol at the Rhode Island School of Design Museum in 1969. Perhaps this work provides a richer lens through which to consider our relation to the Web than the ideas about planes of pure imagery — perpetual and liquid exchange from a place of disembodiment — which more closely characterise, and are influenced by, the post-modern reception of Warhol's painting. In

Raid the Icebox I, Warhol's work of browsing, liking, sharing and recycling describes today's internet user.

One other recent work that shares much with *Raid the Icebox I*, but makes explicit the relationships between collecting, curation and Web use, is *The Pale Fox* (2014), by the French artist Camille Henrot. Henrot's work, like Warhol's, developed from her time behind the scenes at a major American museum, in this case, the Smithsonian. Yet, again in parallel with *Raid the Icebox I*, while the evolution of the exhibition began with her findings at the museum, and the experience of being lost in it, the shelves of eclectic objects, images and music that are exhibited in *The Pale Fox*, in a 'blue-screened' gallery space, are the result of patterns of thought and association circulating as much around Henrot's subjecthood as the organising principals of the museum. In being so, crucially, this work is also to do with the Web, and the orchestration of this work matches Marisa Olsen's description of a 'post-internet' condition of subjecthood, influenced by experience online.[77] Henrot presents her thinking as filtered through a contemporary experience of internet searches and eBay purchases but, equally, works in the mode of these systems, recycling her own ideas and material in her work so that 'nothing gets lost.'[78] In *The Pale Fox*, what caught Henrot's eye in the museum has been reworked and reinterpreted in the mind of the artist habituated to time online, accompanied and embellished by technologies that arbitrate over the direction of thought. Like Warhol's experience in the museum stores, Henrot's work recasts the voices and narratives that the museum holds in an idiosyncratic, crucially opaque unfolding, onto or through images and objects from the Web. Equivalent to the intrusion of the contents of the cold storage space into the museum in Warhol's earlier intervention, and with that space's accommodation of Warhol's off-register sense of things, in Henrot's work there is a disruption of the contained coherence of the museum by the alternative space of the Web. But there is also a challenge to the Web to contain the coherence of its commercial frameworks when triangulated by the obscurities of the museum and the bizarre relational connections that the objects make when presented together in the gallery. Both Warhol and Henrot's rearrangements, therefore, are consequences of a hijacking by the artists of the agendas of Web, artworld and museum alike: structures which essentially offer frameworks of interpretation. Out of these emerge re-understandings of the content belonging to those frameworks determined by idiosyncratic, highly subjective approaches that hold chaos and order in a more delicate balance than before.

If there is, here, a suggestion of the kind of solipsism by which Warhol is characterised in the literature on *Raid the Icebox I*, and that I have wanted to reclaim for a Benjaminian vision of the historical-materialist subject, this solipsism reappears more problematically in readings of the post-internet subject. Thanks to 'cookies' and the information included in our digital tail, companies can manipulate content so as to advertise specifically to us, and customise our experience according to our historical use of the Web. This is a museum of commodities that wraps itself around us; one in which we neither need confront those spaces, like the stores or the arcade where the material of history lies indeterminate, nor develop capacities by which we might benefit from doing so.

Recycling, in the work of Warhol, Benjamin, de Antonio and Henrot, is a process of renewal and is, therefore, something temporal. But this temporal operation also determines how the objects are encountered in space. In the cases of Henrot and Warhol's museum works, this is a spatiality in which the subject is surrounded, a formation connected to the idea of solipsism and the themes of 'worlds' of Benjamin's collector. We might, therefore, think of this process of renewal today also in terms of a transition from 2D to 3D, whether or not things, in actuality, make any transition. Renewed nonetheless, objects can speak to audiences so that their own place in the world is 'sweetly adjusted', as Robbins described. But renewal can also threaten to destabilise. In *The Philosophy*, Warhol's solution to the threat objects present (his ever-encroaching sea of possessions, like Kane's, like Big Daddy's) is to re-instigate the order of the museum and create a holographic virtual reality for his stuff; perhaps so that he could order things from it should the desire take him. This virtual reality of holographic wafers was never realised, but by the time *The Philosophy* had been published, another storage project had begun.

Time Capsules

What you should do is get a box for a month, and drop everything in it and at the end of the month lock it up. Then date it and send it over to Jersey. You should try to keep track of it, but

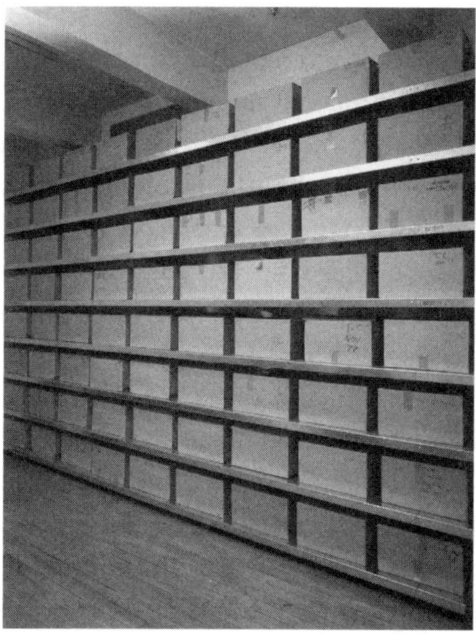

Fig. 5.9. Installation of 72 of Andy Warhol's *Time Capsules* at The Andy Warhol Museum, 1994. Collection of The Andy Warhol Museum, Pittsburgh.

if you can't and you lose it, that's fine, because it's one less thing to think about, another load off your mind.

Tennessee Williams saves everything up in a trunk and then sends it out to a storage place. I started off myself with trunks and the odd pieces of furniture, but then I went around shopping for something better and now I just drop everything into the same-size brown cardboard boxes that have a color patch on the side for the month of the year. I really hate nostalgia, though, so deep down I hope they all get lost and I never have to look at them again. That's another conflict. I want to throw things right out the window as they're handed to me, but instead I say thank you and drop them into the box-of-the-month. But my other outlook is that I really do want to save things so they can be used again someday.[79]

Warhol's account of his *Time Capsules* describes some of the difficulties, as he says 'conflicts', with recycling. Renewal, as in Benjamin, required the care and attention of the collector, impossible if he had become sub-sumed by his collection or was repulsed. The whole enterprise could be jeopardised by the sheer amount of material belonging to the past that needed sorting out but was not necessarily of any immediate value. Of course, it was precisely this kind of difficulty that Warhol had brought to the space of the museum in *Raid the Icebox I*, exposing how museums dealt with the past by 'tidying it up'. Michael J. Golec has observed of the passage above that, in it: 'the interplay between nothing and everything and losing and finding […] constitutes a theory of the archive itself—a load off the mind.'[80] For him, the *Time Capsules* are an equivalent of the cold storage spaces of the Museum of the Rhode Island School of Design. However, while they are surely related, we should not see the *Time Capsules* as merely about preservation and protection, about a consolidation and fixing of value in the object. This suggestion underestimates the importance of recycling for Warhol's project, how integral an idea of future use and value was to it.

The 612 *Time Capsules* have acted like an epilogue for Warhol's practice since 1994 when their contents began to be archived, a task that has now been completed (fig. 5.9 and plate 5.10). Begun in 1974, during a move of address, Warhol continued thereafter to fill removal boxes with papers, drawings, prints, cards, invitations, tickets and bills, that is to say, mostly things in 2D. Nevertheless, the *Time Capsules* also included objects: stolen crockery, food, fashion, leisure accoutrements, the massive spirit level used in the publicity photos for *Shadows*, and a whole host of other knick-knacks; in fact, nearly everything he had to hand and which he had no immediate use for. It was a work of clearing space, as the passage above describes. But if it had only been the monthly act of simultaneous recording and wiping, which the passage from *The Philosophy* makes it out to have been, there would have only been 156 *Time Capsules*, as Ronald Jones has pointed out.[81] Clearly the project had a life of its own, as long time Warhol Enterprises employees Vincent Fremont and Brigid Berlin agree:

> FREMONT: *Time Capsules* were growing…
> BERLIN: They were fucking alive, those *Time Capsules*.[82]

The *Time Capsules* reflect the sense, now familiar, that objects were a problem for Warhol and that he saw their relation to the spaces they occupied as problematic; both the socially reflective and hierarchical places of the artworld and the collection, and, disastrously, his limited personal space. The *Time Capsules* address the latter. Indeed, as their own institution under Warhol's curatorship, they became a container for the degree of threat that Warhol sensed objects and things presented:

> FREMONT: Andy liked getting a present, but he'd want to keep it as a collectable immediately.
> BERLIN: He didn't want to open anything that he got because he thought there was a bomb in it, so he'd give it to us to open. He always thought he was going to get poisoned or shot or blown up [...].[83]

Fremont, whose inspiration the project had been, made a note of the period each capsule covered on the boxes. The space that the *Time Capsules* helped clear, on and around Warhol's desk and office space, was, as a significant piece of uptown real estate, valuable. Yet, as much as it cleared space, the project, having become a curatorial and collecting endeavour, filled space elsewhere and filled-in time: past, present and future. Thus they had a value in their own right. They prevented loss; something that perhaps determined Warhol's hoarding in the first place (Fremont describes Warhol as a 'recording angel'). The *Time Capsules* both formalised and marketized the operations, in Warhol's day-to-day life, of recycling, collecting and re-evaluation that were so central to Warhol's practice.[84] Warhol had considered the value of the *Time Capsules* and expressed in *The Diaries* how he:

> took a few time capsule boxes to the office. They are fun – when you go through them there's things you really don't want to give up. Someday I'll sell them for $4000 or $5000. I used to think $100, but now that's my new price.[85]

It remains to be seen if the *Time Capsules* will ever be sold off one by one, or, if they are, whether they reach the kind of prices that Warhol imagined. But what I would like to consider with regard to this statement, and these works, is the *action* that Warhol describes. Seeing the value of the work as determined by the experience of opening the box, I would suggest, is not just another means of appreciating what the work is, but signifies a transformation: Warhol was giving the work a new value here because he recognised a new aesthetic experience *in unboxing*. This is crucial because my argument has been in this chapter that, like in the example of *Raid the Icebox I*, his approach to the art-object, to sculptural space and to the institution amounted to a critique of the traditional values invested in them by destabilising their protection and preservation of that value. As Benjamin Buchloh described of Warhol's work, he 'unsettled for a considerable amount of time any secure notion about the object status of his artistic production.[86] Part of the security Warhol targeted was the way in which the artworld sheltered, or contained, its special objects in museums and galleries against America's larger culture of persistent novelty and renewal. In the case of *Time Capsules*, Warhol finds a way of resisting this subjection by objects that piled up on his desk in such a way as to be able to throw them out and re-access them afresh later on. And, of course, this emphasis on renewal is crucial to what I have argued in terms of Warhol's longstanding operation of recycling. *Time Capsules* deal with the pressure of excess material, making space for recycling in time by offsetting it to the future. Opening the boxes becomes part of the work and part of its value.

These moments of unboxing are moments of uncertainty, of chance, of anticipation: of time having become an agent. The *Time Capsules* are novelty machines. Yet they are also intimate moments of revisitation of one's past. They are separate from the more structural states, defined on the one side by the original context of the object's possession and, on the other, by the category into which the object is archived and its historical meaning. Here, again, we might think of *Raid the Icebox I* with regard to this liminality. For a short while the object is new, curious, defamiliarised: neither with a determined place in the world, nor a position in the archive. It is from this nakedness that the experience of boxing and unboxing gains its own aesthetic effect.

It is the work of Jeff Koons, however, that has best made the argument for newness as an aesthetic experience of its own. And it is important that he did this, alongside Warhol and others, precisely at the time more established figures in the artworld attacked the concept and power of the new in critiques of ideas such as originality, authorship, and later of the slew of 'neo' movements of the early 1980s. Koons foregrounded newness as the subject of his first major project, *The New* (fig. 5.10), his 1980 series

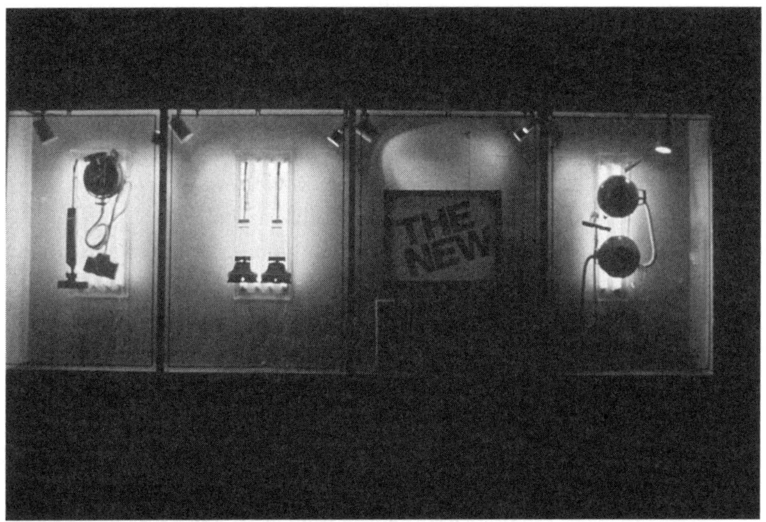

Fig. 5.10. Jeff Koons, *The New* (Installation View), 1980. Courtesy of the New Museum, New York. Photo: New Museum.

of fluorescent-lit Plexiglas boxes containing out of the box, store bought, brand name appliances, most famously Hoover vacuum cleaners. In writings on his website, Richard Prince recalls the moment, in 1980, when Koons showed him the work in development during a visit to Koons's sparsely furnished apartment:

> So what's getting me is the washer/dryer. This "tag-team" even has the labels still attached.
> And I'm saying "so uh […] What-Is-Up?"
> And Jeff says, "The New."
> Everything is brand new.
> That's his turn. His twist. His contribution. His continuation. His "third place."
> And his "new," immediately makes sense. I like the sense and I like what it makes. Making sense is something that good art does.
> Sometimes.
> The apartment is a showroom.
> And even though what he's showing are store bought

appliances [...] that small gesture of not touching what is generally [...] immediately, unpacked and "plugged in," is, in the words of Madison Ave., " a big bright flash of white light."
Turn On, Drop Out, Plug In.
That's what happened at the New Museum.
When Jeff was invited to make a show in the windows. (This was when The New Museum was on 6th Ave. and 14th St.). He somehow got the museum to buy him four vacuum cleaners and the story goes [...] that one of them got plugged in and he found out and told the staff that he couldn't use it. It was "used." Old. "No good." Its integrity had been compromised. He told them they would have to go out and buy another. The same. The same kind. A whole new vacuum cleaner. And of course the New Museum had no budget, but what could they do?
Jeff's foot was down and unless the object was BRAND NEW [...] the object became irrelevant, second hand, garbage.[87]

These are the aesthetics of physical newness, of being 'box-fresh'. Suspended in the moment of their unpackaging, before being plugged-in, Koons's work developed the aesthetic of unboxing that Warhol discovers reopening the *Time Capsules*.[88] More generally, the exploration of commodity aesthetics in Warhol's work, especially the pristine boldness of the *Campbell's Soup Cans'* and *Brillo Boxes'*, was a crucial platform from which Koons was able to pursue the taut impeccable surface of newness.

In an interview between Koons and Warhol's long-time associate Gerard Malanga, published for the 2004 exhibition *Andy Warhol: 5 Deaths*, Koons speaks of his high regard for Warhol's sculpture before going on to talk of his own work. In relation to *The New*, he describes how the most banal of commodities becomes the site of heightened aesthetic feeling. While it is important, as we have seen, that the object was brand new, Koons reveals the vacuum cleaner also symbolises an encounter that is in other ways unfamiliar, and this, in turn, adds a dimension to the significance of its being new. For him, the vacuum cleaner drew his attention when he was an infant. He describes it as 'anthropomorphic' and the 'first aggressive object' he encountered as a child, seen from a position in the immediate vicinity of his mother and from the lowered perspective of the floor. Certainly we might consider this in terms of a kind of fetishism other than commodity fetishism. But, what is important about these relations is the extent to which they have to do with the alteration of scale and perspective through the memory of a child's view and how, following the logic of fetish but not (reductively) its conclusions, this encounter revolves around all kinds of absence and loss associated with childhood. Additionally, the aesthetic is one set askance by a medium (memory) which re-places the commodity in the home. Indeed, Warhol's 'unboxing', and Koons's aesthetic of the untouched, straight out of the box commodity, balance between homeliness and the uncanny. Though it might not have been apparent, *The New*, therefore, suggests a quality of intimacy that is also crucial to both the aesthetics of *Raid the Icebox I* and *Time Capsules*.

The same dynamics of newness and structural order, aesthetic strangeness and the domestic are also true of the contemporary YouTube sub-culture of 'unboxing' videos. This I want to offer as a final context for thinking through the relevance of Warhol's collecting strategies and for thinking contemporary culture through Warhol's work. 'Unboxing' user-uploaded videos were first popular with technology aficionados filming themselves taking newly bought gadgets from their packaging, usually giving some commentary to the camera at the same time.[89] In the lifeless machines and toys, whose first moments are recorded in unboxing videos, the limitless potential that their advertisers promise is latent. Usually the commodities are not even demonstrated. Instead, we only see the blank, unanimated screens of the uncharged machines while the gadget's functionality goes largely unevaluated. The appeal of the videos is, rather, in the excitement of unboxing itself, in the fleeting moments before new commodities become ubiquitous. This, again, is an arena where commodity fetish is as much to do with temporality as it is the thing. In fact, these videos combine the gesture of presenting the commodity as emergent and untouched, which Koons made with *The New*, with Warhol's processes recycling the by-products of other businesses. Like Koons's work and, indeed, Warhol's, the content of the work emerges from the apparently non-commercial, real world environment of the home, however, in this case, it is YouTube rather than the gallery that does the work of reframing and redistribution. The videos have now begun to inform television adverts and marketing campaigns, but it was the consumers themselves who captured and distributed what had previously escaped un-monetised. Unboxing video authorship, and

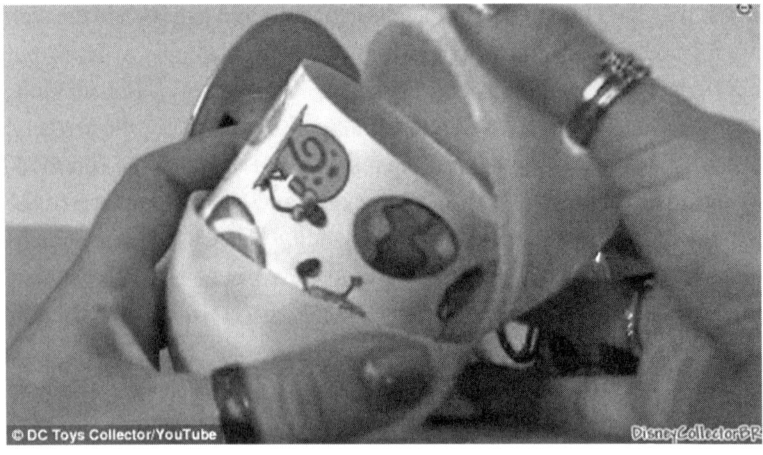

Fig. 5.11. Still from DisneyCollector, 'Angry Birds Toy Surprise Jake NeverLand Pirates Disney Pixar Cars2 Spongebob Huevos Sorpresa' available at http://youtube/aoc8d0gcf08 (accessed 11 December 2014).

viewership, has gained popularity with a wider public and today total viewership is in the hundreds of millions. The unboxing phenomena has now found its largest audiences with videos, made for children, of toys being unpackaged. One single unwrapping video (uploaded by YouTube user DisneyCollector, and featuring the unwrapping of a variety of surprise plastic eggs with film-themed toys inside) had had 95,167,291 views at the time of writing this book (fig. 5.11).[90]

Unboxing videos, because of their setting in people's homes and their non-professional presenters, are seen as real in a way advertisements are not. In contrast to the artifice of commercial presentation, where subject and object are shown as completely integrated, the videos communicate an explicit and unembellished moment of contact with what is both unfamiliar and, initially, separate. This might also be said to have been the case with Pop, which intervened in an artworld that, at the time of Abstract Expressionism, presented the integration of subject and object in paint in a way that we might see as analogous to the integration of subject and object in the car or iPod advert. Yet, if Abstract Expressionism, like advertising, offered a fantasy of aesthetic experience that was unalienated, that, like advertisements, guaranteed a quality of being 'in touch', it would be equally fantastical to suggest the unboxing video or Warhol's *Campbell's Soup Can,* offers anything more real. Rather, we might think of these encounters in terms of a hyperreality in which experience is itself simulacral, an 'other' phenomenology without distinct referent to normal conditions of experience. The videos' soundscape of packaging noises and close-up first person camera work makes the videos points of entrance into phantasmic phenomenological worlds in which new forms of object relations take place.[91]

In the unboxing video and in Jeff Koons's work *The New*, the mass produced commodity has become a platform for aesthetic investigations into newness that add extra dimensions, indeed extra value, beyond what the companies that produce the products can account for. But newness is a fragile state, a last frontier of commodity aesthetics perhaps, a territory where value might still escape, where experience might yet go without a price tag. In this work, aesthetic enquiry emerges and re-evaluation takes place, perversely, on the site of prescribed and determined aesthetic value. These are works in which newness is a distinct aesthetic state. Meanwhile, we might think of the renewals of *Raid the Icebox I* and *Time Capsules* as providing an alternative to precisely the structures of value that constrict the aesthetic possibilities of our encounters with objects.

In Warhol's personal spaces objects inflicted a pressure, not just on a limited space, but on his sense of his own freedom. Their spatial and temporal presence was a burden, it restricted possibilities. The *Time Capsules* responded to this dual burden, preventing the past, as much as the things from the past, from spilling out all over the place. Warhol saw museums and the institutions of art as problematically nurturing this un-freedom of pastness and clutter in the name of historical value. He responded by recycling, a process of renewal already intrinsic to the development of Pop Art in America in the early 1960s. In these practices, recycling is about re-entering circulation across the divides between world and artworld, it is a re-making present, imperative, that which has been discarded or disregarded.[92] And, as in the case of the Navajo blankets Warhol collected, discussed above, recycling was something that was related to sculpture's identity. In being made from what is leftover, having accumulated social footprints, recycling becomes politicised and emerges in Warhol's work in the framework of sculpture.

Conclusion

One-Dimensional Man – In 3D!

This book began with portraits and the famous portrait ascribed to Andy Warhol, in 1966, by Gretchen Berg, who located everything there is to know about Andy Warhol on the two dimensional surface of his paintings, films and his one dimensional self. Warhol's work *Silver Clouds* is mentioned more than once in that interview, explicitly as sculpture, but, in adding sculpture to the list of those surfaces that define him, it has been my hope that this book has added another dimension to this portrait of Andy Warhol and his work. If this book qualifies the attention that has been paid to Warhol's painting by looking at his sculpture, it does so, not to produce another Warhol, but to deepen our understanding of the Warhol that already exists. Yet, at the same time, and as I will explore in this conclusion, this understanding has no less to do with surface.

Such an understanding of Warhol's practice is, therefore, three-dimensional in terms beyond those which distinguish sculpture from painting. The third dimension, here, relates to the quality of Warhol's work being between things: between the physical properties of the work and the readings ascribed by the spectator. It is a concern for surface, but here the surface is felt between the surfaces of matter and thought, between the contours of history. It is defined by virtue of its ability to hold the formally two-dimensional and three-dimensional together, and develop a register between the material and immaterial, illusion and reality.

This polymorphic surface coincides with the idea of post-modern image culture and its scale-less, object-less economy of exchange and equivalence, an idea that, indeed, is important in theoretical understandings of Warhol's art and personhood. The one-dimensional Warhol is a figure akin to that assimilated subject described in Herbert Marcuse's book: *One-Dimensional Man: Studies in the Ideology of Advanced Industrial Society* (1964). Yet, the picture of the world so important to the readings in this book is different to that in which we find Marcuse's subject. Crucially, for my readings the artworld does not represent that 'oppositional, alien, and transcendent' alternative dimension of reality that Marcuse describes of high art, but only an extension of the social world, an elite territorial outpost, metaphysically altered but not by any means offering an alternative to social order.[1] It is precisely these conditions that require us to consider Warhol's three-dimensionality *as a surface*, and as a between space, rather than a transcendental alternative. Warhol, in three-dimensions, refuses to present either any other reality, or something that might function as a fixable, tangible alternative to the status quo. Instead, his work defended a form of social representation posed in opposition to the artworld's idealism.

As I have discussed in this book, with the emergence of influential positions such as those taken by Arthur Danto and Donald Judd in the 1960s, this form of idealism took the shape of discourses that attempted to bracket illusionistic space and pose a rarefied form of reality against the territories of ambiguity and relative value outside of the museum. It is precisely amongst these territories, however, and in opposition to these discourses, that Warhol's surface operates. If post-modern visual culture jettisons scale, the positivist object and the 'specificity' of its materials and medium, these are characteristic concerns of Minimalism. Yet I have argued in this book that the dichotomy that considers Warhol's work as seamlessly assimilated to postmodern image culture on one side, and positions Minimalism on the other, or else reads Warhol as following in the footsteps of Minimalism's innovations, is contrived for the benefit of historical narrative. By extending his work beyond a notional and defined objecthood, Warhol cast viewer-space in illusory environments that reflected how class registered through the conditions of vision, even in the arena of a putative 'real space'.

This book began with a comparison between the three-dimensional, ghostly presence of the 'factory fresh' *Campbell's Soup Cans* (1962) and what I described as the 'sculptural' condition of *Torn Campbell's Soup Can* (1962). Leaning on readings by Benjamin Buchloh and Roland Barthes, the 'clean' works, I argued, substitute the relationship between the painting and its viewer for a single, hovering sublation of the two in the commodity image. In contrast, I posed sculpture as the category defined by a materiality incommensurate with the conditions of the commodity, and thus the appropriate category through which to view the *Torn* paintings. They, and sculpture in this sense, signify a fall from circulation and a loss of value. Yet it was the sense of an uncanny presence, like that of the 'clean' *Campbell's Soup Can* paintings, that first brought Warhol to experiment, in the same year, with sculpture in actuality, in the form of *Campbell's Soup Box* (plate 2.1). This was a painting-object, or image-sculpture, whereby the repeated *Campbell's* painting was transferred onto the three dimensions of a plywood box. This work failed, Warhol claimed, but it led to the total immersive environment of *The Personality of the Artist* installation in 1964.

Suggested by the examples above is an idea of sculpture in pursuit of a three-dimensional presence already established by the commodity image, rather than three-dimensionality as necessarily a result of sculpture.[2] New grounds for sculpture emerge here, while at the same time those conditions traditionally associated with sculpture have served to stand for the fall-out from commodity aesthetics. In the examples of more recent work, images become sculptural objects when printers snarl up, when circulation is impeded. Seth Price's dispersed Mylar image rolls and Wolfgang Tillmans' *Lighters*, like Warhol's *Abstract Sculpture*, *Crushed Newspaper* and his early *Crumpled Paper Show*, is work that has fallen out of, and become incompatible with, prescribed frameworks for, and assumptions about, image display and relay.

In the work of the other artists that I have related to my discussion of Warhol in this book there is a more general sense of fluidity that, likewise, contours the surface between embodied space and representation. It speaks, for example, of the transitions in Camille Henrot's work from the museum to the gallery, through images on eBay and the internet. It speaks, also, of the work of Keith Haring and Jean-Michel Basquiat, who developed new iconology and a new image-ground on the surfaces of a crumbling New York City. And it speaks of the work of Paul Thek, who filled mock-Minimal incantations of modern life with life-like waxworks of rotting hunks of flesh. But, mostly, it speaks of Warhol and his persistent suggestion that the image is never not in real space and real space is never not an imaging environment. Warhol's work was the work of re-presentation, whereby social context became aesthetic content and the aesthetic content became the social context. Instead of creating an illusory plane of reality, in which subject and object registered perfectly, Warhol brought the two dimensions of the social viewer and the aesthetic object into the space of mis-registration between them, causing collapse, ambiguity and trespass.

In introducing Warhol's sculpture and the undertaking of this book, I described sculpture for Warhol, and readings of Warhol, as off-register. Indeed, the off-register, I argued, is something pervasive and fundamental to all Warhol's work, not just sculpture's relation to the existing discourse on Warhol in art history. But if the idea of Warhol's sculpture, understood in terms of its position outside established frameworks of understanding, is easy to get to grips with, an idea of the off-register *in itself*, and what that means for Warhol's art, is harder to fathom. If to register is to ascertain something, to form a correlation, the off-register is a mark of dislocation and expresses uncertainty; deviance more often than not in the case of Warhol's work. Yet, no less than registration, the off-register suggests presence, and though, in itself, says 'nothing', means nothing, it *stages* where meaning occurs.

This is how we might also understand Warhol's three-dimensional surface as it looms above the paintings and commands object-space in the sculptures and installations. The surface of Warhol's art, described at the start of this conclusion, is a stage of encounter between the sign and the signified; between the subject and the world around it. Yet, though this surface reaches across media and is fundamental to Warhol's operations, it is also something the study of Warhol's relation to sculpture especially helps to make clear. I want to now develop this constellation of ideas, of surface and staging, that bear on the off-register, and consider sculpture's place in relation to three last scenarios in which we find Warhol's work. The first is Evelyn Hofer's photographs of Warhol's studio taken immediately

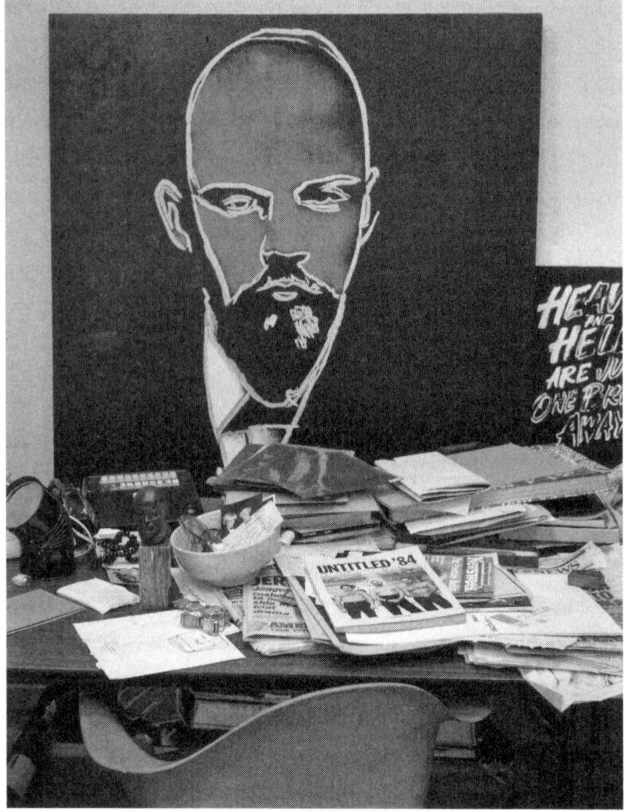

Fig. 6.1. Evelyn Hofer, *Andy Warhol's Studio with Lenin*, N.Y. 1987. Estate of Evelyn Hofer.

after his death (fig. 6.1 and plate 6.1). In these, we find two works belonging to two late series, *The Last Supper* and *Lenin*, which we find each have sculptural counter parts. The second scenario is an interview with Warhol's assistant Ronnie Cutrone in which Cutrone discusses the source material used for Warhol's *Hammer and Sickle* (1976). The third and final scenario is the essay 'Theatrum Philosophicum' (1970), by Michel Foucault. Here, Foucault discusses Warhol's work and, in relation to it, proposes the theoretical model of the 'phantasm' which, finally, I shall read my understanding of Warhol's three-dimensionality through.

***

If, as I have described of Warhol's paintings, object presence haunts image space, the sense of work in progress in Hofer's photographs is that of life pervading the space of the dead. Warhol's beautiful, grand studio was busy right up until the last days. It is a room with areas of clutter rather than a cluttered room, and, generally, there is a sense of knowing where things are put and of organization. In it, a variety of different artistic projects seem to be in progress all at the same time. Amongst the recent work set against the walls of the studio are the two works I shall go on to discuss. They form a backdrop before which are signs of Warhol's interests and concerns at the sides, on the floor and other surfaces, while papers and acetates are dotted here and there in the clear space in the centre. Warhol had been lifting weights with Jean-Michel Basquiat, there are two weight benches in the studio and a 'Computrim 900' exercise bike; there are books on astrology and tarot; there is, on the right, a huge statue; there are shopping bags; and there are boxes, tons and tons of boxes.

The image of Lenin (fig. 6.1) is based on an early photograph of the revolutionary from 1897, which was cropped for Stalin's purposes in 1948. But this is not the only source material Warhol used for this work, he also consulted a small statuette of Lenin, which we see in the photograph left beside the Lenin painting. The tiny sculptural Lenin is a later portrait than the 1897 one used for the image: the head is bowed, the features now heavily set. Warhol did not photograph this object for the silkscreen. It is difficult to see how this later, small, monochrome, three-dimensional rendering of Lenin informed the final work: it surely would only have complicated the issue of likeness: it is *unlike* the image of the youthful Lenin. Yet it seems that Warhol worked on the portrait with the statuette as a reference close by. My suggestion is that Warhol invited this unlikely sculpture to sit with the images as a recalcitrant, off-register presence, as something to complicate the picture; to intervene and bring contingency to precisely that seamless process of duplication so often associated with Warhol's work.

In the case of the second studio shot (plate 6.1), in which Warhol's last great series *The Last Supper* provides the point of focus, there are more details to consider. In *The Diaries* we learn that, at an early stage of the commission, Warhol went to considerable effort, if not expense, to procure a 3D model of Leonardo's famous design:

Thursday, April 25th, 1985.

I'm trying to find another store that sells the sculpture of the Last Supper that's about one-and-a-half feet—they're selling it in one of those import stores on Fifth near Lord & Taylor but it's so expensive there, about $2,500. So I'm trying to find it cheaper in Times Square. I'm doing the Last Supper for Iolas. For Lucio Amelio I'm doing the Volcanoes. So I guess I'm a commercial artist. I guess that's the score.

Tuesday, July 9, 1985.

Sent Benjamin out on a simple errand and it cost me a thousand dollars! I'd given him $2,000 to go get the large-size sculpture of the Last Supper that we'd bargained the guy down from $5,000 to $2,000 on. So he went there and it wasn't there anymore. The Last Supper comes in small, medium, and large. So, then at this other place, I'd gotten the guy down from $2,500 to $1,000 for the medium. But Benjamin forgot we'd gotten them *down*, and he bought the medium one for $2,000! He *didn't remember*! It was actually the size I really wanted, anyway, but he wound up giving the second store for the medium one what he was supposed to buy the large one for. So this means he hasn't got a head for figures—a thousand dollars is a lot of waste. I just couldn't believe it, after I'd haggled so hard.[3]

These diary entries provide the reader with a vivid snapshot: the image of a two dimensional Warhol with which this book began. He self-mockingly admits to being 'a commercial artist' and seems to justify the popular critique of himself as cynical and overwhelmingly concerned with money, confirmed by the petty despair at his assistant's lack of nous. As much as 'commercialism' is a contentious issue between Warhol's detractors and those that come to his defence, it was also a central and generative struggle for Warhol himself. While he devised a practice that was arguably more proximate to commerce than any before, as his *Diaries* and interviews attest, his own feelings in relation to this fluctuated. He frequently expresses a wish to be seen as avant-garde, or be associated in such a way, and we read his conceding to being a commercial artist in the passage above as indicative of a loss of avant-garde status in this respect. At the same time, however, the period in which he makes *The Last Supper* was a period in which a new wave of artists harnessed the powers of the entrepreneur, the adman, the stockbroker, and the pop star. So it is perhaps the kind of commercial work that he is engaged with in the case of *The Last Supper* that causes consternation. The work was a commission by his old acquaintance the gallerist Alexandre Iolas, a person who links Warhol to artists such as Max Ernst and Jean Tinguely. So, in Warhol's mind, perhaps the commission made him look older than he would like. Or, indeed, perhaps Warhol's attitude of surrender is a mark of finally leaving these questions behind: for *The Last Supper*, Warhol worked uninhibited. This, his last major project, comprised over 100 variations and 40 preparatory drawings.

Warhol had only recently undertaken the commission for *The Last Supper* at the time of the diary entries. The importance of the model, here, is highlighted by the efforts we hear that Warhol undergoes to get it. However, any schematic relationship to the final image is utterly imprecise, it is certainly not the source of the image Warhol reproduced. Warhol used a variety of sources for this work since, according to David Bourdon, reproductions of the original were too dark.[4] Instead, Warhol worked from multiple print copies, and another, cheaper, model in white plastic. The different sources used depended on which of the two different painting techniques he used in the series. The works shown at the opening of *The Last Supper* exhibition, in Milan, in spring 1987, were silkscreened, but, possibly influenced by Jean-Michel Basquiat, Warhol also returned to a variant of his early freehand tracing technique for another series of *The Last Supper*. These were not included in the Milan exhibition but the painting in the studio photograph is an example of one. In these, the figures are rearranged, with symbols of a later era—brand images and price tags—accompanying it.[5]

Trying to understand the role of this sculptural source material what seems absurd is the notion of veracity to the original in these negotiations of image and object, copy and master, and painting and sculpture. Having been so damaged and restored so many times, to different degrees of success, Leonardo's *Last Supper* is itself no original: the image does not even register with itself. Even so, the high-kitsch porcelain sculpture of *Last Supper* that Warhol acquired is a kind of obscenity of misregistering values as well as verisimilitude. Yet perhaps *difference* is again the role sculpture played in the making of this work: it diverts the transition of the image to the canvas through an object that acts in different ways to complicate and intervene in the registration of image-to-image. Sculpture intervenes to 'stage' the process of representation. Literally intervening in the space between the artist and the canvas in the studio, its difference and difficulty contributes to the sense of presentness that we also find in the 'clean' *Campbell's Soup Cans* and, for example, in the *Shadows'* invasive and yet negative presence.

This is equally what is at stake in Ronnie Cutrone's description of the *Hammer and Sickle* series of paintings. Warhol originally had attempted to make a silkscreen of already existing images of the hammer and sickle symbol but, as Cutrone describes:

> the symbols were flat, stencilled. And I thought, well, maybe I could find something that had more depth to it, like an etching or an engraving. But that wasn't too successful. Then eventually, one of us said, 'Well, let's just buy the hammer and sickle and take photos of it.' […] So I bought them back, cast large shadows on them with side lighting, and shot them. Then we did paintings with a sponge mop—big, white, thickly painted backgrounds—and then we screened over them in red and black or just black. To me, those paintings were successful because they just weren't very communist; they weren't so dead-end. There was something architectural and almost semi-abstract about them.'
>
> You mean sculptural?
>
> Actually sculptural is more the word. They looked like they could be an amusement park ride somewhere, in Disneyland even.[6]

In Cutrone's account, sculpture's role is vital. It acts as a force that causes the painting to deviate from a symbol of communism towards abstraction, but at the same time, in its mis-registration, translates that ambiguity powerfully, makes it present. It is a force of differencing and de-familiarisation (and, thinking of Disneyland, perhaps of carnival). Much of Warhol's work was informed by this sense of something sculptural not necessarily bound to objecthood but, between registers, difference. Perhaps this is why the story of Warhol's sculpture is also the story of attempts to represent immateriality: the invisible sculptures, shadows and holograms that ironically end up producing a whole slew of matter, of things leftover. The real hammer and sickle, and the *Last Supper* model and Lenin bust in Hofer's photograph, are each examples of this matter.[7]

This sense of sculpture as three-dimensional surface, as presence and as a force of difference that I have been suggesting is, however, nowhere on view in Hofer's photograph itself. Instead, here is representation that fails to account for difference or allow for mis-registration. Without Warhol, the studio's clashing registers, its jumble of Jesus, the logo for General Electric and Lenin, reflects misunderstandings of Warhol's work as a superficial, post-modern hodgepodge.

And so to the final scenario in which we encounter 3D Warhol. Michel Foucault's 1970 essay 'Theatrum Philosophicum', in which Foucault describes exactly this state of apparently empty difference:

> of Warhol with his canned foods, senseless accidents, and his series of advertising smiles: the oral and nutritional equivalence of those half-open lips, teeth, tomato sauce, that hygiene based on detergents; the equivalence of death in the cavity of an eviscerated car, at the top of a telephone pole and at the end of a wire, and between the glistening, steel blue arms of the electric chair.[8]

But does that mean that we find this work arrested in a state of one-dimensional superficiality for Foucault? This is that same idea implied by the words put into Warhol's mouth in Gretchen Berg's 1966 article 'Andy Warhol: My True Story': 'If you want to know all about Andy Warhol, just look at the surface: my paintings and my films and me, and there I am.'[9] No, though Foucault might have agreed that looking at surfaces is important, he would, however, not have agreed with the suggestion of simplicity, or that these surfaces can be collapsed back into any 'true story'. Instead, Foucault's surface acts as an antidote to the idea of Warhol as superficial and this marries it with what I have hoped to present in the previous chapters on Warhol's sculpture. For Foucault, the enfolding of difference and repetition in Warhol's work—its 'stupidity'—has the consequence of releasing meaning from the weave of 'words and things', and describes instead what Foucault calls 'the phantasm'.[10] In his description of this concept, Foucault collects many of the ideas that I have used in describing sculpture, and I want to develop this parallel, finally, as it expands on the significance of the three-dimensional for Warhol as something beyond parochial categories pertaining to media.

'Theatrum Philosophicum' is ostensibly a review of the writing of Gilles Deleuze. Yet it is also a piece of critical writing that as much advances Foucault's own thinking as it is a celebratory endorsement of Gilles Deleuze's project; a project of discovering difference within thought—as a form of free-thought—within its own aesthetic spectrum.[11] Foucault reclaims surface as a site of a radical aesthetics through the conception of the 'phantasm'. The phantasm is thought without object; an unconstellated, surface-thought that, Foucault writes, functions 'at the limit of bodies; against bodies and protrudes from them': phantasms 'topologize the materiality of the body.'[12] It is the intermediary surface which thinking breaks when it distinguishes between ideas and materials, images and objects. The phantasm announces the presence of thought without pertaining either to its object or its subject, instead it is paired with the event—what we might understand as the thought-occurrence of phantasmic thinking. This idea of the phantasm, I want to suggest, is what Warhol's sculpture expresses through the anti-objects, charged spaces and three-dimensional paintings considered in these pages: it is the three-dimensional surface of Warhol's aesthetic vision. It is 'atmosphere'. It is the corollary of the 'eerie concreteness' Benjamin Buchloh senses in the *Campbell's Soup Can* series, and it is the latent sense of presence Danto feels when he sees the spectre of the 'stock-boy' in his ruminations on *Brillo Boxes*. It is newness, ever renewing, ever emerging and continual; it is the thought equivalent of an *Invisible Sculpture*. These presences animate the surfaces of the works, the spaces of invisibility and installation. Foucault proposes a philosophy that attends to the phantasm and, in coming to regard Warhol's practice as phantasmic, we have an art form that accompanies this. For Foucault, a force of differencing beams out from Warhol's repetitions of images, duplications of objects and his perverse, subversive deferral to the logic of categorisation. Warhol's phantasmic art remains undifferentiated, unconnected, on the surface. Like the phantasm, it is all surface without being two-dimensional. It registers with the three-dimensional presence of the phantasm, not an object in space but an in-between surface on which representation figures.

For Foucault, the phantasm is understood as an alternative to a particular set of discourses that subordinate the surface to underlying structures: neopositivism, phenomenology and the philosophy of history.[13] These, Foucault writes, fail to account for the event, for surface. They (respectively) either confuse it with the 'state of things' and the object; treat it as only accountable within the framework of subjective meaning; or, lastly, place its ongoing within a structure of past and present. Foucault's critique correlates with the opposition to temporal, phenomenological and positivist orders in Warhol's art. It is negative, ambiguous and ever concerned with renewal. Moreover, confirming the parallel between the philosophy of phantasm and Warhol's art of surface, Foucault's philosophy of surface, as a critique, maps perfectly onto Warhol's critical engagement with Minimalism. Foucault's description of positivism's substitution of surfaces for depths; the 'domain of primal significations' of phenomenology; and the 'pattern of time' emergent from the philosophy of history, pertain directly to the ways in which Minimalist art is received. Here the politics of the phantasm extend the parallel with the politics I have argued are at the heart of Warhol's work. What Foucault does to philosophy, Warhol does to the artworld: undoing its self-image as a place apart from superficiality, embedded in structures organised around social value. Through Foucault's phantasmic surface, we have a means to think Warhol's surfaces without jettisoning his criticality, releasing surface from an understanding whereby it only serves to make realisms seem more precious, more valuable.

The importance of the phantasm, then, is that it elucidates a condition that disrupts attempts at disambiguation in response to a larger culture that creates inequality through such intolerance of ambiguity. Through sculpture, we understand the phantasm of Warhol's art: to encounter it is to feel the resonance of those difficult relations with objecthood that, despite the image plane, linger no less. And the phantasm in turn helps us understand what sculpture meant for Warhol's work. It intervenes in the spaces of disambiguation, distinction and taste; it trespasses across the boundaries, spatial and discursive, that define them. In its resistance to these means of ascertaining and maintaining value, the phantasm of Warhol's work takes on a political dimension, a third dimension of surface and perpetual trespass: we should all be strangers in the artworld *together*, it says.

Notes

Introduction: Portraits

1   Matt Wrbican, 'The True Story of My True Story', in Eva Meyer-Hermann, *Andy Warhol: A Guide to 706 Items in 2 Hours 56 Minutes: Other Voices Other Rooms* (exh. cat.), NAi Publishers, Rotterdam, 2008, pp. 56–7, p. 57.

2   Neil Printz and Sally King-Nero, *Andy Warhol Catalogue Raisonné (Vol. 3)*, Phaidon Press, New York, 2004, p. 20. There are three projects listed in this time period that have sculptural elements: *Rain Machines*, three Plexiglas Mylar cases (*c.*1970), and a vacuum cleaner work. For the latter, Warhol vacuumed a gallery space at Finch College, New York, for *Art in Process*, a show held in February 1972.

3   Developed by Briony Fer in relation to Eva Hesse. Briony Fer, *Eva Hesse: Studiowork*, Yale University Press, London, 2009.

4   Andy Warhol, Pat Hackett (ed), *The Andy Warhol Diaries*, Penguin Modern Classics, London, 2010, p. 749. On Saturday 12 November 1983, Warhol jokes with a neighbour about doing land art in order to 'freak him out' about his property investment being spoilt: 'I told him that I was planning to do a "big earth work with parked trailers."'

5   John O'Connor and Benjamin Liu, *Unseen Warhol*, Rizzoli, New York, 1996, p. 119.

6   Andy Warhol, *The Philosophy of Andy Warhol: From A to B and Back Again*, Penguin, London, 2007, p. 144.

7   Gretchen Berg, 'Andy Warhol: My True Story', in Kenneth Goldsmith (ed), *I'll be Your Mirror: The Selected Andy Warhol Interviews: 1962–1987*, Carroll & Graf,

New York, 2004, pp. 85–97, p. 92. The interview appeared in differing versions in *The East Village Other*, *The Los Angeles Free Press* and *Cahiers du Cinema*.

8 Wrbican, 'The True Story of 'My True Story'', pp. 56–7. Here is what was actually said during the conversation between Berg and Warhol:

> Gretchen Berg: It's all there on the surface then; it's what we can see.
> Andy Warhol: Well, I like – I guess, yeah.
> Gretchen Berg: What do you like?
> Andy Warhol: The surface.
> Gretchen Berg: Then that's all we can see; if you want to know about Andy Warhol, we just look at your paintings and your films and that's –
> Andy Warhol: Yeah.
> Gretchen Berg: There's nothing profound underneath –
> Andy Warhol: No.

Berg then wrote up the interview as though the words were Warhol's and published them.

9 Brian O'Doherty, *Inside the White Cube: The Ideology of the Gallery Space*, University of California Press, Berkeley, 1999, p. 93.

10 Three volumes were available at the time of writing, the fourth was published in September 2014, too late for my research:

> George Frei and Neil Printz, *The Andy Warhol Catalogue Raisonné: Paintings and Sculpture 1961–1963 Vol. 1* Phaidon Press, New York, 2002. George Frei and Neil Printz, *The Andy Warhol Catalogue Raisonné: Paintings and Sculpture 1964–1969 Vol. 2A* Phaidon Press, New York, 2004. George Frei and Neil Printz, *The Andy Warhol Catalogue Raisonné: Paintings and Sculpture 1964–1969 Vol. 2B*, Phaidon Press, New York, 2004. Neil Printz and Sally King-Nero, *The Andy Warhol Catalogue Raisonné: Paintings and Sculpture 1970–1974 Vol. 3*, Phaidon Press, New York, 2010.

11 O'Connor and Liu, *Unseen Warhol*, p. 119.

12 This is true of many of Crow's observations but the term specifically refers to, Thomas Crow, 'The Absconded Subject of Pop', *Anthropology and Aesthetics*, No. 55/56, Spring–Autumn 2009, pp. 5–20.

13 Branden W. Joseph, 'One-Dimensional Man', *Art Journal*, Vol. 57, No. 4, Winter, 1998, pp. 105–09.

14 Douglas Crimp, 'Getting the Warhol We Deserve', *Social Text*, No. 59, 1999, pp. 49–66, p. 60.

15 Benjamin H. D. Buchloh, 'Drawing Blanks: Notes on Andy Warhol's Late Works', *October*, 127, Winter 2009, pp. 3–24, p. 3.

16 Paul Taylor, 'The Last Interview', in Goldsmith (ed), *I'll be Your Mirror*, pp. 383–394, p. 387.

17 Hal Foster, *The Return of the Real*, The MIT Press, London, 1996, p. 134.

18 William S. Wilson, 'Prince of Boredom: The Repetitions and Passivities of Andy Warhol'. Available at http://www.warholstars.org/andywarhol/articles/william/wilson.html (accessed 21 November 2014).

19 Michael J. Golec, *The Brillo Box Archive: Aesthetics, Design and Art*, University Press of New England, Lebanon, 2008, p. 86–7.

20 Thomas Crow, Merce Cunningham, Robert Whitman, Michelle Kuo, Trisha Brown, 'Social Register', *Artforum International*, 47.1, September 2008, pp. 426–31, 484, 492.

21 On Rauschenberg, the closet and the context of 1950s homophobia see: Jonathan Katz, 'Lovers and Divers: Picturing a Partnership in Rauschenberg and Johns', *Frauen/ Kunst/ Wissenschaft*, June 1998, pp. 16– 31. For a completely different take on the stakes involved in *Now Let Us Praise Famous Men* see Nan Rosenthal, 'Now Let Us Praise Famous Men', in Gary Garrels (ed), *The Work of Andy Warhol*, Bay Press, Seattle, 1989, p. 35–52.

22 Andy Warhol and Pat Hackett, *POPism: The Warhol Sixties*, Penguin, London, 2007, p. 3.

23 Rainer Crone, *Andy Warhol*, trans. John William Gabriel, Thames & Hudson, London, 1970, p. 29.

24 Warhol and Hackett, *POPism*, p. 6.

25 Ibid.

26 Ibid.

27 For example, the final portrait of America in the Epilogue of Ralph Ellison's *Invisible Man*:

> Whence all this passion towards conformity anyway? Diversity is the word. Let man keep his many parts and you will have no tyrant states. Why, if they follow this conformity business, they'll end up by forcing me, an invisible man, to become white, which is not a color but the lack of one. Must I strive towards colorlessness? But seriously and without snobbery, think of what the world would lose if that should happen. America is woven of many strands. I would recognize them and let it so remain. It's winner take nothing that is the great truth of our country or of any country. Life is to be lived, not controlled, and humanity is won by continuing to play in face of certain defeat. Our fate has become one and yet many. This is not prophecy, but description.

Ralph Ellison, *Invisible Man*, Penguin Modern Classics, London, 2001, p. 577.

28 See Anthony E. Grudin, ' "Except Like a Tracing": Defectiveness, Accuracy, and Class in Early Warhol', *October*, 140, Spring, 2012, pp. 139–64.

29 Ibid., p. 142.

30 Benjamin H. D. Buchloh, 'Andy Warhol's One-Dimensional Art, 1956–1966', in Kynaston McShine (ed) *Andy Warhol: A Retrospective* (exh. cat.), New York Museum of Modern Art, 1989, pp. 39–61, p. 54.

31 Rainer Crone, 'Discussion', in Garrels, *The Work of Andy Warhol*, pp. 124–41, p. 128.

32 Charles F. Stuckey, 'Warhol in Context', in Garrels, *The Work of Andy Warhol*, p. 3–34, p. 24.

33 Ibid., p. 15.

1 Locating the Sculptural

1 Benjamin H. D. Buchloh, 'Andy Warhol's One-Dimensional Art, 1956–1966', in Kynaston McShine (ed), *Andy Warhol: A Retrospective* (exh. cat.), Museum of Modern Art, New York, 1989, pp. 39–61, p. 55.

2 Roland Barthes, 'That Old Thing Art', in Paul Taylor (ed), *Post-Pop Art*, The MIT Press, Cambridge, 1989, pp. 21–31, p. 24.

3 David Bourdon, *Warhol*, Harry Abrams Inc., New York, 1995, p. 99. Bourdon refers to an interview he conducted with Warhol's brother in 1987 as the source of the account.

4 David Joselit, 'Yippie Pop: Abbie Hoffman, Andy Warhol, and Sixties Media Politics', *Grey Room*, No. 8, Summer, 2002, pp. 62–79, p.73.

5 Ibid., p. 74.

6 John O'Connor and Benjamin Liu, *Unseen Warhol*, Rizzoli, New York, 1996, pp. 20–2. Warhol's next two contributions to shows at the Loft Gallery were regularly mounted drawings.

7 Ibid., p. 31. See also Victor Bockris, *Warhol*, Penguin, London, 1990, pp. 125–26.

8 The procedure for producing marbleised paper that Warhol used was to dip individual sheets into a solution, where water-based and water-repellent pigments came together, so that swirls and shapes of colours permeated the paper. Suggesting the accuracy of Giallo's account, in the archives of the Warhol Museum in Pittsburgh there are examples of marbleised paper with creases where folds had been made, but with no ink drawings and folded in no discernible pattern. Papers folded in such a way as to bring to Giallo's mind 'paper fortune tellers', though, perhaps reflects an interest in chance. With or without this invocation of 'fortune', the marbleising technique is 'chancy', the word Warhol would later use to describe his silkscreen painting technique. This early technique can therefore be categorised alongside a whole range of Warhol's later uses of chance, and of photographic and photographic-like processes to create abstract effects, perhaps especially the *Shadows* (1979) and *Yarn* (1983) series. In his work in the 1950s, Robert Rauschenberg also used marbleising effects, though as was the case with Warhol's later use of marbling in, for example, *Big Torn Soup Can* (1962), here marbleised passages and moments are achieved more locally, and would have required a greater degree of handwork. For reference to 'chancy' see: Andy Warhol and Pat Hackett, *POPism: The Warhol Sixties*, Penguin, London, 2007, p. 22.

9 Now at Philadelphia Museum. I am indebted to Gary Comenas for this insight.

10 Peter Gidal, *Andy Warhol Films and Paintings: The Factory Years*, De Capo, London, 1971, p. 102.

11 These works were all started after Warhol made *Fate Presto* a huge, monumental triptych occasioned by the Neapolitan earthquake in 1981. It is painted in three different registers (black on black, white on white and black on white). There are also other editions of Mylar crumpled works made at this time and from this print, I have chosen these two partly to curtail confusion partly because of access to the work during my research. These late newspaper works all recall the hand painted *192 Die in Jet* of 1962. See: Molly Donovan, 'Where's Warhol? Triangulating the Artist in the Headlines', in Molly Donovan (ed), *Warhol Headlines*, Prestel, London, 2011, pp. 2–25.

12 Benjamin H. D. Buchloh, 'Drawing Blanks: Notes on Andy Warhol's Late Works', *October,* 127, Winter 2009, pp. 3–24, p.3.

13 For a vivid account of the circumstances of Stewart's death and those which followed see: Jennifer Clement, *Widow Basquiat: A Memoir*, Canongate, London, 2000, pp. 117–32.

14 Matt Wrbican, 'Warhol research', December 19 2010. Online. Email: wrbicanm@warhol.org. Wrbican's notes on the work are as follows:

> Large sculpture in 4 pieces. Acrylic, oil stick, collage, and paper on stretched canvas. (a) is a large, broken up canvas, predominately pink, with a face at the top left, and "smoked eel" written twice at upper right. (b) is a small painting of a figure, grey on white on paper (footprints on verso), (c) is a smaller, broken up and shredded canvas, predominately red and with a blue splotch on it, (d) is another smaller broken canvas predominately blue with dirty brown yarn on it, with caption "Artist could have been choked: Doc" at upper left corner. Clemente contributed a drawing of a face, placed on the sculpture.

15 Ibid.

16 Such as in the following extract from 29 June 1983, about a bridge that had collapsed and was holding up traffic: 'They say that it was a seven inch pin that caused the whole thing to go. It's so abstract. People just kept driving onto it even when it was there.' Andy Warhol, Pat Hackett (ed), *The Andy Warhol Diaries*, Penguin Modern Classics, London, 2010, p. 709.

17 Briony Fer, *Eva Hesse Studiowork*, Yale University Press, London, 2009, pp. 33–4.

18 Ibid., p. 137.

19 All quotes, Luke Skrebowski, 'Productive Misunderstandings', in Diarmuid Costello and Margaret Iversen (eds), *Photography After Conceptual Art*, Wiley Blackwell, London, 2010, pp. 86–107, p. 101.

20 Wolfgang Tillmans and Dominic Eichler, *Wolfgang Tillmans Abstract Pictures*, Hatje Cantz, Ostfildern-Ruit 2011, pp. 8–11.

21 Wolfgang Tillmans and Hans Ulrich Obrist, *The Conversation Series*, Verlag der Buchhandlung Walther König, Köln, 2007, pp. 91–2.

22 Wade Guyton, Rachel Kushner, 'To Build a Fire: Wade Guyton in conversation with Rachel Kushner', in Jeffrey Deitch, *The Painting Factory: Abstraction After Warhol*, Skira Rizzoli Publications, Inc., New York, 2012, pp. 133–43, p. 143.

23 Roland Barthes, *Image-Music-Text*, Fontana, London, 1977, p. 39.

24 Scott Rothkopf, 'File Sharing: Scott Rothkopf on Kelley Walker's Untitled, 2006', *Artforum*, Vol. 51, No.1, September 2012, pp. 454–7, p. 457.

25 David Joselit, 'What to Do with Pictures', *October*, 138, Fall 2011, pp. 81–94.

26 Price is careful to include the video image's time stamp in his print and to draw attention to it in the title, which I read as an irony indicative of the failure to preserve authenticity in digital economies.

2 'Sublime but compulsive negation': *Brillo Boxes*

1 Victor Bockris, *Warhol*, Penguin, London, 1989, p. 233.

2 Though this is the case with Warhol's later series of *Campbell's Soup Cans* from 1964, the same year as the *Brillo Boxes*.

3 Warhol used Wallowitch's images in his drawings and prints in the 1950s. Charles F. Stuckey collects the numerous other references Warhol's work of this time makes to the work of his peers. Charles F. Stuckey 'Warhol in Context', in Gary Garrels (ed), *The Work of Andy Warhol*, Bay Press, Seattle, 1989, pp. 3 – 34.

4 Glenn O'Brien, 'Interview: Andy Warhol', in Kenneth Goldsmith (ed), *I'll be Your Mirror: The Selected Andy Warhol Interviews: 1962–1987*, Carroll & Graf, New York, 2004, pp. 233–64, p. 243.

5 I will return to similar optical effects in Warhol's work in the next chapter, where I will discuss Warhol's long fascination with holography and Warhol's 1970 sculpture *Rain Machine*, with its 3D images of daisies.

6 Benjamin H. D. Buchloh, 'Andy Warhol's One-Dimensional Art: 1956–1966', in Kynaston McShine (ed), *Andy Warhol: A Retrospective*, Museum of Modern Art, New York, 1989, pp. 39–61, p. 48.

7 Arthur C. Danto, 'The Artworld', *Journal of Philosophy*, Vol. 61, No. 19, 1964, pp. 571–84, p. 581.

8 Ibid., p. 580.

9 Arthur C. Danto, *Andy Warhol*, Yale University Press, London, 2009, p. 66.

10 Danto, 'The Artworld', p. 580. My italics.

11 Ibid.

12 Ibid. Victor Bockris claims that Warhol intended to make the gallery look like 'the interior of a warehouse'. Bockris, *Warhol*, p. 233.

13 For a deeper discussion of the contradictions and inconsistencies of Danto's work on Warhol's boxes, see Paul Mattick, 'The Andy Warhol of Philosophy and the Philosophy of Andy Warhol', *Critical Inquiry*, Vol. 24, No. 4, 1998, pp. 965–87, p. 967.

14 Anthony E. Grudin, ' "Except Like a Tracing": Defectiveness, Accuracy, and Class in Early Warhol', *October*, 140, Spring 2012, pp. 139–64, p. 140.

15 Ibid., p. 142.

16 Ibid., p. 140.

17 Andy Warhol and Pat Hackett, *POPism: The Warhol Sixties*, Penguin, London, 2007, p. 6.

18 Anthony E. Grudin, "A Sign of Good Taste": Andy Warhol and the Rise of Brand Image Advertising', *Oxford Art Journal*, Vol. 33, No. 2, 2010, pp. 211–32, p. 211.

19 John O'Connor and Benjamin Liu, *Unseen Warhol*, Rizzoli, New York, 1996, p. 35.

20 Sidney Tillim, 'Andy Warhol', in Alan R. Pratt (ed), *The Critical Response to Andy Warhol*, Greenwood Press, London, 1997, pp. 7–8.

21 Iconographic readings 'have oversimplified his intricate reflections on the status and substance of the painterly object and have virtually ignored his efforts to incorporate context and display strategies into the work themselves. Features that were aggressively antipictorial in their impulse and evidently among Warhol's primary concerns in the early exhibitions have been obliterated in the process of the acculturation of his art.' Benjamin H. D. Buchloh, 'Andy Warhol's One-Dimensional Art', in McShine (ed), *Andy Warhol*, p. 54.

22 George Frei and Neil Printz, *Warhol: Paintings and Sculpture 1964–1969 Vol. 2A: The Andy Warhol Catalogue* Raisonné, Phaidon Press, New York, 2004, p. 55.

23 Ibid.

24 Michael J. Golec, *The Brillo Box Archive: Aesthetics, Design and Art*, University Press of New England, Lebanon, 2008, p. 114.

25 Ibid., p. 103.

26 Ibid., p. 85.

27 Ibid., p. 116.

28 Ibid., p. 113.

29 Ibid., p. 87.

30 Like the Stable opening, *Sleep's* premiere on 17 January 1964 at the Grammercy Arts was a carefully orchestrated affair. Warhol placed on the stage two transistor radios, each tuned at top volume to different rock stations. According to the *New York Post*, the screening was attended by only nine people, two of whom left during the first hour. See, David Bourdon, 'Warhol as Filmmaker', *Art in America*, 59, 1971, pp. 12–6.

31 Gretchen Berg, 'Andy Warhol: My True Story', in Goldsmith (ed), *I'll Be Your Mirror*, pp. 85–96, p. 92.

32 Golec, *The Brillo Box Archive*, p. 114.

33 Joseph Gelmis, 'Andy Warhol', in Goldsmith (ed), *I'll Be Your Mirror*, pp. 160–69, p. 168.

34 Andy Warhol and Pat Hackett, *POPism: The Warhol Sixties*, Penguin, London, 2007, p. 3.

35 Gerard Malanga, *Archiving Warhol: Writings and Photographs*, Creation Books, New York, 2002, p. 148.

36 Tillim, 'Andy Warhol', in Pratt (ed), *The Critical Response to Andy Warhol*, p. 7.

37 Ibid.

38 Grace Glueck, 'Art Notes: Boom?', in Pratt (ed), *The Critical Response to Andy Warhol*, pp. 6–7, p. 7.

39 Brian O'Doherty, *Inside the White Cube: The Ideology of the Gallery Space*, University of California Press, London, 1999, p. 49.

40 He later does, referring to 'Warhol's Airborne Pillows', a 'sight of the sixties', which 'untied happiness with didactic clarity.' Ibid., p. 93. In my reading of this work in the following chapter, I again offer a darker reading to writers belonging to the American tradition. Though we are all indebted to O'Doherty's contribution, the theme of trespass is a coincidence. As I explain, the notion came to me through researching Warhol's sculpture, in particular his burglar alarm works.

41 Ibid., p. 52.

42 Donald Judd, 'Specific Objects', in Charles Harrison and Paul Wood (eds), *Art in Theory*, Blackwell, London, 2002, pp. 824–28, p. 827.

43 Ibid.

44 This is the same Sam Wagstaff that later became the mentor and benefactor of photographer Robert Mapplethorpe.

45 I take this information from James Meyer's *Minimalism Art and Polemics in the Sixties*, Yale University Press, London, 2001, p. 78 and 283. The exhibition and the relationship to Judd and Minimalism is also considered in Charles F. Stuckey, 'Warhol in Context', p. 13. Meyer's account of the Wagstaff show balances Donald Judd's account of it which is disparaging, though he conceded that, even without his work, the exhibition displayed a 'new attitude' (p. 283, n2). The letter to Warhol is quoted in Frei and Printz, *Warhol Catalogue Raisonné*, pp. 54–5:

> At the end of 1963, the idea of box sculptures was very much on Warhol's mind. While preparing an exhibition for the Wadsworth Atheneum, Sam Wagstaff wrote to Warhol on December 11, 'I'm enclosing a third set of [loan] forms in hopes that you will be able to make a sculpture of a pile of white boxes with silkscreen sides as we talked about one day. How is that project coming?' Wagstaff's exhibition, 'Black, White and Gray', opened in January and focused on the absence of colour. It included two of Warhol's *Car Crash* paintings […] but no box sculptures.

46 *Minimal Art: A Critical Anthology*, Gregory Battcock (ed), University of California Press, London, 1995. David Bourdon, *Warhol*, Harry N. Abrams Inc., New York, 1989, pp. 186–87.

47 While framing his account of Warhol within a Minimalist historiography (which I shall come to), Hal Foster writes that Pop began 'another trajectory of art since 1960… often displaced by the Minimalist genealogy in the critical literature (if not the marketplace).' Hal Foster, *Return of the Real*, MIT Press, London 1996, p. 127.

48 David Raskin, *Donald Judd*, Yale University Press, London, 2010, p. 13.

49 Ibid., p. 12.

50 See, Anna C. Chave, 'Minimalism and the Rhetoric of Power', *Arts Magazine*, Vol. 64, No. 5, January 1990, pp. 44–63.

51 Jo Baer, *Jo Baer: Broadsides and Belle Lettres, Selected Writings and Interviews 1965–2010*, Roma Publications, Amsterdam, 2010, p. 27.

52 The idea that Warhol 'acquiesced' when others offered opinions of his work is discussed in Reva Wolf's sensitive essay 'Through the Looking Glass' in, Kenneth Goldsmith (ed.), *I'll be Your Mirror*, pp. xi–xxxii.

53 For example, Mark Godfrey, 'From Box to Street and Back Again: An Inadequate Descriptive System for the Seventies', in Donna de Salvo (ed), *Open Systems Rethinking Art c.1970*, Tate Publishing, London, 2005, pp. 24–49.

54 James Meyer, 'Bochner's *Measurement Series*', in Peter Weibel (ed), *Kontext Kunst*, DuMont Buchverlag, Cologne, 1994, pp. 129–33. Available at http://zoolander52.tripod.com/theartsection3.5/id1.html (accessed 19 November 2014).

55 Anne Rorimer, *New Art in the 60s and 70s: Redefining Reality*, Thames and Hudson, London, 2001, pp. 184–85.

56 The weak sales of the work perhaps suggest that the ploy did not quite turn out the way Warhol imagined. Warhol had been sure the boxes would sell well but they did not. We might imagine Warhol making an assumption that potential buyers would perceive that they could re-appropriate this act of trespass by claiming the work for the artworld and buying it up. The miscalculation was—if this had been the case—that the artworld did not act as one, or have any collective self-awareness; but at the same time, the exhibition was considered a single-spectacle, so that this invasion of product packaging could only conceivably be overcome, and turned into an asset, through being acquired as one.

57 Foster, *Return of the Real*, p. 247, n. 37.

58 This is not to say that the work is particularly redemptive. Although exchange between the real world and the artworld is preserved at the level of the spectator's experience, rather than unrealistically enfranchising the artworld, this experience then comes to take on the zero value ascribed to the comparable conditions between one world and the other. One might say the only critical value of Warhol's art lies in this possibility of misregistration, in this case between artworld and real world.

3 Atmosphere

1 Andy Warhol, *The Philosophy of Andy Warhol (From A to B and Back Again)*, Penguin, London, 2007, p. 160.

2 David Bourdon, *Warhol*, Harry N. Abrams Inc., New York, 1989, p. 228–29.

3 Benjamin H. D. Buchloh, 'Andy Warhol's One Dimensional Art: 1956–1966', in Kynaston McShine (ed), *Andy Warhol: A Retrospective*, Museum of Modern Art, New York, 1989, pp. 39–61, p. 47.

4 Rosalind Krauss, 'Madness of the Day', in Jeffery Deitch (ed), *The Painting Factory: Abstraction After Warhol* (exh. cat.), Skira Rizzoli, London, 2012, pp. 23–9, p. 27.

5 Andy Warhol and Pat Hackett, *POPism: The Warhol Sixties*, Penguin, London, 2007, p. 113.

6 Warhol's own accounts frequently call the works *Silver Pillows*, particularly in *POPism*.

7 Warhol and Hackett, *POPism*, pp. 211–12.

8 Such sensitivity also links them to the alarm works that will be considered in the following chapter.

9 This account is based on a conversation between Klüver, George Frei, Neil Printz and S. King-Nero, 18 May 1994. George Frei and Neil Printz, *Warhol: Paintings and Sculpture 1964–1969 Vol. 2A: The Andy Warhol Catalogue Raisonné*, Phaidon Press, New York, 2004, p. 207.

10 'I did my first tape recording in 1964.' Warhol, *The Philosophy of Andy Warhol*, pp. 94–5.

11 There is another distinct work that emerged from the *Clouds* project, that is the installation of massive transparent cushions of air resting on the floor, referred to as 'Plastic Bags', installed by the entrance at Warhol's famous Stockholm show in 1969. These works might be considered as obstacles in the way I have considered the boxes installed at *Personality of the Artist* in 1964. Spectators had to push past these objects which quickly became disgusting by dint of their static charge attracting dust. In a chapter for a publication for a recent Warhol retrospective Matt Wrbican describes these as 'related' to the *Clouds* but 'entirely new works'. Matt Wrbican, 'Time Capsule 61 Goes to the Movies', in Eva Meyer-Hermann, Matt Wrbican, Andy Warhol and Geralyn Huxley, *Andy Warhol: Other Voices, Other Rooms*, NAi Publishers, Rotterdam, 2008, p. 115–19, p. 118.

12 Victor Bockris, *Warhol*, Penguin, London, 1990, p. 234.

13 Warhol and Hackett, *POPism*, p. 204.

14 Ibid., p. 186.

15 Ibid., p. 83.

16 Warhol told Alan Solomon in a 1966 interview on CBS: 'Since I didn't want to paint any more, I thought… that I could give that up and do the movies. And then I thought that there must be a way that I have to finish it off, and I thought

the only way is to make a painting that floats.' Quoted in Rainer Crone, *Andy Warhol*, trans. John William Gabriel, Thames & Hudson, London, 1970, p. 30.

17 Ibid.

18 David Joselit, 'Yippie Pop: Abbie Hoffman, Andy Warhol, and Sixties Media Politics', *Grey Room*, No. 8, Summer 2002, pp. 62–79, p. 75.

19 Mark Francis, '*Horror Vacui*: Andy Warhol's Installations', in Mark Francis (ed), *Andy Warhol: the Late Work, Vol. 1 Texts*, Prestel, Munich, 2004, pp. 10–20.

20 Robert Rosenblum, 'Saint Andrew', *Newsweek*, 7 December 1964, pp. 100, 103–04, p.103.

21 Lane Slate, 'USA Artists: Andy Warhol and Roy Lichtenstein', in Kenneth Goldsmith (ed), *I'll be Your Mirror: The Selected Andy Warhol Interviews: 1962-1987*, Carroll & Graf, New York, 2004, pp. 79–84, p. 80. Interview conducted in 1966.

22 Warhol, *The Philosophy of Andy Warhol*, p. 144.

23 Gretchen Berg, 'Andy Warhol: My True Story', in Goldsmith (ed), *I'll Be Your Mirror*, pp. 85–96, p. 92.

24 'Art and film have nothing to do with each other, film is just something you photograph, not to show painting on.' Ibid.

25 Charles F. Stuckey, 'Warhol in Context', in Gary Garrels (ed), *The Work of Andy Warhol*, Bay Press, Seattle, 1989, pp. 3– 34, p. 21,

26 See, for example, Barbara Rose (1965), 'A B C Art', in Gregory Battcock (ed), *Minimal Art: A Critical Anthology*, Dutton, New York, 1968, pp. 274–97, p. 293.

27 Bockris, *Warhol*, p. 207.

28 By which I am referring, of course, to Patti Astor's New York Fun Gallery, open 1981–1985.

29 Nancy Spector, Richard Prince, Glenn O'Brien, Jack Bankowsky, *Richard Prince* (exh. cat.), The Solomon R. Guggenheim Foundation, New York, 2007, p. 326–33.

30 Ibid., p. 331.

31 Ibid., p. 228

32 Ibid., pp. 328–33.

33 Warhol and Hackett, *POPism*, p. 41. Callie Angell writes of Collins: 'The actor Rufus Collins, whose friendship with Warhol began in the 1950s, trained at the Actors Studio in New York and was a member of the Living Theatre in the 1960s […] Collins was also one of the earliest stars of Warhol's cinema, beginning in August 1963 with *Naomi and Rufus Kiss*, the film from which Warhol's Plexiglas sculpture *The Large Kiss* was derived' Callie Angell, *Andy Warhol Screen Tests: The Films of Andy Warhol Catalogue Raisonné (Vol. 1)*, Abrams/ Whitney Museum of American Art, New York, 2006, p. 54.

34 Like the silkscreens on Plexiglas, the Gerard Malanga poetry-portrait book *Screen Tests/A Diary* used multiple consecutive frames taken from Warhol's

Screen Tests to accompany the poems on the other side of the page. The *Screen Test* poetry book and the Plexiglas sculptures have a common formal component, aside from their use of direct copies of segments of film reel. Both the Plexiglas works and the book present their images on a transparent medium, further emulating their original source (the pictures in the book are on individual leaves of transparent paper, like tracing paper). Gerard Malanga and Andy Warhol, *Screen Tests/A Diary*, Kulcher Press, New York, 1967.

35 Marco Livingstone, 'Do It Yourself: Notes on Warhol's Techniques', in McShine (ed), *Andy Warhol*, pp. 63–80, p. 73.

36 Stephen Koch, *Stargazer: Andy Warhol's World and His Films*, Marion Boyers, London, 1985, p. 56.

37 Anne d'Harnoncourt has written that it is 'of all Duchamp's creations, the most accessible (to the point of being literally transparent) as well as the most abstruse. We see through [it] more than we see [it]. The viewer becomes part of the view.' Anne d'Harnoncourt and Walter Hopps, 'Reflections on a New Work by Marcel Duchamp', *Philadelphia Museum of Art Bulletin*, Vol. 64, No. 299–300, April–September 1969, pp. 6–58, p. 8.

38 In 1971, Gerard Malanga interviewed Warhol about his printing technique, and the parallel is discussed, although resisted at first by Warhol.

> Malanga: Is there a relationship between your prints and your involvement with film?
> Warhol: At the time I wasn't aware of any relationship. They were for me at that time and still are two distinct expressions. But you did point out to me the similarity in the repetition of images in both media. I'm speaking here in regard to the early films, like *Sleep* and *Empire*.
> Malanga: Yes. I remember holding up to the light a clip from *Sleep* and taking notice how each frame was exactly the same; each frame was static because the film was static in its actual projection.

Gerard Malanga, 'A Conversation with Andy Warhol, in Goldsmith (ed), pp. 191–96, p. 195.

39 *Large Kiss*, like the film from which it came, is important nonetheless because it gave visibility to explicitly homosexual contact, and because that contact involved a black man, Rufus Collins.

40 Joseph's is by far the most sophisticated analysis of *Sleep*. Branden W. Joseph, 'The Play of Repetition: Andy Warhol's *Sleep*', *Greyroom*, No.19, 2005, pp. 22–53.

41 Ibid., p. 33.

42 Richard Meyer, 'Warhol's Clones', in Monica Dorenkamp and Richard Henke (eds), *Negotiating Lesbian and Gay Subjects*, Routledge, New York, 1995, pp. 93–122, p. 108.

43 Annette Michelson, '"Where is Your Rupture?": Mass Culture and the *Gesamtkunstwerk*', *October*, 56, Spring 1991, pp. 42–63, p. 55.

44 Ibid., p. 56.

45 Ibid., p. 58.

46 See, for further discussion and source, John Jervis, *Transgressing the Modern*, Blackwell, London, 1999, p. 25.

47 To quote Wayne McGuire, referred to in Branden W. Joseph, "'My Mind Split Open': Andy Warhol's Exploding Plastic Inevitable'. *Grey Room* No. 8 Summer 2002 pp. 80–107, p. 81.

48 Victor Bockris and Gerard Malanga, *Uptight: the Story of the Velvet Underground*, Omnibus Press, London, 1983, p. 124.

49 Joseph, 'My Mind Split Open', p. 80.

50 Koch, *Stargazer*, p. 72.

51 Actually Warhol made two other works during this period that are described in the *Catalogue Raisonné* as sculpture, although my analysis will concentrate on *Rain Machine*. These works are the Plexiglas Mylar rollers—which were made to dispense Mylar in the Factory, although they had very definite artistic properties—and the 'vacuum cleaner work', mentioned above, a part-sculpture, part-performance piece for the exhibition *Art in Process* (1972).

52 Bockris, *Warhol*, p. 164.

53 *A Report on the Art and Technology Program of the LA County Museum of Art 1967–1971*(exh. cat.), Los Angeles County Museum of Art, 1971, p. 330. Warhol's section is on pp. 330–37.

54 *Report*, p. 335.

55 Ibid., p. 330.

56 Ibid., pp. 268–69.

57 Anne Goodyear, 'From Technophilia to Technophobia: the Impact of the Vietnam War on the Reception of "Art and Technology"', *Leonardo*, Vol. 41, No. 2, April 2008, pp. 169–73.

58 As Andrew Ross has argued, in his investigation of the 'no-collar' environment of media and tech companies in the New Economy, the emergence of the open plan artist's workspace, the nurture of creativity and inspiration, and the relatively unstructured, fluid tasking of employees were all imported from the artist's studio. Indeed Ross even mentions Warhol's factory model, and his preparation of the ground of 'business art', as enabling reciprocation on the part of the artist invited into the corporate world, following the art boom in the 1980s. Andrew Ross, *No-collar: The Humane Workplace and Its Hidden Costs*, Temple University Press, Philadelphia, 2004. The New Economy is associated with both a broad shift from manufacturing based economies to service based ones, and the emergence of dotcom and digital industries in the 1990s.

59 In April, 1969, Jane Livingston went to New York and saw the three mock-ups at Warhol's studio. In one of them, small polyethelene particles were agitated in a circular motion by air blowers to simulate whirling snowflakes; this was

encased between two glass faces embedded in an approximately six by eight foot rectangular wood frame. There was also a rain machine of similar size, but not enclosed by glass; it consisted of a simple pump system through which water circulated, falling in strands from apertures in a top section of pipe into a trough concealed beneath an artificial grass bed. The rain was side lighted to create an effect of sparkling beads. There was also a wind machine, simply a wooden box encasing an air blower. Each of these was intended to work in conjunction with a 3D image; behind the rain, for example, would be a hologram or video screen; the snow machine would incorporate a holographic image in the centre, through and around which the plastic flakes would circulate; the wind machine would vibrate and a 3D holographic sphere would vibrate as well.

60 Indeed Rauschenberg's EAT-related work might have been a source of more literal inspiration for *Rain Machine*. Rauschenberg's sculpture *Oracle* had an electric air pump going into a large tub of water, making a bubbling/gurgling sound. In 1967, and also for EAT, Fujiko Nakaya, who was close to Rauschenberg during the 1960s, made her first *Fog Sculpture*. *Report*, p. 330.

61 Warhol, *The Philosophy of Andy Warhol*, p. 158.

62 The Frank-Ratchye Studio for Creative Enquiry, 'Previously Unknown Warhol Works Found on Floppy Discs from 1985'. Available at http://studioforcreativeinquiry.org/events/warhol-discovery (accessed 13 August 2014).

63 Jason Sapan, 'Warhol', 30 April 2014. Online. Email: drlaser@holographer.com. According to Sapan, during the shoot Warhol included in his small entourage a 3D cinematographer, 'He brought along his 3D cinematographer. Interestingly enough, this man shot 3D slides on what I believe was a Stereo Realist camera.'

64 Ibid.

65 Ibid.

66 Ibid.

67 Ibid.

4 The Artwork Across the Street

1 Yasmil Raymond, brochure for exhibition of *Shadows* at the Hirschhorn Museum, *September 25, 2011–January 15, 2012*, unpaginated.

2 Lynne Cooke, 'Andy Warhol: *Shadows*', in Lynne Cooke, Karen J. Kelly and Bettina Funcke (eds), *Robert Lehman Lectures on Contemporary Art*, Dia Art Foundation, New York, 2004, pp. 87–93, p.90. Cooke also compares the painting installation *To the People of New York City* (1976) by Blinky Polermo, also shown at the Heiner Friedrich space. For the Judd quotation see: David Raskin, *Donald Judd*, Yale University Press, London, 2010, p. 13.

3 Yasmil Raymond, brochure for *Shadows*.

4 Andy Warhol, Pat Hackett (ed), *The Andy Warhol Diaries*, Penguin Modern Classics, London, 2010, pp. 66–67 and p.280. Warhol mentions greeting 3000 people at the opening of *Shadows*. The first reference is to Warhol's take on the Paris show.

5 Arguably shadows had always been an important part of Warhol's work. During the 1970s, Warhol's use of his own studio-shot imagery and his working relationship with Ronnie Cutrone, gave him licence to explore the impact of shadows in paintings with a greater sense of purpose. This is in evidence in work such as the *Hammer and Sickle* and *Skull* series (both 1976). John O'Connor and Benjamin Liu, *Unseen Warhol*, Rizzoli, New York, 1996, pp. 55–71.

6 Mark Francis, '*Horror Vacui*: Andy Warhol's Installations', in Mark Francis (ed), *Andy Warhol: The Late Work*, Prestel, Munich, 2004, pp. 10–20, p. 11.

7 Ibid. With regard to Minimalism, we might also consider the attempts inside and outside of the gallery to invoke high values with a 'less is more' aesthetic, for example, in the window displays of upmarket shops. This Minimalism, which is repressed in discussions of the movement in art history, is the opposite to the *horror vacui*, which describes the crowded environments such as that Warhol emulated with *The Personality of the Artist*.

8 Andy Warhol, 'Painter Hangs Own Paintings', *New York Magazine*, Vol. 12, No. 6, 5 February 1979, pp. 9–10, p. 10.

9 Ibid., p. 9.

10 Another Photorealist, Chuck Close, was an important exhibitor at the 1979 Whitney Biennial, and yet another, Don Eddy, was showing at the Nancy Hoffman Gallery that year.

11 Warhol fails to mention the John Gibson Gallery which, strictly speaking, was the gallery across the street from the Heiner Friedrich. It housed conceptual and Minimalist work broadly in concert with the Heiner Friedrich agenda.

12 Dieter Roelstraete, 'Modernism, Postmodernism and Gleam: On the Photorealist Work Ethic', *Afterall: A Journal of Art, Context, and Enquiry*, No. 24, Summer 2010, pp. 5–15, p. 8.

13 Indeed, like many of Warhol's late works, these large-scale abstract paintings recall the New York School artists Warhol's Pop work had helped supersede in 1962–3. In Warhol's versions, however, the designs for works such as the *Shadows, Rorschach Tests* (1984) and *Oxidation Paintings* (1977–78) are achieved by means of mediation; chance; factory and housework; and bodily emission, rather than the masterful handling of paint.

14 Harold Rosenberg, 'The American Action Painters', *ARTnews*, December 1952, pp. 22–50. In relation to the same quote, Benjamin Buchloh describes how Warhol's strategies act more generally as a 'deliberate transgression of those sacred limits' of the canvas edge. Benjamin H. D. Buchloh, 'Andy Warhol's One Dimensional Art: 1956–1966', in Kynaston McShine (ed), *Andy Warhol: A Retrospective*, Museum of Modern Art, New York, 1989,

pp. 39–61, p.56. This framing in the context of high modernist painting kept at a mop-length distance, however, maintains the kinship with the art across the street. So, for example, the manifesto-like essay, 'Art Hysterical Notions of Progress and Culture', by Valerie Jaudon and Joyce Kozloff, abounds with reference to Clement Greenberg, Willem de Kooning and Barnett Newman. Yet many, if not all, of the negative descriptions of works would suit Minimal Art as much as it would suit Abstract Expressionist work: 'purity', 'industrial', 'reductive' and 'rational'. Valerie Jaudon and Joyce Kozloff, 'Art Hysterical Notions of Progress and Culture', *Heresies*, 4, 1978, pp. 38–42. In other ways this indictment of Abstract Expressionism by Jaudon and Kozloff can be seen as still implicating Minimalism: throughout the decade, figures associated with Minimalism continued in the tradition of their forebears by allowing their work to represent an image of American advancement and power. No more was this the case than at the sixth International Exhibition at the Guggenheim in 1971. See Alexander Alberro, 'The Turn of the Screw: Daniel Buren, Dan Flavin, and the Sixth Guggenheim International Exhibition', *October*, 80, Spring 1997, pp. 57–84.

15 For Warhol's account of the scene at the preview, see Warhol, *Diaries*, p. 279. For more on Warhol and decoration see Charles F. Stuckey, 'Warhol in Context', in Gary Garrels (ed), *The Work of Andy Warhol*, Bay Press, Seattle, 1989, pp. 3–34, pp. 18–9.

16 Warhol was very impressed by the film, praising it unreservedly over the phone to Pat Hackett. Warhol, *Diaries*, pp. 129–130. Though disco would be said to have 'died' later in the year *Shadows* opened, following the barely concealed racism and homophobia of the 'disco sucks' backlash from predominantly white middle-class America, *Shadows* had already been in development for over a year at that time and, in New York, the parties continued. See: Tim Lawrence, *Love Saves the Day: A History of American Dance Music Culture, 1970–1979*, Duke University Press, Durham, NC, 2004, pp. 363–433.

17 *Interview* magazine, No. 4, April 1979, pp. 22–3. Lauren Walker and Janis Savitt model clothes by Yves Saint Laurent and Thierry Mugler.

18 Elisa Auther, 'Wallpaper, the Decorative, and Contemporary Installation Art', in Maria Elena Buszek (ed), *Extra/Ordinary: Craft and Contemporary Art*, Duke University Press, Durham, NC, 2011, pp.121–22, pp.115–35. Auther writes: 'As the ultimate attack on the sanctity of painting, wallpaper overturned the privileged place of originality, uniqueness, and autonomy essential to painting's superiority to decoration. While recognizing that Warhol's wallpaper transgressed the boundaries of fine art, it is crucial to bring to light that this transgression was abetted by wallpaper's association with the decorative, the domestic, and the feminine… his wallpaper productions repositioned the artist as an interior decorator, feminizing him through the medium's intimate association with the home and popular taste. With this brazen celebration of decoration, Warhol's wallpapers can be read as a rejection of the heterosexual bravado relished in the image.' See also Stuckey, 'Warhol in Context', p. 20.

19 Anna C. Chave, 'Minimalism and the Rhetoric of Power', *Arts Magazine*, Vol. 64, No. 5, January 1990, pp. 44–63.

20 Yet the success of the installation was compromised by the necessity that the work sit above floor level. Had it been able to do so, *Shadows* would have been entirely contiguous with the architectural elements of the gallery, its floor and wall space. Like so many installations that relied on the ground Minimalism had laid, indeed, like Walter De Maria's *Broken Kilometer* that proceeded *Shadows* at the Heiner Friedrich Gallery, on the floor it would have provided a perfect continuity with the space, with no slip of register between it and the paintings: just a wholesale elevation.

21 Lawrence, *Love Saves the Day*, p.1.

22 Hal Foster, 'Figment in a Factory', in Eva Meyer-Hermann, Matt Wrbican, Andy Warhol and Geralyn Huxley (eds), *Andy Warhol: Other Voices, Other Rooms*, NAI Publishers, Rotterdam, 2008, pp. 105–09, p. 108.

23 Not italicised. I take Warhol to mean working on the idea of an invisible sculpture, not the *Invisible Sculpture*.

24 Claes Oldenburg, Andy Warhol, Robert Morris and Benjamin H. D. Buchloh, 'Three Conversations in 1985', *October*, 70, 1994, pp. 33—54.

25 The physical elements of *Invisible Sculpture* are in the Warhol Museum collection: a plastic siren, one or two motion detectors, two large batteries, and many feet of insulated electrical wire. A photo of these objects is published in *Andy Warhol: 365 Takes*, The Andy Warhol Museum, Harry N. Abrams Inc., New York, 2004, pp. 203–4.

26 O'Connor and Liu, *Unseen Warhol*, pp. 65–6. In February 1986 the shoe was on the other foot:

'Monday, February 17, 1986.
I screamed at the interview girls because one of them set off the alarm and it costs $50 every time the alarm company comes. Even if you call them one second after it starts and say it was a mistake, they want the $50 so they tell you 'The guy already left', and he comes'.
Warhol, *Diaries*, p. 993.

27 In the exhibition *Twisted Pair: Marcel Duchamp/Andy Warhol* (2010), curated by Matt Wrbican, a comparison is made between Warhol's alarm work and Duchamp's *Sixteen Miles of String* installation at *First Papers of Surrealism* (1942), the first Surrealist exhibition in the US. Both works invade the spectators' space 'while also forcing them to keep their distance'. Matt Wrbican, 'Invisible Sculpture', 6 September 2012. Online. Email: wrbicanm@warhol.org.

28 Ibid.

29 Warhol, *Diaries*, p. 301.

30 The Warhol Museum collection includes other such empty jars for commercial products, upon which a tiny alarm has been glued. The pickle jar was shown to the public at a one-day event in 1978.

31 Bockris, *Warhol*, p. 179.

32 Warhol, *Diaries*, p. 1094.

33 Ibid., p. 975.

34 O'Connor and Liu, *Unseen Warhol*, p. 119. For a fuller version of this text see Chapter 4.

35 'I was amused at the idea of meat under Plexiglas because I thought it made fun of the scene—where the name of the game seemed to be 'how cool you can be' and 'how refined.' Nobody ever mentioned anything that seemed real. The world was falling apart, anyone could see it…' Richard Flood, 'Paul Thek: Real Misunderstanding', *Artforum*, Vol. 20, No. 2, October 1981, pp. 48–53, p. 49.

36 Margit Brehm, Axel Heil and Roberto Ort, *Paul Thek: Tales the Tortoise Taught Us*, Konig, London, 2009, p. 32. This is one of many acts of what is frequently considered appropriation that appears in this book. However, I will argue in Chapter 4 for appropriation's inadequacy as a critical term.

37 George Frei and Neil Printz, *The Andy Warhol Catalogue Raisonné: Paintings and Sculpture 1964–1969 Vol. 2B*, Phaidon Press, New York, 2004, p. 469.

Ronnie Cutrone, Warhol's assistant during the 1970s, has recalled that Warhol showed him paintings with 'blue and red footprints', and at least one of the early *Piss Paintings* of 1961–1962. The latter, Cutrone noted, were 'rather small, like 40' x 50' or 30' x 40'. But then we did some very big ones at the same time we did the *Oxidation Paintings* in 1978.' The painting [shown in the *Unmuzzled Ox*] measures 54 by 84 inches and surely belongs to the later body of work.

38 'Tuesday, August 14, 1984: Brigid's pug walked across the painting I'd just done. He had orange and purple feet. Madame Defarge kept knitting away.' Warhol, *Diaries*, p. 827.

39 Ibid., p. 482.

40 This is from 1971/early 1972. I am indebted to Thomas Kiedrowski for this information. Thomas Kiedrowski, 'Warhol request', 14 December 2012, Online. Email: kiedrowski@gmail.com.

41 See, for example, Bockris, *Warhol*, p. 207.

42 Robert Reilly, 'Untitled Interview', in Kenneth Goldsmith (ed), *I'll be Your Mirror: The Selected Andy Warhol Interviews: 1962–1987*, Carroll & Graf, New York, 2004, pp. 110–17, pp. 111–12.

5 A Waste of Space

1 Andy Warhol, *The Philosophy of Andy Warhol: From A to B and Back Again*, Penguin, London, 2007, p. 145.

2 Neil Printz and Sally King-Nero, *Andy Warhol Catalogue Raisonné (Vol. 3)*, Phaidon Press, New York, 2004, p. 31.

3 'Being the right thing in the wrong place and the wrong thing in the right place is worth it because something interesting always happens.' Warhol, *The Philosophy of Andy Warhol*, p. 158.

4 Another version of these negotiations is given in Bob Colacello's *Holy Terror*, in which Pivar is recorded as having made a deal with the inventor of a portrait bust machine, which was expected to go ahead. Bob Colacello, *Holy Terror: Andy Warhol Close Up*, Harper Collins, New York, 1990, p. 482. Pivar's claims have been undermined recently through his association with an exhibition of plaster works erroneously attributed to Warhol.

5 Catherine Johnson, *Thank You Andy Warhol*, Glitterati Books, London, 2012, p. 185.

6 Colacello, *Holy Terror*, p. 482.

7 Of this moment, Christopher Makos recalls:

The thing that started off his sculptures was the idea of making big cardboard boxes and filling them up with cement. He had hired a friend of mine, Mark Burkett, who was in the group called the Pedantics. Mark was one of the musicians looking for freelance work, and I said, 'Here's a job, Mark. We've got this idea of filling up these boxes with cement.' Well, if you take a box that's three feet by four feet and maybe four feet tall, it's a nice strong box. But you fill it with cement, it gets wet and expands and finally explodes.

The first couple of tries were disasters. And then they got the idea of lining the box with plastic. Line it in plastic and then fill it up. Of course these projects made an enormous mess. It drove everybody crazy—this white powder flying everywhere. And they mixed it with something that stunk. And so it stank up the whole area. It was wet. It was messy. In those days, the Factory was at 860 Broadway. It was smaller—all that shit was being done in the back not far from the interview offices. So people were always whining, whether it was the piss paintings stinking up the back or the naked boys being photographed. Everybody whined all the time about Warhol's other stuff.

Anyway, they let the cement harden and dry. And then they *couldn't move* these boxes. They didn't know what the hell to do with them. Now *my* gift is a tiny little version that's four inches by about three inches by about two inches tall. And it's a Whitman's box of chocolates that's been emptied of its chocolate and filled with cement. The punch line is that, even though it's filled with cement, it's very, very lightweight. It fulfils the original idea of cement. It's very nihilistic. It doesn't mean anything. I think he signed it on the inside. Sealed the box up. Resealed it in the cellophane wrap. And that's it. No one knows what's in the box. I know it's a little bit heavy.

John O'Connor and Benjamin Liu, *Unseen Warhol*, Rizzoli, New York, 1996, p. 119.

8 Warhol, *The Philosophy of Andy Warhol*, p. 196.

9 Another way in which the problem of art and wasted space is resolved is not by making art out of waste, or out of clearing space, but by making art

on a ground already in use. Warhol did this in one case by recycling paper already used for print. In one poster for his *Ladies and Gentlemen* series we find the image of a drag queen above a print of fish and, beneath that, an image of a couple at a bench. The Andy Warhol Museum has three such works, all with unique features, and head archivist Matt Wrbican has remarked that, according to Jay Shriver, Warhol's assistant in the 1980s, these works are not alone in exhibiting this inclination to reuse and recycle. What the works produce is a maxed-out off-register effect that goes with the subject matter of cross-dressing. Matt Wrbican, 'RE: crumple newspaper 'abstract sculpture'', 3 May 2013. Online. Email: wrbicanm@warhol.org.

10 I refer to the quotation used previously: 'My favourite piece of sculpture is a solid wall with a hole in it to frame the space on the other side.' Warhol, *The Philosophy of Andy Warhol*, p. 144.

11 *Andy Warhol's Folk and Funk* (exh. cat.), Museum of American Folk Art, New York, 1977, p. 7.

12 Colacello, *Holy Terror*, p. 496.

13 Here is Berlin talking with Vincent Fremont, one of the founding directors of the Andy Warhol Foundation for the Visual Arts:

> FREMONT: After he died, we went up to his house, and the guest room that used to be empty was floor-to-ceiling with stuff. He was the proverbial pack rat.
>
> BERLIN: His whole dining room was nothing but a bunch of shopping bags filled with batteries for tape recorders.

Vincent Fremont, 'Brigid Berlin', *Interview*, June/July 2008, pp. 92–3.

14 Some accounts of Warhol's collecting—the shops he frequented, his specific interests in different eras and makers and the company he kept when doing the 'Saturday stroll' around the antique shops and galleries in New York—are to be found in John Smith (ed), *Possession Obsession: Andy Warhol and Collecting* (exh. cat.), The Andy Warhol Museum, New York, 2002. Arguably, Warhol collected Americana before his arrival in New York and before Pop. Famously Warhol had written to Shirley Temple and was rewarded with an autographed picture of the childhood star.

15 See, for example, Anthony E. Grudin, ' "Except Like a Tracing": Defectiveness, Accuracy, and Class in Early Warhol', *October*, 140, Spring 2012, pp. 139–64.

16 Quoted in Branden W. Joseph, '1962', *October*, 132, Spring 2010, pp. 114–34, p. 119.

17 Ibid., n. 14.

18 Joseph, '1962', p. 123.

19 For more on Warhol's early subject's roots in the 1950s, see Chapter 1.

20 Andy Warhol and Pat Hackett, *POPism: The Warhol 1960s*, Penguin, London, 2007, p. 71.

21 Warhol, *The Philosophy of Andy Warhol*, p. 93.

22 Ibid., p. 146:

> I think about people eating and going to the bathroom all the time, and
> I wonder why they don't have a tube up their behind that takes all the
> stuff they eat and recycles it back into their mouth, regenerating it, and
> then they'd never have to think about buying food or eating it. And they
> wouldn't even have to see it—it wouldn't even be dirty. If they wanted
> to, they could artificially color it on the way back in. Pink. (I got the idea
> from thinking that bees shit honey, but then I found out that honey isn't
> bee-shit, it's bee regurgitation, so the honeycombs aren't bee bathrooms
> as I had previously thought. The bees therefore must run off somewhere
> else to do it.)

23 Artist Rachel Harrison puts celebrity culture and recycling together in her evaluation of Warhol's influence. Rachel Harrison, and Bob Nickas, 'Empire State',
Artforum, Vol. 43, No. 2, 2004, pp. 146–47, p.146.

24 Rosalind E. Krauss, *The Originality of the Avant-Garde and Other Modernist
Myths*, The MIT Press, London 1986, p. 168.

25 Nancy Spector, *Richard Prince*, Guggenheim Museum Publications, New York,
2007.

26 Andrew Ross, 'The Uses of Camp', in David Bergman (ed), *Camp Grounds: Style
and Homosexuality*, University of Massachusetts Press, Amherst, 1993,
pp. 54–77, esp. 'Postscript', p. 75; Evan Watkins, *Throwaways: Work Culture and
Consumer Education*, Stanford University Press, Stanford, CA, 1993, p. 159.

27 Richard Prince's status as a pioneer of appropriation art might be qualified,
to an extent, given that the 'first wave' of appropriation art in America was
advanced by Elaine Sturtevant. See Elisa Schaar, 'Spinoza in Vegas, Sturtevant
Everywhere: A Case of Critical (Re-)Discoveries and Artistic Self-Reinventions',
Art History, Vol. 33, No. 5, 2010, pp. 886–909.

28 Warhol, *The Philosophy of Andy Warhol*, p. 93.

29 'Daniel Robbins, 'Confessions of a Museum Director', in *Raid the Icebox I with
Andy Warhol* (exh. cat.), Rhode Island School of Design Museum, Providence, RI,
1969, pp. 8–16, p. 14.

30 Lisa Graziose Corrin, 'The Legacy of Daniel Robbins' *Raid the Icebox I*', *Rhode
Island School of Design Museum Notes 1996*, Rhode Island School of Design
Museum, Providence, RI, June 1996, pp. 54–61, p. 56.

31 Robbins, 'Confessions of a Museum Director', p. 14.

32 Briefly, the catalogue can be sketched as follows: of a 404-item inventory, shoes
number 198, of which the majority are described as 'American'. The 22 Mound
Builder ceramic pieces, the 11 textile pieces and the 13 woven baskets all can be
described as Native American, and these stack up against 49 works of drawing,
watercolour and oil on canvas, half of which (definitely the less notable half) are
described as 'American'.

33 Including the American Mound Builders, responsible for most of the ceramics shown. Their history stretched from around 3000 BCE to the sixteenth century CE.

34 Brando and Littlefeather's protest was made in response to the Wounded Knee incident of 1973 and more broadly the misrepresentation of American Indians in film and television. Brando's involvement with the cause of the Native American peoples preceded the Wounded Knee incident and came at a time of increased awareness and sympathy as a consequence of the civil rights movement.

35 Warhol had a painful ingrown toenail during his visit to the Rhode Island School of Design Museum and was limping, with a hole cut in his shoe to relieve pressure. In that state, he may have had Paul Newman's character in *Cat on a Hot Tin Roof* in mind. He too hobbled around a store of dusty forgotten antiques in the film's last scenes. Also of note, Warhol himself collected Navajo rugs and other works.

36 Perhaps this gesture refers to the attempt Warhol made, earlier in the 1960s, to acquire 'floating chairs' from a supplier of magic trick props for a work that was never realised but has been linked to *Silver Clouds*. See Ronald Jones, 'Living in a Box', *Frieze*, Issue 82, April, 2004. Available at http://www.frieze.com/issue/article/living_in_a_box/ (accessed 14 August 2015).

37 David Bourdon, 'Andy's Dish', in *Raid the Icebox I with Andy Warhol*, pp. 17–24, p. 18.

38 Ibid., p. 20.

39 Ralph T. Coe, 'American Indian Art', in Smith, *Possession Obsession: Andy Warhol and Collecting*, Andy Warhol Museum, Pittsburgh, PA, 2002, pp. 112–25, p. 122.

40 Ibid., p. 124.

41 The levelling effect of a natural history had been earlier demonstrated by Warhol's participation in the Hallmark Gallery Children's Aid celebrity Christmas tree design of 1964. Here the division between the natural and the cultural is brought into stark relief. At the end of 1964, the 'famous friends' of the charity, among whom were Cecil Beaton, Joanne Woodward and Paul Newman, were given Christmas trees to decorate for a charity fundraiser organised by the greetings card company. Warhol's tree was returned by the artist as blank as he had received it.

42 One of many instances of this comes in Warhol's interview with Glenn O'Brien. Glenn O'Brien, 'Interview: Andy Warhol', in Kenneth Goldsmith (ed), *I'll be Your Mirror: The Selected Andy Warhol Interviews: 1962–1987*, Carroll & Graf, New York, 2004, pp. 233–64, p. 237.

43 The painting is William Merritt Chase's *Woman in Pink*, *c*.1888–9 (oil on canvas, H 77.8cm, W 102.8cm). Another aspect that stresses the catalogue's innovative integration with the display is Warhol's image of an elaborate door mechanism, presumably a feature of the museum's storage facility, printed full page on the catalogue's first page, with an image of the back of the same door on the other side.

44 Deborah Bright, 'Shopping the Leftovers: Warhol's Collecting Strategies in *Raid the Icebox I* ', *Art History*, Vol. 24, No. 2, 2001, pp. 278–91, pp. 279–80.

45 Michael Lobel, 'Warhol's Closet', *Art Journal*, Vol. 55, No. 4, 1996, pp. 42–50, p. 45. Lobel is referring to Eve Kosofsky Sedgwick, *Epistemology of the Closet*, University of California Press, Oakland, CA, 1990.

46 Lobel, 'Warhol's Closet', p. 46.

47 This is not to say that Warhol's home did not include some rooms that were beautifully presented, but so much of the stuff in it was stored in one or two rooms that were full to bursting.

48 The source for this report is John W. Smith, 'Andy Warhol's Art of Collecting', in Smith (ed), *Possession Obsession*, p. 17.

49 Cathleen McGuigan, 'The Selling of Andy Warhol,' *Newsweek*, 18 April 1988; Corrin, 'The Legacy of Daniel Robbins', p. 61, n. 2.

50 Ibid., p. 56.

51 Robbins, 'Confessions of a Museum Director', p. 15.

52 Peter Wollen, *Raiding the Icebox: Reflections on Twentieth Century Culture*, Verso, London, 2008, p. 166.

53 Robbins, 'Confessions of a Museum Director', p. 14.

54 Corrin, 'The Legacy of Daniel Robbins', p. 57.

55 Ibid., p. 55.

56 The myth of the *yurodivy* (holy fool) has been used by some commentators to describe Warhol's personality—in ways that are similar to Robbins's description. The figure of the *yurodivy* is connected to the area in what is now north-eastern Slovakia, from which Warhol's family emigrated before his birth.

57 More generally, Corrin's assessment of *Raid the Icebox I* in relation to later artists' in-the-museum work is full of contradictions. On the one hand, she impresses on the reader the importance of *Raid the Icebox I* in the history of Institutional Critique, going so far as to suggest that Fred Wilson directly references the arrangement of Windsor chairs in the famous section of *Mining the Museum* (1992) in which similar chairs were gathered around a whipping post (this section of Wilson's *Mining the Museum* was labelled 'Cabinetmaking, 1820–1960'). Yet, on the other, this influence is 'mythical', writing that there is 'little mention of it as key to the context in which they are working.' Corrin also describes that Warhol 'paid no heed to visual distinctions [...] originals or fakes', as if his radicality was a consequence of unselfconsciousness. This is not true. As I have already argued, Warhol paid great attention to fakes, and to issues of visual distinction. Corrin, 'The Legacy of Daniel Robbins', p. 55–6.

58 Ibid., p. 57.

59 Bright, 'Shopping the Leftovers', pp. 284–98.

60 Robbins, 'Confessions of a Museum Director', p. 14.

61 That Warhol saw this work as a means of representing femininity in the elite context of the museum is still an idea worth considering. When in 1977 he was

interviewed for the *New York Times* about *Folk and Funk*, he matter-of-factly went on record to say that: 'the reason I like folk art is that most of the best of it—the quilts, the painted furniture—is done by women… It's the best woman-art around.' Rita Reif, 'Warhol the Collector: A Taste for the Commonplace', *New York Times*, 22 September 1977, p. 55.

62 Bright, 'Shopping the Leftovers', p. 282. If anything, Warhol was taking a risk with his role in orchestrating the show.

63 Wollen, *Raiding the Icebox*, p. 166.

64 Ibid., p. 168.

65 Robbins, 'Confessions of a Museum Director', p. 14.

66 Jonathan Flatley, 'Like: Collecting and Collectivity', *October*, 132, Spring 2010, pp. 71–98, p. 83.

67 Walter Benjamin, *Illuminations*, trans. Harry Zorn, Pimlico, London, 1999, p. 253.

68 Flatley, 'Like: Collecting and Collectivity', p. 80.

69 Benjamin, *Illuminations*, p. 63.

70 Ibid., p. 69.

71 Walter Benjamin, *The Arcades Project*, quoted in David Frisby, *Fragments of Modernity*, Routledge, London, 2013, p. 188–89.

72 Robert Hobbs, 'Kelley Walker's Continuum: Consuming and Recycling as Aesthetic Tactics', in Suzanne Cotter (ed), *Seth Price/Kelley Walker: Continuous Project*, Modern Art Oxford, Oxford, 2007, pp. 1–25, p. 13.

73 In her book *Pop or Populus*, Bettina Funcke has also addressed this work within the context of an analysis of Warhol's strategic mobilisation of media as a meeting point of mass and high culture. She makes plain the importance for her of Warhol's work: 'the radicality of Warhol's art lies in its direct expression of the process of production.' For her, recycling is the means of representation of these processes. She describes Walker's 'attitude as an artist' similarly, elaborating with a list of his artistic activities: 'finding, stealing, copying, appropriating, inverting, repossessing, and redistributing in a new context'. Creeping back in here is a sense of separation: recycling is a means of representation, while appropriating, stealing and so on are means of production that are being represented. I am arguing slightly differently: Warhol saw that recycling was to become part of the capitalist machinery, and that this is further explored by Walker. Bettina Funcke, *Pop or Populus: Art between High and Low*, Sternberg Press, London, 2009, p. 152.

74 Vincent Pécoil, 'Kelley Walker' *Flash Art*, no. 247, March/April 2006, pp. 62–4.

75 However, the integration of production and consumption was already explicit in what came to be used for the recycling logo, designed, tellingly, at the same time as *Raid the Icebox I* and therefore just before the publication of *The Philosophy of Andy Warhol*.

76 Enquiry into the relationship between virtual systems and real space, and the effects of that relationship, was the territory of many of Dan Graham's experiments

with feedback, beginning at the same time as *Raid the Icebox I*, in which subjects were required to locate selfhood within information systems that by their nature were constantly shifting and morphing. The site of such work might not be spatial per se, but it takes the idea of 'location' and applies it to real space and screened sources of information. Graham's work is pertinent because, as part of a critique of Minimalism's assured and unitised moment of encounter, it highlighted that the subject was never mentally contained by its apparent physical situation.

77 Régine Debatty, 'Interview with Marisa Olson', *We Make Money Not Art*, 2008. Available at http://we-make-money-not-art.com/archives/2008/03/how-does-one-become-marisa.php#.VXqoAkbZCDk (accessed 12 June 2015).

78 Tate 'Camille Henrot: Grosse Fatigue', 28 February 2014. Available at http://www.tate.org.uk/context-comment/audio/camille-henrot-grosse-fatigue (accessed 15 August 2015).

79 Warhol, *The Philosophy of Andy Warhol*, p. 145.

80 Michael J. Golec, *The Brillo Box Archive: Aesthetics, Design and Art*, University Press of New England, Lebanon, 2008, p. 120.

81 Ronald Jones, 'Living in a Box'. He writes:

> The sheer magnitude of accumulation is startling here. Some examples: Warhol's hospital bracelet from the 1968 shooting, receipts from Max's Kansas City, four maids' uniforms, a 1941 photograph of Shirley Temple inscribed to Andrew Warhola, a letter from Philip Johnson reminiscing about police arriving at his Connecticut home to put a stop to the Velvet Underground playing, an announcement for a memorial exhibition for James Harvey (the designer of the Brillo box), fan letters, a pair of shoes that once belonged to Clark Gable, the Raymond Loewy-designed dinner service from Concorde, a 1956 letter from Alfred Barr turning down Warhol's offer to donate one of his shoe drawings to the Museum of Modern Art, a letter from Irving Blum encouraging him to leave the Stable Gallery for Leo Castelli, a Christmas card from Paul and Linda McCartney and some of Warhol's mother's clothes.

82 Vincent Fremont, 'Brigid Berlin', *Interview*, June-July, 2008, pp. 92–3.

83 Ibid., pp. 92–3.

84 Kat Murrell, 'Vincent Fremont on Andy Warhol: He was an energy force', 27 October 2009. Available at http://thirdcoastdaily.com/2009/10/vincent-fremont-on-andy-warhol-he-was-an-energy-force/ (accessed 21 November 2014).

85 Andy Warhol, Pat Hackett (ed), *The Andy Warhol Diaries*, Penguin Modern Classics, London, 2010, p. 1060.

86 Benjamin Buchloh, 'The Andy Warhol Line', in Gary Garrels (ed), *The Work of Andy Warhol*, Bay Press, Seattle, 1989, pp. 52–69, p. 67.

87 Richard Prince, 'Bird Talk', 17 September 2014 [Richard Prince]. Available at http://www.richardprince.com/contact/ (accessed 14 August 2015).

88 Though this isn't to suggest a direct influence. In other ways Koons's work owes a great deal to Warhol, Warhol's pristine, overwhelming presentation of *Brillo Boxes*; the flighty impermanence of *Silver Clouds* (with their silver-Mylar appearance emulated by Koons's cast inflatable *Rabbit* of 1986); and his paintings, that do more than record, but go some way to preserving the contemporaneity of images from specific times—newspapers, police records and movements within art history.

89 If unboxing came to be understood as part of the significance of the *Time Capsules* project by Warhol, then it is fitting that the video blogs posted online by the archivists at the Warhol Museum have a lot in common with unboxing videos. The *Time Capsules* are carefully unboxed by members of the archival team at the Andy Warhol Museum in Pittsburgh, who offer a commentary on the contents of the box and the work of unboxing and categorisation being undertaken. For example: Warhol Museum, 'Out of the Box August 15, 2014', 26 January 2015 [Warhol Museum Blog]. Available at http://blog.warhol.org/museum/tc86-opening-a-warhol-time-capsule/ (accessed 14 August 2015).

90 DisneyCollector, 'Angry Birds Toy Surprise Jake NeverLand Pirates Disney Pixar Cars2 Spongebob Huevos Sorpresa', 11 May 2013 [YouTube]. Available at http://youtube/aoc8d0gcf08 (accessed 11 December 2014). This kind of hit count is worth millions in advertising revenue.

91 In speaking of the image as a platform for a new kind of object relations, I want to distinguish my ideas from the 'image-object' of Guy Debord. For Debord, the spectacle screens relations to objects, wrapping them up as it were, the viewer always situated on the other side of this screen. I am describing changed phenomenology, as if we had entered the world on the other side of the screen and had to negotiate new object relations. It has been much of the argument of the book that the reception of Warhol solely in terms of images and the screen of spectacle (without enquiring into what those images give forth) reduces the artist, as well as the work, to two dimensions. For reference to the term 'image-object' see Guy Debord, *Society of the Spectacle*, trans. D. Nicholson-Smith, Zone Books, New York, 1995, p. 16 (Thesis 15).

92 Perhaps we can understand Warhol's portraiture technique in this way too: making luminous, loud, larger than life, cutting out the noise, the distractions: an ideality that is also a realism.

Conclusion: One Dimensional Man – In 3D!

1 Herbert Marcuse, *One-Dimensional Man: Studies in the Ideology of Advanced Industrial Society*, Beacon Press, Boston, 1964, p. 57.

2 True, also, of Richard Prince. Both artists treated the images that they intended for their two dimensional work as objects. In the fifth round of the involved

process of re-photography, Prince 'works' the camera in front of his already heavily manipulated reproduction, shooting it from many angles and with different frames and focal points.

3 Andy Warhol, Pat Hackett (ed), *The Andy Warhol Diaries*, Penguin Modern Classics, London, 2010, p. 896 and p. 921.

4 David Bourdon, *Warhol*, Harry N. Abrams Inc., New York, 1989, p. 406.

5 According to the Guggenheim, the two sources for the image were a cheap black and white photograph of a widely circulated nineteenth-century engraving and a schematic outline drawing found in a 1913 *Cyclopedia of Painters and Painting*. The former served as model for the silkscreens, the latter for the so-called hand-drawn paintings, which were made by tracing the simplified contours of the encyclopaedia illustration as they were projected onto the canvas. According to David Bourdon, Warhol used 'kitsch, secondary sources' including 'a white plastic maquette of the Last Supper that was reportedly found in a gas station on the New Jersey Turnpike, a published line drawing based on the composition, and a large, Italian Capo-di-Monte bisque figural group that was found in a midtown shop.' Claudia Schmuckli, 'Andy Warhol: *The Last Supper*', no date [Guggenheim Past Exhibitions]. Available at http://pastexhibitions.guggenheim. org/warhol/ (accessed 12 November 2014). See also, Bourdon, *Warhol*, p. 406.

6 John O'Connor and Benjamin Liu (eds), *Unseen Warhol*, Rizzoli, New York, 1996, p. 63.

7 Around this time, Warhol increasingly began to make his silkscreen paintings and prints using images produced in-house. One good reason for this development was to avoid being culpable of copyright infringement, something that had caused problems on multiple occasions during the 1960s. It has been suggested that, where Warhol did not have permission to use the source image, he may have photographed models, toys or statues of a similar likeness to the image he wanted to avoid directly reproducing copyrighted material. In this case, copyright was not an issue, and nor can the statues of Lenin and *Last Supper* be considered to have been acquired with the intent of swerving copyright.

8 Michel Foucault, 'Theatrum Philosophicum', in Donald F. Bouchard (ed), *Language, Counter-Memory, Practice*, Cornell University Press, Ithaca, 1977, pp. 165–96, p. 189.

9 Gretchen Berg, 'Andy Warhol: My True Story', Kenneth Goldsmith (ed), *I'll be Your Mirror: The Selected Andy Warhol Interviews: 1962–1987*, Carroll & Graf, New York, 2004, pp. 85–97, p. 92.

10 Foucault, 'Theatrum Philosophicum', p. 174.

11 Deleuze also mentions Warhol in *Difference and Repetition*, though in a way that is not so nearly as well integrated into the depths of his text. Gilles Deleuze, *Difference and Repetition*, Continuum, London, 2004, p. 366.

12 Ibid. p. 170.

13 Foucault, 'Theatrum Philosophicum', p. 175.

Bibliography

American Folk Art Museum, *Andy Warhol's Folk and Funk* (exh. cat.), Museum of American Folk Art, New York, 1977.

Angell, Callie, *Andy Warhol Screen Tests: The Films of Andy Warhol Catalogue Raisonné (Vol. 1)*, Abrams/Whitney Museum of American Art, New York, 2006.

Baer, Jo, *Jo Baer: Broadsides and Belle Lettres, Selected Writings and Interviews 1965–2010*, Roma Publications, Amsterdam, 2010.

Barthes, Roland, *Image-Music-Text*, Fontana, London, 1977.

______ 'That Old Thing Art', in Paul Taylor, ed., *Post-Pop Art*, The MIT Press, Cambridge, MA, 1989, pp. 21–31.

Battcock, Gregory (ed.), *Minimal Art: A Critical Anthology*, University of California Press, London, 1995.

Benjamin, Walter, *Illuminations*, trans. Harry Zorn, Pimlico, London, 1999.

Bockris, Victor, *Warhol*, Penguin, London, 1990.

______ and Gerard Malanga, *Uptight: the Story of the Velvet Underground*, Omnibus Press, London, 1983.

Bourdon, David, 'Warhol as Filmmaker', *Art in America*, 59, 1971, pp. 12–16.

______ *Warhol*, Harry N. Abrams Inc., New York, 1989.

Brehm, Margit, Axel Heil and Roberto Ort, *Paul Thek: Tales the Tortoise Taught Us*, Konig, London, 2009.

Bright, Deborah, 'Shopping the Leftovers: Warhol's Collecting Strategies in *Raid the Icebox I*', *Art History*, Vol. 24, No. 2, 2001, pp. 278–91.

Buchloh, Benjamin H. D., 'Andy Warhol's One Dimensional Art: 1956–1966', in Kynaston McShine (ed.), *Andy Warhol: A Retrospective*, Museum of Modern Art, New York, 1989, pp. 39–61.

________ 'Drawing Blanks: Notes on Andy Warhol's Late Works', *October*, Winter 2009, pp. 3–24.

Chave, Anna C., 'Minimalism and the Rhetoric of Power', *Arts Magazine*, Vol. 64, No. 5, January 1990, pp. 44–63.

Clement, Jennifer, *Widow Basquiat: A Memoir*, Canongate, London, 2000.

Colacello, Bob, *Holy Terror: Andy Warhol Close Up*, Harper Collins, New York, 1990.

Cooke, Lynne, 'Andy Warhol: *Shadows*', in Lynne Cooke, Karen J. Kelly, and Bettina Funcke (ed), *Robert Lehman Lectures on Contemporary Art*, Dia Art Foundation, New York, 2004, pp. 87–93.

Corrin, Lisa Graziose, 'The Legacy of Daniel Robbins' *Raid the Icebox I*', *Rhode Island School of Design Museum Notes 1996*, Rhode Island School of Design Museum, Newport, RI, June 1996, pp. 54–61.

Crimp, Douglas, 'The Photographic Activity of Post-modernism', *October*, 15, Winter, 1980, pp. 91–101.

________ 'Getting the Warhol We Deserve', *Social Text*, No. 59, 1999, pp. 49–66.

________ 'The Photographic Activity of Post-modernism', in Fogle, Douglas (ed.), *The Last Picture Show: Artists Using Photography, 1960–1982*, Walker Art Centre, D.A.P. /Distributed Art Publishers, New York, 2003, pp. 204–07.

Crone, Rainer, *Andy Warhol*, trans. John William Gabriel, Thames & Hudson, London, 1970.

Crow, Thomas, 'Saturday Disasters: Trace and Reference in Early Warhol', in Guilbaut, Serge (ed.), *Reconstructing Modernism: Art in New York, Paris, and Montreal, 1945–1964*, MIT Press, Cambridge, MA, 1990, pp. 311–26.

________ *Modern Art in the Common Culture* Yale University Press, London, 1996.

Danto, Arthur C., 'The Artworld', *Journal of Philosophy*, Vol. 61, No. 19, 1964, pp. 571–84.

Debatty, Régine, 'Interview with Marisa Olson', *We Make Money Not Art*, 2008, available at http://www.we-make-money-not-art.com/archives/2008/03/how-does-one-become-marisa.php (accessed 23 August 2014).

Debord, Guy, *Society of the Spectacle*, trans. Nicholson-Smith, D., Zone Books, New York, 1995.

Donovan, Molly (ed.), *Warhol Headlines*, Prestel, London, 2011, pp. 2–25.

Feldman, Frayda, and Jorg Schellmann, *Andy Warhol Prints: a Catalogue Raisonné, 1962–1987*, D.A.P. /Distributed Art Publishers in association with R. Feldman Fine Arts, Inc., New York, 1997.

Fer, Briony, *Eva Hesse Studiowork*, Yale University Press, London, 2009.

Flatley, Jonathan, 'Like: Collecting and Collectivity', *October*, 132, Spring 2010, pp. 71–98.

Flood, Richard, 'Paul Thek: Real Misunderstanding', *Artforum*, Vol. 20, No. 2, October 1981, pp. 48–53, p. 49.

Foster, Hal, *Return of the Real*, MIT Press, London 1996.

_______ 'Figment in a Factory', in Meyer-Hermann, Eva, Wrbican, Matt, Warhol, Andy and Huxley, Geralyn (eds), *Andy Warhol: Other Voices, Other Rooms*, NAI Publishers, Rotterdam, 2008, pp. 105–09.

Francis, Mark, '*Horror Vacui*: Andy Warhol's Installations', in Mark Francis (ed.), *Andy Warhol: the Late Work, Vol. 1 Texts*, Prestel, Munich, 2004, pp. 10–20.

Frei, George and Printz, Neil, *The Andy Warhol Catalogue Raisonné: Paintings and Sculpture 1961–1963 Vol. 1*, Phaidon Press, New York, 2002.

_______*The Andy Warhol Catalogue Raisonné: Paintings and Sculpture 1964–1969 Vol. 2A*, Phaidon Press, New York, 2004.

_______*The Andy Warhol Catalogue Raisonné: Paintings and Sculpture 1964–1969 Vol. 2B*, Phaidon Press, New York, 2004.

Frisby, David, *Fragments of Modernity*, Routledge, London, 2013.

Funcke, Bettina, *Pop or Populus: Art between High and Low*, Sternberg Press, London, 2009.

Garrels, Gary (ed.), *The Work of Andy Warhol*, Bay Press, Seattle, 1989.

Gidal, Peter, *Andy Warhol Films and Paintings: The Factory Years*, De Capo, Studio Vista, London, 1971.

Giles, Paul, 'The Allure of Iconography: Andy Warhol and Robert Mapplethorpe', *American Catholic Arts and Fictions: Culture, Ideology, Aesthetics*, Cambridge University Press, Cambridge, 1992, pp. 273 – 95.

Godfrey, Mark, 'From Box to Street and Back Again: An Inadequate Descriptive System for the Seventies', in de Salvo, Donna (ed.), *Open Systems Rethinking Art c.1970*, Tate Publishing, London, 2005, pp. 24–49.

Goldsmith, Kenneth, *I'll Be Your Mirror: The Selected Andy Warhol Interviews*, Da Capo Press, Boston, 2004.

Golec, Michael J., *The Brillo Box Archive: Aesthetics, Design and Art*, University Press of New England, Lebanon, 2008.

Goodyear, Anne, 'From Technophilia to Technophobia: the Impact of the Vietnam War on the Reception of "Art and Technology"', *Leonardo*, Vol. 41, No. 2, April 2008, pp. 169–73.

Grudin, Anthony E., "A Sign of Good Taste': Andy Warhol and the Rise of Brand Image Advertising', *Oxford Art Journal*, Vol. 33 No. 2, 2010, pp. 211–32.

_______'"Except Like a Tracing": Defectiveness, Accuracy, and Class in Early Warhol', *October*, 140, Spring 2012, pp. 139–64.

Halley, Peter, *Wolfgang Tillmans*, Phaidon Press, London, 2002.

Hapgood, Marilyn Oliver, *Wallpaper and the Artist: from Durer to Warhol*, Abbeville Press, New York, 1992.

Harnoncourt, Anne d' and Walter Hopps, 'Reflections on a New Work by Marcel Duchamp', *Philadelphia Museum of Art Bulletin*, Vol. 64, Nos. 299–300, April–September 1969, pp. 6–58.

Harrison, Rachel and Bob Nickas, 'Empire State', *Artforum*, Vol. 43, No. 2, 2004, pp. 146–47.

Hobbs, Robert, 'Kelley Walker's Continuum: Consuming and Recycling as Aesthetic Tactics', in Cotter, Suzanne (ed.), *Seth Price/Kelley Walker: Continuous Project*, Modern Art Oxford, Oxford, 2007, pp. 1–25.

Jaeggi, Rahel, *Alienation*, trans. Neuhouser, Frederick and Smith, Alan E., Columbia University Press, New York, 2014.

Jervis, John, *Transgressing the Modern*, Blackwell, London, 1999.

Johnson, Catherine, *Thank You Andy Warhol*, Glitterati Books, London, 2012.

Jones, Ronald, 'Living in a Box', *Frieze* Issue 82, April, 2004, available at http://www.frieze.com/issue/article/living_in_a_box/ (accessed 21 November 2014).

Joselit, David, 'Yippie Pop: Abbie Hoffman, Andy Warhol, and Sixties Media Politics', *Grey Room*, No. 8, Summer 2002, pp. 62–79.

______'What to Do with Pictures', *October*, 138, Fall 2011, pp. 81–94.

Joseph, Branden W., 'One-Dimensional Man', *Art Journal*, Vol. 57, No. 4, Winter, 1998, pp. 105–9.

______'"My Mind Split Open": Andy Warhol's Exploding Plastic Inevitable'. *Grey Room* No. 8 Summer 2002 pp. 80–107.

______'1962', *October*, 132, Spring 2010, pp. 114–34.

Judd, Donald, 'Andy Warhol', in Pratt, Alan R. (ed.), *The Critical Response to Andy Warhol*, Greenwood Press, London, 1997, pp. 2–3.

______'Specific Objects', in Charles Harrison and Paul Wood (eds), *Art in Theory*, Blackwell, London, 2002, pp. 824–8.

Katz, Jonathan, 'Lovers and Divers: Picturing a Partnership in Rauschenberg and Johns' in *Frauen/ Kunst/ Wissenschaft*, Berlin, June, 1998, pp. 16–31.

Koch, Stephen, *Stargazer: Andy Warhol's World and His Films*, Marion Boyers, London, 1985.

Krauss, Rosalind E., *The Originality of the Avant-Garde and Other Modernist Myths*, The MIT Press, London 1986.

______'Madness of the Day', in Deitch, Jeffery (ed.), *The Painting Factory: Abstraction After Warhol* (exh. cat.), Skira Rizzoli, London, 2012, pp. 23–9.

LA County Museum of Art, *A Report on the Art and Technology Program of the LA County Museum of Art 1967–71* (exh. cat.), Los Angeles County Museum of Art, Los Angeles, CA, 1971.

Lawrence, Tim, *Love Saves the Day: A History of American Dance Music Culture, 1970–1979*, Duke University Press, Durham, NC, 2004.

Livingstone, Marco, 'Do It Yourself: Notes on Warhol's Techniques', in McShine, Kynaston (ed.), *Andy Warhol: A Retrospective*, Museum of Modern Art, New York, 1989, pp. 63–80.

Lobel, Michael, 'Warhol's Closet', *Art Journal*, Vol. 55, No. 4, 1996, pp. 42–50.

Malanga, Gerard, *Archiving Warhol: Writings and Photographs*, Creation Books, New York, 2002.

Marcuse, Herbert, *One-Dimensional Man*, Routledge, London, 1994.

Mattick, Paul, 'The Andy Warhol of Philosophy and the Philosophy of Andy Warhol', *Critical Inquiry*, Vol. 24, No. 4, 1998, pp. 965–87.

McGuigan, Cathleen, 'The Selling of Andy Warhol,' *Newsweek*, 18 April 1988.

Meyer, Richard, 'Warhol's Clones', in Dorenkamp, Monica and Henke, Richard (eds), *Negotiating Lesbian and Gay Subjects*, Routledge, New York, 1995, pp. 93–122.

Michelson, Annette, '"Where is Your Rupture?": Mass Culture and the *Gesamtkunstwerk*', *October*, 56, Spring 1991, pp. 42–63.

______(ed.), *October Files 2*, MIT Press, London, 2001.

Murrell, Kat, 'Vincent Fremont on Andy Warhol: He was an energy force', October 27th, 2009, available at http://thirdcoastdaily.com/2009/10/vincent-fremont-on-andy-warhol-he-was-an-energy-force/ (accessed 21 November 2014).

O'Brian, John (ed.), *Clement Greenberg: Collected Essays and Criticism Vol. 2*, University of Chicago Press, London, 1995.

O'Brien, Glenn, 'Interview with Andy Warhol, *High Times* 24 (Aug. 1977)', in Kenneth Goldsmith(ed.), *I'll be Your Mirror: the Selected Andy Warhol Interviews: 1962–1987*, Carroll & Graf, New York, 2004, pp. 233–64.

O'Connor, John and Benjamin Liu, *Unseen Warhol*, Rizzoli, New York, 1996.

O'Doherty, Brian, *Inside the White Cube: the Ideology of the Gallery Space*, University of California Press, London, 1999.

Oldenburg, Claes, Andy Warhol, Robert Morris and Benjamin H. D. Buchloh, 'Three Conversations in 1985', *October*, 70, The Duchamp Effect, Autumn 1994, pp. 33–54.

Pécoil, Vincent, 'Kelley Walker', *Flash Art*, no. 247, March/April 2006 pp. 62–4.

Printz, Neil and Sally King-Nero, *The Andy Warhol Catalogue Raisonné: Paintings and Sculpture 1970–1974 Vol. 3*, Phaidon Press, New York, 2010.

Raskin, David, *Donald Judd*, Yale University Press, London, 2010.

Reif, Rita, 'Warhol the Collector: A Taste for the Commonplace', *New York Times*, 22 September 1977, p. 55.

Ritzer, George, Paul Dean, and Nathan Jurgenson, 'The Coming of Age of the Prosumer', *American Behavioral Scientist*, No. 56, 2012, pp. 379–98.

Robbins, Daniel, 'Confessions of a Museum Director', in *Raid the Icebox I with Andy Warhol* (exh. cat.), Rhode Island School of Design Museum, Newport, RI, 1969, pp. 8–16.

Roelstraete, Dieter, 'Modernism, Post-modernism and Gleam: On the Photorealist Work Ethic', *Afterall: A Journal of Art, Context, and Enquiry*, No. 24, Summer 2010, pp. 5–15.

Rorimer, Anne *New Art in the 60s and 70s: Redefining Reality*, Thames and Hudson, London, 2001.

Rose, Barbara, 'A B C Art' (1965), reprinted in the more or less contemporary anthology Battcock, Gregory (ed.), *Minimal Art: A Critical Anthology*, Dutton, New York, 1968 pp. 274–97.

Rosenblum, Robert, 'Saint Andrew', *Newsweek*, 7 December 1964, pp. 100–6.

Ross, Andrew, *No-collar: The Humane Workplace and Its Hidden Costs*, Temple University Press, Philadelphia, 2004.

Rothkopf, Scott, 'File Sharing: Scott Rothkopf on Kelley Walker's Untitled, 2006', *Artforum*, Vol. 51, No.1, September 2012, pp. 454–57.

Schaar, Elisa, 'Spinoza in Vegas, Sturtevant Everywhere: A Case of Critical (Re-) Discoveries and Artistic Self-Reinventions', *Art History*, Vol. 33, No. 5, 2010, pp. 886–909.

Skrebowski, Luke, 'Productive Misunderstandings', in Diarmuid Costello and Margaret Iversen (eds), *Photography After Conceptual Art*, Wiley Blackwell, London, 2010, pp. 86–107.

Smith, John (ed.), *Possession Obsession: Andy Warhol and Collecting* (exh. cat.), The Andy Warhol Museum, New York, 2002.

Spector, Nancy, Glenn O'Brien, Jack Bankowsky, and Richard Prince, *Richard Prince* (exh. cat.), Solomon R. Guggenheim Museum, New York, 2007.

Staff of the Andy Warhol Museum, *Andy Warhol: 365 Takes*, The Andy Warhol Museum, Harry N. Abrams Inc., New York, 2004.

Stoichita, Victor, "Beyond the Peter Pan complex: Warhol's *Shadows*", in Cooke, Lynne, Kelly, Karen J. and Funcke, Bettina (eds), *Robert Lehman Lectures on Contemporary Art*, Dia Art Foundation, New York, 2004, pp. 95–107.

Swenson, Gene R., 'What is Pop Art?: Answers from 8 Painters, Part 1', *Art News*, Vol. 62, November 1963, pp. 24–7 & 60–3.

Tillim, Sidney, 'Andy Warhol', in Alan R. Pratt (ed.), *The Critical Response to Andy Warhol*, Greenwood Press, London, 1997, pp. 7–8.

Tillmans, Wolfgang and Hans Ulrich Obrist, *The Conversation Series*, Verlag der Buchhandlung Walther König, Köln, 2007.

______ and Dominic Eichler, *Wolfgang Tillmans Abstract Pictures*, Hatje Cantz, Ostfildern-Ruit, 2011.

Warhol, Andy, 'Painter Hangs Own Paintings', *New York Magazine*, Vol. 12, No. 6, 5 February 1979, pp. 9–10.

______*The Philosophy of Andy Warhol: From A to B and Back Again*, Penguin, London, 2007.

______*POPism: the Warhol 1960s*, Penguin, London, 2007.

______Hackett, Pat (ed), *The Andy Warhol Diaries*, Penguin Modern Classics, London, 2010.

Wilson, William, 'Prince of Boredom: The Repetitions and Passivities of Andy Warhol', available at http://www.warholstars.org/andywarhol/articles/william/wilson.html (accessed 21 November 2014).

Witkovsky, Matthew, 'Another History', *Artforum International*, Vol. 48, No. 7, March 2010.

Wollen, Peter, *Raiding the Icebox: Reflections on Twentieth Century Culture*, Verso, London, 2008.

Wrbican, Matt, 'Time Capsule 61 Goes to the Movies', in Eva Meyer-Hermann (ed.), *Andy Warhol: Other Voices, Other Rooms* (exh. cat.), NAi Publishers, Rotterdam, 2007, p. 115–19.

______'The True Story of "My True Story"' in Eva Meyer-Hermann (ed.), *Andy Warhol: A Guide to 706 Items in 2 Hours 56 Minutes: Other Voices Other Rooms* (exh. cat.), NAi Publishers, Rotterdam, 2007, pp. 56–7.